AN AMERICAN BETRAYAL

AN AMERICAN BETRAYAL

———◆———

CHEROKEE PATRIOTS
AND THE TRAIL OF TEARS

DANIEL BLAKE SMITH

A JOHN MACRAE BOOK   HENRY HOLT AND COMPANY   NEW YORK

Henry Holt and Company, LLC
Publishers since 1866
175 Fifth Avenue
New York, New York 10010
www.henryholt.com

Henry Holt® and ® are registered trademarks of
Henry Holt and Company, LLC.

Library of Congress Cataloging-in-Publication Data

Smith, Daniel Blake.
   American betrayal: Cherokee patriots and the Trail of Tears / Daniel
Blake Smith.—1st ed.
      p. cm.
   Includes bibliographical references.
   ISBN: 978-0-8050-8955-4 (hardcover)
   1. Cherokee Indians—History.   2. Cherokee Indians—Relocation.
3. Trail of Tears, 1838–1839.   I. Title.
   E99.C5S632 2011
   975.004'97557—dc22   2010052594

Henry Holt books are available for special promotions and
premiums. For details contact: Director, Special Markets.

First Edition 2011

Designed by Kelly S. Too

Printed in the United States of America

1   3   5   7   9   10   8   6   4   2

For Lorri

CONTENTS

AN AMERICAN BETRAYAL

Prologue

The assassins boldly rode up at daybreak, not bothering to disguise their faces.

The night before, June 21, 1839, more than one hundred angry Cherokees had met at the Takatoka Council Grounds, near present-day Tahlequah, Oklahoma. Amid boiling tempers, a group of men scribbled three names on a list: Major Ridge, John Ridge, and Elias Boudinot. None of the accused was present and no defense was mounted, so all three were quickly found guilty in a mock trial staged by the supporters of Chief John Ross. Their crime? Betraying the Cherokee Nation by selling tribal lands without approval—and the penalty was death. Numbered lots were drawn from a hat, with an *X* beside the number of each man designated as an assassin.

Early on June 22, three assassination parties of twenty-five armed men each headed toward their separate destinies: Honey Creek, the home of John Ridge; Park Hill, where Elias Boudinot lived and worked with his friend the missionary Samuel

Worcester; and Little Rock Creek near the Arkansas border, where Major Ridge, John's father and Elias's uncle, would soon be crossing. Certain of the justice of their mission, they feared no retribution. In their minds, the history of their people not only sanctioned but demanded their actions: Elias Boudinot and Major and John Ridge had to die. On a single day the assassins—all members of the party who had fiercely resisted removal out West—targeted the three men who had sold the Cherokees' sacred land to cooperate with President Andrew Jackson's forced relocation of the tribe to Oklahoma. All the years of outrage over removal and the bitter quarrels between Chief Ross and the Boudinot-Ridge party erupted in a violent day of blood revenge that was nearly operatic in sweep and tone.

The murderous reprisals of June 22, 1839, were a violent coda in the haunting and powerful story of heartbreak and loss, conflict and controversy that is the Trail of Tears. Arguably the most tragic interracial event in American history, the Trail of Tears has sometimes been called an American holocaust or genocide. It was neither—no one wanted, let alone planned for, Cherokees to die in the forced removal out West—but it did dramatize not only the loss of sacred lands in the Southeast but also the failure of democracy and justice for an entire people, ironically, the most successful, "civilized" tribe. Few stories from the American past reveal in such devastating terms the consequences of unchecked greed and racial oppression.

The Cherokees were hardly the only Indians to experience the pain and loss of forced removal. Dozens of other tribes in the United States underwent similar suffering, but because of the Cherokees' unique accomplishments as a well-educated people (they had a written language and, thanks largely to Elias Boudinot and Samuel Worcester, set up the first Indian-language newspaper, the *Cherokee Phoenix*), we have come to view their anguish as emblematic for all native peoples who faced forcible removal in the 1830s. Few tribes had so fully accepted the promise of democracy as the Cherokees. (Their 1827 constitution was modeled after the U.S. Constitution.) So in some ways the principal tragedy of the Trail of Tears lies in the heart-wrenching treachery they felt at the hands of the United States.

Most accounts of this powerful story focus on the easily identifiable villains, victims, and heroes. From the Indian-fighting Andrew Jackson to his land-hungry southern white coconspirators, the villains are easy to spot. The Cherokees themselves are often depicted as hopelessly naive in their belief that, thanks to their successful embrace of a "civilized" life, they would be spared from the relentless determination among white leaders and settlers to take over Indian lands in the Southeast. Center stage as the main protagonist in this traditional account is Chief John Ross for his laudable, tenacious struggle to save the homeland and keep the tribe together.[1]

Such a narrative is accurate as far as it goes. But it does not go far enough. A fuller perspective on the Trail of Tears takes us into the minds and hearts of those Cherokees who fought each other just as fiercely as they took on Andrew Jackson over what they saw as the very soul of the Cherokee people. What they were fighting over in Cherokee country and beyond in the 1820s and 1830s was nothing less than what it meant to be a good Cherokee, a patriot, amid the critical struggle over removal.

The removal crisis plunged the Cherokees into a profound and sometimes violent quarrel over the issue of patriotism. From the 1820s on, a series of painfully difficult questions haunted the Cherokee people: Was it possible for a Cherokee to be a full citizen of the American nation and yet remain connected to tribal traditions and ancestral land? Given the obvious hunger among southern whites for Indian land, should Cherokees have placed their hopes on assimilation in their homeland or the independence of the Cherokee Nation, regardless of geography? What could a patriotic Cherokee do to save his people if the only choices were clinging to a homeland that white settlers were bent on overrunning or re-creating the nation in a distant land? In short, if you could not save both your homeland and your people, which one mattered most, which one could you possibly surrender? And what made you the more faithful Cherokee, the more loyal patriot—fighting to save your home or to save your people?

Early on, Cherokees attempted to answer these questions by following the lead of those white politicians from the Washington administration who insisted they become "civilized" and adopt Anglo ways. By assimilating into "enlightened" white culture and its notions of private property and commercial agriculture, they would prove their worth as "red citizens" of the American republic and maintain their presence in their ancestral homeland. But as Elias Boudinot and John Ridge so bitterly discovered, even well-educated, sophisticated Cherokees who did everything "right" that white Americans expected could not escape racism. And the relentless intrusion of white settlers into Indian country, aided and abetted by President Andrew Jackson, revealed that soon, very soon, the Cherokee people would have to surrender something fundamental: either the land they had lived on for thousands of years or their very identity as Cherokees living under their own sovereign government.

Among the ironies of this devastating choice hanging over the Cherokee people was that it took the "civilization" program inaugurated under the presidency of George Washington to reveal to the young and brilliant Boudinot and Ridge that their people's future lay in establishing independence from, not assimilation into, American society. Most everything they valued—their faith, friends, spouses, and education—came from white culture. And yet they came to believe that whites were destroying their people through a violent land grab and moral degeneracy sparked by greed, immorality, and the spread of alcohol. To Boudinot and the Ridges, the Cherokee people faced not simply the threat of losing their homeland but the loss of their own independent culture.

Convinced by the mid-1830s that the Cherokee Nation was teetering on the edge of collapse, Boudinot and the Ridges insisted that removal represented the only realistic means to save their people. And while they understood the deep bond between the land and the Cherokee people, they also grasped that sometimes patriotism required a very hard choice. By choosing removal, Boudinot and Ridge placed important distance between themselves and their missionary friends who had done so much for the Cherokee cause. Samuel Worcester, perhaps Boudinot's closest white friend, believed, like John Ross, that advocating removal was a mistake, and he did not shrink from criticizing Boudinot for what he considered a misguided, fateful decision.[2]

Stung by the criticism leveled at them from their missionary friends, Boudinot and the Ridges erupted in anger when their patriotism was challenged. And when Ross called them traitors who cared nothing for their ancestral homeland, Boudinot struck back, arguing that he too loved the land of their fathers but preferred being exiles to witnessing the degradation and ruin of the Cherokee people.

If Boudinot and the Ridges eventually decided to pursue the patriot call for removal out West where, they believed, moral renewal could be accomplished, Ross and the mass of the Cherokee people focused exclusively on protecting the homeland as the critical work of the true patriot. When he was not attacking pro-removal forces for their traitorous conduct, Ross fought to find a way for his people to remain in their homes, to publicize the unfair plight of the Cherokees, and, in the end, to negotiate better financial terms for removal. Keeping his people united and together—to be sure, strictly under his own leadership—became Ross's unwavering goal. And in taking on men like Boudinot and the Ridges, Ross could point to the vast majority of Cherokees who supported him in resisting removal. Ross spoke for the many traditionalist Cherokees among his supporters when he argued that removal would tear the Cherokee people from their ancient and intimate connections to ancestral mountains and streams. A loyal Cherokee, Ross insisted, would never trade away the homeland without tribal approval. Where Boudinot saw removal as salvation, Ross viewed it as destroying a distinctive, time-honored Cherokee identity.[3]

These clashing notions of patriotism that informed much of the war of words in the removal crisis represented fundamentally colliding visions over the future of the Cherokee people. For Ross and his supporters, standing up against an oppressive federal government allied with greedy white settlers in the South was inextricably linked to saving the homeland and preserving the traditional life ways of the people. But for Boudinot and his friends, such a perspective falsely assumed that Cherokee society was in a sound and prosperous state *before* the crisis over removal. What distinguished the vision of Boudinot and friends from Ross's party was not simply the choice of saving the people over the land but the focus as well on what, exactly, needed "saving."

Deeply inspired by the missionary spirit by which they had been raised, Boudinot and the Ridges believed that the Cherokee people were confronting a moral crisis even more pressing than a political one. So when Ross raged about the depredations of the U.S. government, Boudinot responded by wondering if the Cherokee people themselves were participants in their own degradation. Problems of drunkenness, poverty, crime, and hunger, Boudinot insisted, made the condition of the Cherokees a wretched one on the eve of removal. If Ross would but look at the condition of the mass of Cherokees—and not simply the more prosperous and hopeful status of the most acculturated—he would see reason for worry. Given these moral concerns, Boudinot and others reasoned, the patriotic solution lay in the practical decision to remove out West. Removal, Boudinot believed, not only spared the Cherokees from the violent intrusions of their white neighbors but offered the opportunity for renewal.

However faithfully Ross and his adherents clung to the meaningful, ancestral connections to the land, they paid far less attention to what would happen to the Cherokee people if they were to successfully resist removal and remain in the East. Overrun by white settlers and forced to live under the laws of Georgia, North Carolina, and Tennessee, Cherokees would soon lose their distinctive identity, independence, and sovereignty as a nation. To Boudinot, such a fate was simply unacceptable. In that sense, Elias Boudinot and John Ridge were calling attention to the importance of race and the need for a completely independent Cherokee Nation. Thus remaining in their homeland, where Cherokees would soon be inundated by a demonstrably corrupt and racist white world, would only degrade the people and further subordinate them.

When reframed in the context of these colliding versions of

the good patriot, the struggle over removal takes on a different, more revealing shape. To more fully explore how conflicting meanings of patriotism influenced the heated debates over the Cherokees' fate, this book follows several players who contended for influence and power in the removal crisis: Jackson and his white southern supporters, especially in Georgia, who argued that American values *required* removal to safeguard Indians from certain extinction; Chief John Ross and the bulk of the Cherokee Nation, who fiercely fought to stay in their sacred homeland at all costs; Boudinot and the Ridges, who came to believe that removal offered the best means of preserving the Cherokee people; and the missionary friends of the Cherokees such as Samuel Worcester and Reverend Daniel Butrick who found themselves caught in the middle of an epic battle over land, national survival, and patriotic duty. Harassed and jailed for their opposition to removal, Worcester and Butrick faced a difficult ethical dilemma between the apolitical values of their white leaders in the Northeast and their own instincts in Cherokee country.

Among these many strands of the conflict over removal, the story of Boudinot and the Ridges offers an especially compelling glimpse into the battle over removal—not because they were "right" in the position they took (most historians have judged them wrong), but because of the important questions they raised about saving people versus land and the dangers of assimilation.[4] And what prompted those questions were their own painful, lived experiences as young students in philanthropic New England. The uniquely advanced education that Elias and John received through their missionary friends in Cornwall, Connecticut, made them remarkable examples of perfectly acculturated Indians who ironically turned their sophisticated education into a bitter indictment of the white man's "civilization." Following the experiences from their elite schooling to their agonizing choice for removal sheds important light on the most urgent question of the day in Indian country: with President Andrew Jackson bent on removing all Indians from the Southeast, how could Cherokees maintain their identity and patriotism?

At the other end of the spectrum stood John Ross, who commanded the devotion of the majority of the Cherokee people, mostly traditionalists. Ross, along with most Cherokees, remained a staunch adversary of removal, charging that Boudinot and company were not patriots but traitors to the Cherokee Nation for selling tribal land without the Nation's approval. The only good patriot, as he saw it, was one who fought to preserve the homeland. These intensely conflicting forces tell us much about the tragic upheaval in Cherokee country in the early nineteenth century, illuminating an agonizing story of hope and betrayal.

We begin with hope: Long before the Cherokees faced the calamity of forced removal, white leaders offered them the blandishments of "civilization." And their remarkable aptitude for adopting white culture, especially as it played out in the lives of Elias Boudinot and John Ridge, would earn them praise and approval . . . and prepare them for betrayal.

I

Becoming "Civilized"

The Cherokees' tragic saga commenced ironically on a note of progress. The new national government in 1789 that George Washington presided over was determined to reframe the nation's relationship with native peoples. The federal government, Washington insisted, would no longer treat Indians as conquered enemies without any legal rights to their ancestral lands. Washington's secretary of war, Henry Knox, could not have been clearer: "The Indians being the prior occupants, possess the right to soil. It cannot be taken from them unless by their free consent. . . . To dispossess them . . . would be a gross violation of the fundamental laws of nature, and of that . . . justice which is the glory of a nation."[1] Having just concluded a difficult and costly war for independence, Washington and Knox believed that the nation could ill afford a belligerent approach to the Native Americans on its frontiers. The Revolutionary War had also dislocated many Indian nations. The Cherokees were left reeling from the devastations of war, with more than fifty towns destroyed, fields

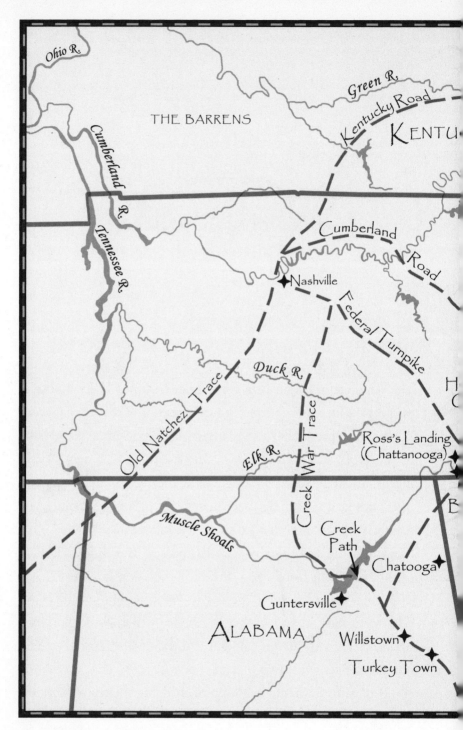

Cherokee country prior to removal

Map by Rebecca L. Wrenn

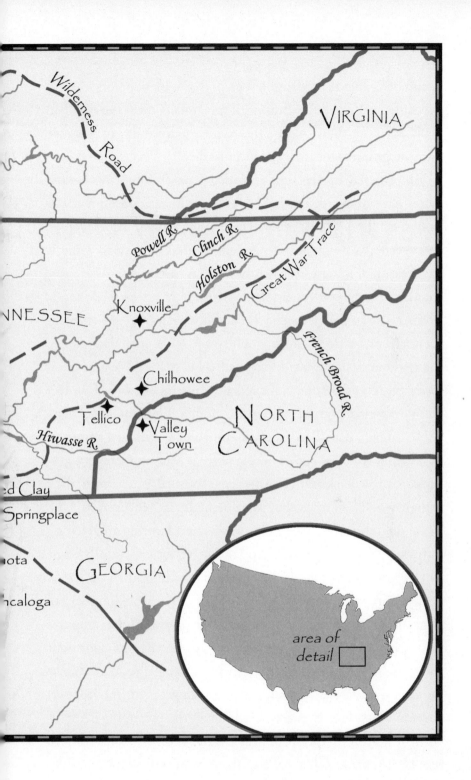

decimated, livestock slaughtered, and population loss due to exposure and starvation from military incursions. The war had depleted more than twenty thousand square miles of valuable hunting grounds for their deerskin trade.[2]

Empowered by the newly ratified Constitution, the United States government determined to redefine its relationship with its Indian neighbors. Guided by federal policy, Indian tribes were to be viewed as sovereign, independent nations entitled to respectful treatment by the new American government. Aggressive encroachment upon Indian lands that had often sparked bloody frontier warfare was to end because the national government promised protection against troublesome white intruders—or so the nation's first president expected. Not only did Washington foster peace with Indians; his federal government would protect Native Americans from extinction, though most thought it inevitable, when "uncivilized" people confronted "civilized" ones.[3]

There was a catch: upon taking office, President George Washington made it clear that Americans wanted peace with their Indian neighbors once they were remade as "red citizens" of a white republic. The first condition was that hunting and trading in furs—the principal livelihood of most tribes, especially those in the Southeast—would be replaced by the more "civilized" occupation of raising crops and livestock. Abandonment of huge Indian hunting grounds for small farming plots guaranteed whites the strategic advantage of freeing up enormous tracts of Indian land—land that whites (from President Washington down to the smallest subsistent farmers on the frontier) coveted. Washington and Knox drew on the prevailing Enlightenment notion that all people can learn and have the ability to reason. They and other Americans also subscribed to the white belief that ultimately Indians would have to surrender their lands to the expanding white population. For reasons never articulated, the founding fathers expected this could happen without conflict or harm to the Indian population. After all, Washington and Knox contended, Indians led "uncivilized" lives not because of some inherent inferiority but because they had not yet been able to imagine a better future for themselves and their children. Ignorance, not race, then, had made them "uncivilized" heathens. But with the right education and proper training they could become respectable citizens, in a fully assi-miliated (excluding black slaves) American society. Thus one of the early treaties of the Washington administration with the Cherokees, the 1791 Treaty of Holston, called for precisely this sort of give and take between the "civilized" and the "uncivi-lized": "That the Cherokee Nation may be led to a greater degree of civilization, and to become herdsmen and cultivators, instead of remaining in a state of hunters, the United States will, from time to time, furnish gratuitously the said nation with useful implements of husbandry." Americans would trade draft animals, plows, and spinning wheels for Indian willingness to abandon the hunt and chase after white civility.[4]

To carry out the new national Indian policy, federal agents were sent out as middlemen between the chiefs and the policy makers in the federal government. The agents were deployed to protect Indian boundaries and set up trading posts where Indians would exchange their furs and skins for seed and hoes, horses and plows.

Just as significantly, missionaries in the late 1790s began arriving as well, armed with the religious values and domestic tools for remaking Native Americans. Beginning in 1799, evangelical Protestants—Moravians, Baptists, Methodists, and Presbyterians—fanned out into Indian country, setting up schools

and missions where Indian boys were taught to become farmers and artisans and Indian girls learned to sew, weave, and
cook. And most important, missionaries hoped to introduce
Christianity—the telltale mark, whites believed, of a "civilized"
people. The Federalists' Indian policy under Washington and
Knox imagined a prosperous world where whites and enlightened Indians would guide their people according to "civilized"
principles and eventually produce a nation that included assimilated Indians as full citizens.[5]

If Washington and Knox believed they could transform
Native Americans with federal Indian agents and Protestant
missionaries, Thomas Jefferson, by the time he became president in 1801, pointed to scientific grounds for the prospects of
such hopeful assimilation. Since a backward life in the forest
was responsible for the Indians' ignorance, a more "civilized"
environment would significantly improve them. And once that
happened, Jefferson argued, "we shall probably find that they
are formed in mind as well as in body, on the same module with
the 'Homo sapiens Europaeus.' "[6]

Jefferson viewed Africans as inferior to whites, but as early as
1785 he observed, "I believe the Indian . . . to be in body and
mind equal to the whiteman."[7] Indians' "vivacity and activity"
of mind, he believed, was the equal of whites, and physically
Indians were brave, active, and affectionate—the full equal to
whites. The orations of Demosthenes and Cicero, he observed,
did not surpass the speech he quoted from Iroquois chief Logan.
Once they exchanged the hunter state for agriculture, once they
gave up the wandering life of the chase for the stable existence
rooted in industry and thrift, Indians, he argued, would make
fully acceptable American citizens. The steps were simple: "1st,
to raise cattle, etc., and thereby acquire a knowledge of the value

of property; 2d, arithmetic, to calculate that value; 3d, writing, to keep accounts, and here they begin to enclose farms, and the men to labor, the women to spin and weave; 4th, to read 'Aesop's Fables' and 'Robinson Crusoe' are their first delight."[8]

This more positive, "enlightened" approach to Indian-white relations may have offered hope to Cherokees—but it was meant to feel like their *last* hope. It could not have been lost on the Cherokees—or any other tribe subject to the civilization program—that becoming "civilized" was their only alternative to destruction. Becoming "civilized" was not, of course, a two-way street; for whites, "civilized" Indians were those willingly submerged into white culture. Early on Jefferson made this point: "Incorporating themselves with us as citizens of the United States, this is what the natural progress of things will, of course, bring on, and it will be better to promote than to retard it. Surely it will be better for them to be identified with us, and preserved in the occupation of their lands, than be exposed to the many casualties which may endanger them while a separate people."[9]

Thinly disguised behind Jefferson's enlightened rhetoric about the malleability of native peoples stood the bedrock determination to acquire their lands. As he noted in 1803 in a letter to an Indian agent: "In keeping agents among the Indians, two objects are principally in view: 1. The preservation of peace; 2. The obtaining lands." For Jefferson, like most white leaders, civilizing the Indians became simply a means for gaining access to their lands. Hence the emphasis he placed on converting Indians from hunters to small-scale farmers. "The Indians," Jefferson wrote, "being once closed in between strong settled countries on the Mississippi & Atlantic, will, for want of game, be forced to agriculture, will find that small portions of land well improved, will be worth more to them than extensive forests unemployed, and will be continually parting with portions of them, for money to buy stock, utensils & necessities for their farms & families." Hunting, Jefferson believed, had already become inadequate for the Indians' self-sufficiency. So he was intent on promoting agriculture and household manufacturing among the Indians—and he was "disposed to aid and encourage it liberally." As Indians learned "to do better on less land," Jefferson predicted, the expanding population of white settlers all around them would soon take over Indian lands.[10]

And Jefferson made good on his plan: during his presidency, he obtained some two hundred thousand square miles of Indian territory in nine states—mostly in Indiana, Illinois, Tennessee, Georgia, Alabama, Mississippi, Arkansas, Louisiana, and Missouri—an acquisition of territory that far exceeded the needs of white settlers or interest of Indians willing to surrender hunting grounds as a step toward becoming "civilized." Jefferson's policy was in part a military strategy aimed at clearing out Indians from the Ohio and Mississippi River valleys, compressing them into an ever-shrinking region between the Appalachian Mountains and the Mississippi River.

At its heart, Jefferson's Indian policy viewed as hopeless all Indians who clung to their "savage" ways as nomadic hunters: their game was becoming extinct, and their peoples were demoralized and depopulated by war, liquor, and disease. Their only hope, he insisted, came from selling their lands, accepting white values, intermarrying with whites, and becoming respectable yeoman farmers and U.S. citizens.[11]

White political leaders from Washington to Jefferson may have had hope for the civilization program, but out West it was a different matter. Most frontiersmen thought Indians could never become the equal of whites. In fact, some westerners feared that once Indians became farmers they would *never* get rid of them. To most frontier settlers, Indians were simple, backward, ignorant, and lazy, prone to lying, begging, and stealing. The two races were never meant to live together. And some Cherokees felt the same way. As one federal agent to the Cherokees, Return J. Meigs, observed, "Many of the Cherokees think that they are not derived from the same stock as whites, that they are favorites of the Great Spirit, and that he never intended they should live the laborious lives of whites."[12]

Those who implemented the civilization program out West often spoke just as bluntly about the challenge they were facing. Lewis Cass, who lived with the Indians on the Northwest frontier as governor of the Michigan Territory, 1813–31, looked on Indians as primitive savages driven by passions, self-interests, and fears. They lacked all proper sense of enterprise, industry, and thrift that had informed Cass's Puritan background. "Like the bear, and deer, and buffalo of his own forests," Cass wrote in 1827, "an Indian lives as his father lived, and dies as his father died. He never attempts to imitate the arts of his civilized neighbors. His life passes away in a succession of listless indolence, and of vigorous exertion to provide for his animal wants, or to gratify his baleful passions. He never looks around him, with a spirit of emulation, to compare his situation and that of others, and to resolve on improving it."[13] And the only hope for the "improvement" of Indians, Cass believed, lay with their youth. The adults and tribal elders simply could not change enough to meet white needs. But perhaps the missionary effort, he speculated, would bear fruit with the rising generation.

Whereas the federal agents who fanned out into Indian country in the 1790s brought Indians a new political and economic message of how they could best assimilate into the new republic, the missionaries following them into the Southeast offered natives nothing less than a cultural transformation. That transformation, of course, was to be conducted strictly in the image of white, "civilized" Protestants. But their attempt, both heroic and arrogant, served notice on the Cherokees that they were facing a very new world, one that offered them ever-shrinking choices about what it meant to be a patriotic Cherokee or an American.

The earliest missionaries arriving in the Southeast were Moravians from Salem, North Carolina, who entered the Cherokee Nation and established a mission at Springplace in 1801. Presbyterian ministers came into eastern Tennessee in 1804; after the War of 1812, Methodists and Baptists moved into Cherokee country. The most organized missionary effort, though, came courtesy of the American Board of Commissioners for Foreign Missions (ABCFM), who moved into Cherokee country in the 1810s. Headquartered in Boston, the American Board was an interdenominational organization, composed mainly of Congregationalists and Presbyterians, that gained strength from the revival fires sweeping the country in the early nineteenth century. Funded by wealthy merchants and textile manufacturers in New England, the board sought to "elevate the aborigines" in the South, starting with the Cherokees. The American Board set up ten mission schools among the Cherokees, while the Baptists established three schools, and the Moravians and Presbyterians two each. Methodists funded six to nine circuit riders per year and ran a handful of "itinerating" schools.[14]

Regardless of denominational connection, all the mission schools focused on two goals with their Indian students (mainly children six to sixteen years old): (1) teaching Indian boys to become farmers and artisans and Indian girls domesticity (sewing, weaving, and cooking); (2) converting Cherokees to Christianity. In their larger goal of conversion, the missionaries mostly failed. By 1830 the Moravians had produced roughly 45 converts, the Baptists 90; the American Board 219, the Presbyterians nearly 200, and the more permissive and egalitarian Methodists 850. (Unlike other denominations, the Methodist missionaries intermarried with the Cherokees, raised families with them, and became adopted members of the Cherokee Nation.) All told, though, fewer than 10 percent of Cherokees left their own native religion for Christianity.[15]

But in the world of education, the missionaries tapped into a far more willing spirit among the Cherokees. The American Board built Brainerd Mission in 1817, in present-day Chattanooga, and sent missionaries there to inculcate Cherokee children in the fundamentals of English, the precepts of Christianity, and the essentials of a "civilized" life.[16] Many of the Cherokee leaders understood early on that their future in the new American nation required English and familiarity with the white man's culture. According to one missionary, in 1818 Cherokee second principal chief Charles Hicks supported his people's need for the training and education offered by the mission schools. "Mr. Hicks says many of the people are very anxious to receive instructions & their anxiety is increased from the conviction that their very existence as a people depends upon it." Hicks approved as well the value of replacing hunting with agriculture, which, he said, "has convinced them [the Cherokees] that they can live much more comfortably by tilling their land & raising stock than they can in their old way."[17]

Little of this cultural transformation, however, came easily.

Much of what the missionaries tried to inculcate in Cherokee children flew in the face of their native upbringing and values. The mission regimen itself required more discipline than the Cherokee students' own parents usually imposed. "We are not allowed to do bad things," one Cherokee girl at Brainerd reported. "When we get angry, we have to stand in the middle of the floor before all the scholars and say the 29 verse of the 14 chap in Prov. When we tell lies, we say the 22 verse of the 12 chap of Prov." How to spend the Sabbath led to puzzlement and punishment. One student noted, "I try to tell them how to spend the Sabbath day and tell them where they will go when they die if they are not good. When they first enter school if they are asked these questions, they often say they don't know." Another student remarked, "When we break the Sabbath, we say the 4 commandment I wish to be a good girl while I live in this world and when I die to go and be where God is."[18]

Brainerd, like Springplace, was designed as a model farm, where after school the boys learned to raise cattle, use the plow, plant cotton, grind corn, chop wood, and become blacksmiths. Cherokee girls, like their white counterparts, focused on cooking and making clothes so they could stay by the hearth. The missionaries also brought radically new values to sex and family life: it was immoral to have sex beyond marriage; men should have only one wife; abortions were not allowed; women who labored in the fields while their men idly hunted in the forest were "uncivilized"; all the witchcraft, tribal rituals, and power of medicine men were simply heathen practices that needed to be replaced by Christianity and Western science.[19]

Such training and schooling turned on its head everything Cherokees had come to know in their own households and villages. Brought up in a matrilineal society—where lineage was

traced through the mother, not the father—girls, like their mothers, worked the fields while boys hunted and grew up to be warriors. Most Cherokee girls, then, had they remained home with
their mothers, would have learned the story of Selu, the first
woman, who taught her people to plant crops, like all other
women in the fields. In this radically different, patriarchal world
of white missionaries, Cherokee children and their parents had
to confront a disturbing reversal of gender roles. With men now
expected to take over agricultural work from women, natives of
both genders sometimes viewed this as a disgrace to masculin-
ity. One Quaker missionary noted that among the Senecas, "if
a man took hold of a hoe to use it the women would get down
his gun by way of derision & would laugh to say such a Warrior
is a timid woman."[20]

This conflict of culture in Indian country revealed itself early
on in the civilization program. When President John Adams
in 1798 was pushing for a right of way through the Cherokee
Nation and a new road-building program, the Cherokee Council fought the very idea of road construction. In fact, the council
censured one of its own, James Vann, a prosperous mixed-blood,
simply for building a wagon. Their concern? "If you have a
wagon," the council noted, "there must be wagon roads—& if
wagon roads, the whites will be in amongst us."[21]

Early on, much of the resistance to the civilization program
came from the more traditional elements in the Cherokee Nation.
These more conservative Cherokees saw the double-edged quality
of the missionaries' Christianity: while it offered hope to some, it
also denigrated Cherokee traditions, created conflict with the
more ambitious Cherokees eager to acculturate, and served to
confuse the notion of Cherokee identity. And from the missionaries' standpoint, there was no question but that they were biased

against "uncultivated" traditionalists. Full-bloods were frequently seen by missionaries as "essentially slovenly, dirty, smelly people."[22] Thus when a new Cherokee student, a full-blood named John Arch, entered Brainerd in 1819, his missionary teachers could not help but point to his "wild and savage aspect [that] seemed to mark him as one unfit for admission to the school." To make matters worse, "he had the dress and dirty appearance of the most uncultivated part of his tribe." But he spoke English, and "his countenance indicated a mind, that might admit of improvement."[23] Arch's tenacity for education turned him into a successful student; indeed, he soon became one of the mission's most trusted interpreters.[24]

Disdain for traditional, "unenlightened" Cherokees grew more prominent by the 1820s as the missionaries made headway with their students and the acculturated mixed-bloods in Cherokee country. Elizabeth Taylor's contemptuous perspective on the behavior of her traditionalist brethren must have brought smiles of approval from her missionary supervisors. "The unenlightened parts of this nation," she noted, "assemble for dances around a fire." Such "dances" and belief in conjurers "who will throw a black cat into the water, hang up a serpent &c" were juxtaposed against the far more civilized world under construction at Brainerd. "Many about this station are more civilized," Elizabeth observed. "Some come to meeting and appear as well as white people. Others dress in the Indian manner with maucassins for shoes, and handkerchiefs round their heads for turbans. But I have learned that the white people were once as degraded as this people; and that encourages me to think that this nation will soon become enlightened."[25]

In truth, the missionaries' holy war against heathenism and "uncivilized" behavior extended beyond race. Savagery, they believed, while primarily an Indian trait, could sometimes also afflict whites. The missionary watchfulness against such a fall from grace was made apparent in a revealing encounter at Brainerd in the fall of 1818:

> We had this evening a melancholy proof of mans proneness to degenerate into the savage state, & loose the knowledge of the truth as it is revealed in the scriptures. A mother advanced in life & a son apparently about 25, who would not from their appearance or their language, be suspected to have one drop of Indian blood in their veins, tarried with us for the night. The[y] said they were part Cherokee, though the son could not speak the language at all, & the mother but poorly. They were free to converse, & manifested almost a total ignorance of every thing relating to religion or a future state, & differed in nothing but colour & speech from the sons of the forest.[26]

Such moments, while showcasing the difficulties missionaries confronted, also seemed to galvanize their religious efforts in Indian country.

Dealing with reluctant parents of mission children constituted yet another challenge for the missionaries. Since a key part of their strategy was to break the powerful—and, to their minds, heathen—hold that Cherokee parents had over their children, it became especially worrisome to ministers when the children they were trying to transform fell back, even briefly, into the control of their excessively attached parents. For example, "Brother Hoyt" was pleased that "the Lord is sending so many of the children of this ignorant people to receive instruction from us," but as he noted in October 1819, "we have to lament that the education of many of them is greatly retarded by their frequent & long visits at home . . . their attachment to their children is so strong, & their desire to have them with them so great, that most of the parents will devise means to get their children home too frequently, & then retain them too long."[27]

To these evangelical missionaries, any absence from their enlightened Protestant message fell like a dark curtain of ignorance and heathenism around their benighted Indian children. After speaking through an interpreter about religion with a Cherokee who arrived at the mission to put his son under the school's care, the missionaries could only lament the degrading ignorance of this Cherokee regarding matters of faith—like so many others they encountered. It was, they noted, "a frank statement of the darkness of their minds. . . . How deplorable must be the state of an immortal mind" who has "not one correct idea" about the next life "or what constitutes a happy preparation for it. Thousands of these are in the bosom of the United States, surrounded on every side by a white population, called Christian." It simply was not true that they could not be civilized, he argued: "They are willing to be taught—they ask for instruction—& if we do not teach them, their blood may justly be required at our hands."[28]

Sometimes it was the missionaries' own blood that was at issue. The anti-mission sentiment that prevailed among some Cherokee traditionalists was occasionally tinged with violence. On a dark night in October 1824, an inebriated Cherokee armed with a gun charged the home of the Reverend Moody Hall, a missionary at the American Board's mission at Carmel. "His purpose, he said, [was] to kill me," Hall insisted. The intruder was disarmed, but months later another armed Cherokee was found prowling outside Hall's house. Hall was now certain that Carmel's heathen wanted him dead and the gospel gone. "Missionaries," he later noted, "will not long be safe in this land unless the government of the United States interferes." In October 1825, two Cherokees threatened Hall's life again. He left Cherokee country and never returned.[29]

More often, Cherokees who disapproved of missionaries and their teachings expressed themselves with mockery, not violence. After Reverend Isaac Proctor repeatedly preached against the Cherokee traditional sport of ball playing as a sinful practice, many of the young men from the mission school "assembled in plain sight of the Mission house, stripped themselves entirely naked, and for some time played Ball."[30]

Despite these cultural conflicts and occasional resistance among the traditionalists, most Cherokees actively participated in the civilization program. As early as 1796, Colonel Benjamin Hawkins, a federal Indian agent journeying to western Georgia, visited Cherokee towns and came away impressed with what he saw. Hawkins reported that the Cherokees he encountered had made huge advances in planting cotton and using spinning wheels. Hawkins, a kind of "secular missionary" to the Indians, observed orchards inside fenced fields, and profitable raising of all manner of livestock—cattle, chickens, hogs, and horses—along with successful crops of corn, peas, and potatoes.[31] A few years later in Tellico, Tennessee, Presbyterian minister Gideon Blackburn built a boarding school that quickly drew students. In 1804 the school began taking in students, and by the following year Blackburn celebrated the graduation of his first class in a ceremony with "little Cherokees, dressed in white clothing, [who] demonstrated their ability to read from books and sing hymns in English." Like other missionaries, Blackburn insisted on a regimen of rigorous study habits, good table manners, hygiene, and obedience to strict deadlines. By 1815 he claimed he had taught some five hundred Cherokees to read English, making the Cherokees he trained more advanced "than any other nation of Indians in America."[32]

More visible was the mission school at Brainerd. Even though Brainerd's church could produce only fourteen Cherokee members in 1821, over one hundred lived and worked at the mission school and showcased a successful effort at educational and cultural assimilation. Brainerd was a small village that included— besides the school—two teachers, a preacher, a doctor, a gristmill, sawmill, blacksmith shop, grain warehouse, barns, stables, and livestock. Both its students and teachers pointed to the encouraging progress of "civilized" labors that were essential to the mission's daily regimen. One Cherokee girl boasted of how the girls had made "fifty hunting frocks, besides hemming a number of handkerchiefs & some other sewing," along with doing their usual milking and washing and ironing—just like the domestic chores that white women performed.[33] Others at Brainerd voiced the same sort of pride in Cherokee advancement. "I will tell you how the Cherokees live," wrote Lucy McPherson. "They generally live in log houses and cabins; though some have framed ones. Some of our neighbors go to the seat of government and to the neighboring states and see how civilized people build houses and they begin to live a little as they do. They have gardens and cultivated fields. Some of them have oxen, sheep, horses, and a great many swine." For Sally Reece, another Brainerd student, the civilization program was an unqualified success. "First I will tell you about the Cherokees. I think they improve. They have a printing press, and print a paper which is called the *Cherokee Phoenix*. They come to meeting on Sabbath days. They wear clothes which they made themselves."[34]

The missionaries grew more certain that they were making

inroads in civilizing the Cherokees. Brainerd school officials in 1818 took heart that Second Principal Chief Hicks expressed "universal satisfaction" in the work they were doing at the school. They also clearly detected support from their students, citing their "increasing confidence in our integrity." And when President James Monroe visited the school in May 1819 and inspected the buildings and farmland, he displayed "approbation of the plan of instruction . . . He thought this the best & perhaps the only way to civilize & Christianize the Indians: and assured us he was well pleased with the conduct & improvement of the children."[35]

Other white political leaders, of course, adopted a much more explicitly patronizing tone regarding expectations for Cherokee advancement. Around the time that Monroe was visiting Brainerd, his secretary of war, John C. Calhoun, was meeting with a Cherokee delegation to remind them that the government envisioned only two options for them: acculturation or removal. "You are now becoming like the white people," he told them. "You can no longer live by hunting but must work for your subsistence." If they continued to work toward private landholding and live like their "white neighbors," they had a future in the new nation. "Without this," he insisted, "you will find you have to emigrate, or become extinct as a people. You see that the Great Spirit has made our form of society stronger than yours, and you must submit to adopt ours."[36]

Earlier, Jefferson himself joined in the admiration for the Cherokees' successful adoption of the civilization program. He told a Cherokee delegation visiting Washington in 1806 that their self-improvement was "like grain sown in good ground, producing abundantly. You are becoming farmers, learning the use of the plough and the hoe, enclosing your grounds and

Vann Family House
Courtesy of Georgia Department of Natural Resources

employing that labor in their cultivation which you formerly
employed in hunting and in war; and I see handsome specimens
of cotton cloth raised, spun and wove by yourselves. . . . Go on,
my children, in the same way and be assured the further you
advance in it the happier and more respectable you will be."[37]

As if in response to such admonitions, the Cherokee people
over the next twenty years developed an increasingly visible
bourgeois culture that looked for all the world just like the southern white planter class that surrounded them. By the mid-1820s
the Cherokee economy had become self-sufficient, trading profitably in cotton, corn, livestock, and poultry with merchants in
New Orleans, Charleston, and Augusta. They managed this
economic growth in part on the backs of black slaves who worked
cotton plantations just like their white brethren in Georgia,
North Carolina, and Tennessee. While only a modest number
of Cherokee planters could afford black slaves, the number of

John Ross
Courtesy of Oklahoma Historical Society

Cherokee-owned slaves nearly doubled from 583 in 1809 to 1,038 in 1825. The Cherokee population itself expanded notably in this period as well, growing by seven thousand. The 1827 census showed that all families had plows and spinning wheels; in the Cherokee Nation there were thirty-one gristmills, fourteen sawmills, six powder mills, eighteen ferries, and nineteen schools.[38]

By the mid-1820s a number of wealthy Cherokee planters and slaveholders had become prominent—men like James and Joseph Vann who lived in an elegant two-story mansion with thousands of acres and scores of slaves, along with large herds of cattle, sheep, and hogs. But two other figures, John Ross and Major Ridge, symbolized the powerful allure of both the civilization program and the desire among the Cherokee elite for acculturation.

John Ross, who would become principal chief, and his brother Lewis Ross owned lucrative mercantile establishments and credit services. The grandson of a Scots Tory agent among the Chicka-maugas, John Ross was only one-eighth Cherokee and had been raised and educated by whites. To most whites, Ross appeared to be one of them; strangers he met in Washington were nearly always surprised to learn he was Cherokee. But he was deter-mined to maintain his popular identity as the relentless sup-porter of the Cherokee people. He helped cement that identity by his marriage to his full-blood wife, Quatie, and by his deci-sion to join the Methodists in October 1829.[39] The American Board had hoped to get his conversion—especially given the organization's strong stand with the Cherokees over the loom-ing removal crisis—but instead the Rosses opted for the Meth-odists out of a different political calculation. The Methodists in 1829 appeared to be the dominant denomination in the Chero-kee Nation and had a more egalitarian approach to "civilizing" Cherokees. It was this religious populism, the Methodists' effec-tive identification with the masses among the Cherokees (not any sort of theological affinity), that appealed to Ross's instincts for galvanizing popular support behind his leadership.[40]

Major Ridge, a distinguished war hero and prominent public figure in the Cherokee Nation, lived, as did most other Cherokee elites, like the plantation gentry of the upland South: he owned several plantations worked by black slaves. In present-day Rome, Georgia, he lived on a 1,500-acre estate in an elegant, two-story home with four brick fireplaces, hardwood paneling, and veran-das on the front and back. Nearby there was a smokehouse with stables and sheds and cribs, peach and apple orchards, and in the distance slave cabins where his thirty slaves lived. The entire estate, valued at over $22,000 (not counting his slaves), was shaded by huge oaks, sycamores, and a road leading down to a ferry.[41]

Major Ridge
Courtesy of Smithsonian Institution

Except for Major Ridge, these rising Cherokee planters and merchants were highly acculturated Indians who were raised to read and write English, don the clothing and manners of white men, send their children to mission schools, adopt the trappings, if not always the spirit, of Christianity, and embrace individual property accumulation and competition. While not large in numbers—this bourgeois middle class probably never exceeded 10 percent of the Cherokee population—its members sat comfortably atop the political and economic power structure.

More traditional values could sometimes also contribute to the Cherokee embrace of "civilization." This was nowhere more evident than in the remarkable efforts of the conservative, traditional Cherokee George Guess, otherwise known as Sequoyah. The son of a Cherokee mother and a white German father who had deserted the family, Sequoyah was left to grow up among the full-bloods in the Lower Town region. He neither spoke nor read English.[42] A poor, middle-aged man with a shrunken leg

Sequoyah
Courtesy of Saint Louis University Libraries Special Collections

who smoked a long-stemmed pipe, Sequoyah had long been fascinated with how whites could communicate by writing. So when he told the head men one day that he could "make a book" by writing down signs connected to individual sounds, they laughed at him. Soon, though, he successfully devised a written language, a syllabary, consisting of individual characters in Cherokee for each distinct sound (totaling eighty-five) that could be combined into written words. Sequoyah wrote down the signs and sounds on bark with pokeberry juice and showed them to his six-year-old daughter. She quickly learned the system. Sequoyah would often showcase this apparently magical world of written language by sending his daughter far down the road with a stranger while back at the house visitors would give Sequoyah a sentence known only to those inside the house with him. His daughter would return and view the marks Sequoyah had made on the paper—and immediately speak the secret sentence.[43]

Sequoyah desperately hoped this new written language would safeguard Cherokee traditions, religion, and history. Sacred myths and rituals were now written down by Cherokee conjurors and medicine men—which, in effect, helped preserve the Cherokee worldview. In 1822 Sequoyah left the Cherokee Nation in the East for the Arkansas Territory, where he spent many years teaching Cherokee children to read and write with his syllabary. He later returned briefly to the East with letters from those children, proving that Indians "could talk at a distance." Preferring the life he found out West to the acculturated, white-dominated world in Cherokee country, Sequoyah moved to Arkansas.[44]

Not only did Sequoyah's remarkable achievement testify directly to the "civilized" status of the Cherokee people—they

Cherokee alphabet from Sequoyah's syllabary

were now the only native people with their own written language—
his syllabary became a powerful tool in the missionaries' hands:
Congregationalist missionaries such as Samuel Worcester and
Daniel Butrick used it effectively in translating the Bible and
other Christian books. And the syllabary would prove critical
for the establishment of the *Cherokee Phoenix*, a biweekly newspaper set up in October 1827, which printed laws, public documents, and articles promoting literature, civics, and religion
among the Cherokees—both in Cherokee and English. The *Cherokee Phoenix* not only served to inform the Cherokee people but
also clearly showcased to white readers everywhere the impressive
achievements of the Cherokee Nation. Not the least of Cherokee
accomplishments in their journey toward "civilization" also
came in the same year: in 1827 the Nation ratified a constitution
modeled on that of the United States.

———

Two of the most promising young men in this increasingly acculturated Cherokee Nation were John Ridge and Buck Watie.
Cousins—their fathers were brothers Major Ridge and Oo-
watie (also known as David Watie)—John and Buck could not
have better symbolized what the civilization program was all
about. Oo-waite and his white wife, Susanna Reese, had left the
town of Hiwassee, after the American Revolution destroyed
much of the region, for Oothcalooga near Rome, Georgia. There,
along with his brother Major Ridge, he cleared and fenced
fields, built a log cabin, and planted orchards, just as the federal
Indian agents had urged Cherokees to do. Life in the Oothcalooga Valley differed radically from what their families had experienced years before in Hiwassee. The communal, clan-based

village life had now been replaced by isolated, self-sufficient patriarchal households. By taking on Watie as the surname for all nine of his children, Oo-watie clearly aligned his family with the repudiation of matrilineality and the old ways of the Cherokee people.[45]

Determined to take advantage of the benefits of the civilization program, Oo-watie in 1811 enrolled the six-year-old Buck in the Moravian school at Springplace Mission, east of present-day Chatsworth, Georgia—the same mission school his cousins John and Nancy Ridge, along with other Indian children, were attending. Except for a brief, unsuccessful experience with a private tutor hired by Major Ridge for him and his cousin John, Buck remained at Springplace until 1817. A Cherokee with a sensitive demeanor, Buck was from the beginning a remarkable, gifted student.

Meanwhile Buck's cousin John, under the ambitious guidance of his father, Major Ridge, who could neither speak nor read English, moved from Springplace to Brainerd, where he quickly developed a reputation as the best student at the school. John was a slim, sensitive young man with a frail constitution and an inquiring spirit. By all accounts a brilliant student, he could sometimes seem arrogant. For example, in July 1817, after his class had been troubled with their spelling, Ridge's teacher decided to give them a shorter lesson. The fifteen-year-old John Ridge, his teacher noted, then piped up, "in a hasty & petulant manner, that he would not have such short lessons, but would get his usual number of columns. This was spoken in such a way that it could not be passed over. Some remarks were made to shew [show] the ingratitude of schollars treating their teachers with disrespect; especially when teachers had labored & done so

John Ridge

Courtesy of Saint Louis University Libraries Special Collections

much for them as we had done." After being reprimanded, John burst into tears and apologized.[46]

The incident prompted a quick visit to the school from an "agitated" Major Ridge. "'I hear,' said he, 'that my children were so bad that you could not manage them, & had just to let them go wild. I came to see if it was true.'" The teachers told him the story was much exaggerated and they were "generally pleased with the conduct of his children. He clasped his hands, & raising his eyes to heaven in a kind of involuting adoration, expressed with strong emotions the gratitude of his heart. He appeared overjoyed at the happy disappointment, exclaiming 'Never was I so glad!'" His final comments as he departed the school suggest that ambitious fathers like Major Ridge joined hands with missionaries in pressing young Cherokees toward a more "civilized" future: "I now leave you with these people [meaning the missionaries] they will take care of you, & you must obey them as you would me."[47]

Later that year larger forces beyond Cherokee country beckoned John and Buck to far more challenging and revealing
encounters with "civilized" white America. In 1817 the Reverend Elias Cornelius of the American Board of Commissioners
for Foreign Missions invited Buck and several other young
Cherokee scholars to continue their studies at the new American Board School at Cornwall, Connecticut. Oo-watie quickly
said yes, and Buck, along with a young Cherokee named Red-
bird, left with Cornelius and American Board treasurer Jeremiah Evarts for New England.

The Reverend Cornelius had also wanted John Ridge to join
the group headed for Cornwall and went to Major Ridge's house
to ask permission. But Ridge was away fighting Seminoles in
Florida alongside General Andrew Jackson. And John, suffering
from a scrofulous condition at the time, was not well enough to
make the long trip to Connecticut. When Major Ridge returned
from Florida and discovered that John had remained at home
with his mother, he became upset at his son missing such an
opportunity to go with Buck and the others. John's health
improved a few months later, so Major Ridge arranged with
another visiting missionary, Daniel Butrick, who was headed
back to New England, to take John with him to Cornwall.[48]

Both Oo-watie and Major Ridge sensed a new and important future was at hand for the Cherokee people. And they fully
expected their sons to play powerful roles in that new world.
Already as young teenagers, Buck Watie and John Ridge had
proven themselves eager and able for the journey that would
bring white and red together. And the first step was Cornwall.

2

Outrage in Cornwall

At the heart of the civilization program lay the conviction that, despite their many deficiencies, native peoples, if immersed in Protestant Christianity and educated to be productive elements of the dominant white culture, could one day become assimilated into "civilized" white America. The energetic missionary outreach into Indian country after 1810, on behalf of both the federal government and the New England–based American Board of Commissioners for Foreign Missions, offered direct testimony to this persistent belief in assimilation. And no place beckoned with a more ardent spirit of hopeful transformation than the new mission school in Cornwall, Connecticut. Established in 1817 by the American Board, primarily composed of Congregationalists and Presbyterians, the school at Cornwall took in students with little or no exposure to the Christian message or the "civilizing" power of education and proper work habits. Cornwall, its founders insisted, would be the crucible for turning young, untutored "heathens" into upstanding

Elias Boudinot
Courtesy of Oklahoma Historical Society

Christians who would then return to their native lands as missionaries.

For their experiment in assimilating young Indians, the leading men of Cornwall could not have hand-selected better prospects than Buck Watie and his cousin John Ridge. They came from homes already exposed to the strong missionary effort in Indian country. And both young men were gifted students intent on broadening their education and becoming as "civilized" as white culture would allow. On the journey to Cornwall in June 1818, Buck, Reverend Cornelius, and the other Cherokee boys rode through eastern Tennessee and stopped at Monticello, where they visited ex-president Thomas Jefferson. Later in the day they rode over to nearby Montpelier to dine with James Madison. In Washington, D.C., they met with President Monroe, who, like Jefferson and Madison, expressed delight in seeing such bright and promising young Cherokee men. Then they journeyed on to Burlington, New Jersey, to visit a wealthy benefactor of the mission school, a man who served as a prominent New Jersey statesman, signer of the Constitution, and well-known philanthropist: Dr. Elias Stockton Boudinot. Buck and Dr. Boudinot established an instant rapport, and Boudinot offered to help support Buck's education. Taken in by Boudinot's influence and abiding interest in Buck's future, the Cherokee boy decided to adopt his benefactor's name. On that day, Buck Watie became Elias Boudinot, a proud, talented young Cherokee, who began a life bent on reconciling two warring cultures, Cherokee and white. It would become a tragic success.

A few months later, Daniel Butrick accompanied John Ridge and a few other Cherokee boys to Cornwall. En route, they stopped for a few days at Salem, North Carolina, where they heard a church choir. Using all of his modest travel allowance, John also bought himself a watch, much to the stern Butrick's chagrin. The watch and the reprimand John received inspired John to compose a poem.

> *Little monitor, by thee,*
> *Let me learn what I should be:*
> *Learn the round of life to fill,*
> *Thou canst gentle hints impart,*
> *How to regulate the heart.*
> *When I wind thee up at night*
> *Mark each fault and set thee right,*
> *Let me search my bosom too,*
> *And my daily thoughts review,*
> *Mark the movements of my mind*

Nor be easy when I find
Latent errors rise to view,
Till all be regular and true.[1]

John Ridge could scarcely imagine that what he would discover in Cornwall would seem so irregular and false.

———

The town of Cornwall, a sleepy village of about sixteen hundred in 1820, lay at the base of a mountain, a cluster of neat, trim houses surrounding the village green—ideal, the school's agents believed, because it was isolated and sheltered. One English visitor described the area as "a deep retired romantic valley" amid much natural beauty.[2] Few places embodied the fervent civilizing ideals white missionaries and federal officials held for native peoples like the Cornwall school. Everything the school stood for—from its work and class regimen to its deliberately diverse student population and religious atmosphere—aimed at nothing less than the inculcation of Christian civilization among native peoples steeped in "pagan" values.

Attending the school were some twenty students from a wide range of backgrounds. Among those Boudinot and Ridge encountered included one Abenaki, two Choctaws, two Chinese, two Malaysians, one Bengalese, one Hindu, several Hawaiians, two Marquesans, three white Americans, as well as all the Cherokees. A rigorous regimen called for morning prayers at the tolling of a bell each day at 6:00 AM, followed by readings in the New Testament. Boudinot and Ridge immersed themselves in an intensive study of history, geography, philosophy, and trigonometry interspersed with working in the garden, plowing fields, and chopping wood. They attended Reverend Timothy

Stone's sermons twice on Sundays at First Church, where students had to sit in a distant corner. Once every year locals observed the mission students go through public-speaking exercises in half a dozen languages. In 1820 Ridge and Boudinot led such declamations, provoking considerable admiration from one Cornwall woman: "The Indian pupils appeared so genteel and graceful on the stage that the white pupils seemed uncouth beside them." Cherokee students even offered a dialogue on the program in 1820 concerning a removal problem to Arkansas.[3]

Both Boudinot and Ridge distinguished themselves early on by their seriousness and well-behaved demeanor. Cornwall teachers especially sensed Boudinot's sophisticated mind and

Cornwall Foreign Mission School
Courtesy of Cornwall Historical Society

grasp of his studies. Some of his teachers were so taken with Boudinot's native intellect that they published his letters in religious journals and sent his proof of a lunar eclipse to the well-known Yale geographer Jedediah Morse.[4]

School officials were sufficiently impressed with both Boudinot's and Ridge's intellectual gifts that they were asked to compose letters to prominent dignitaries on behalf of the school. Elias wrote a letter of thanks to the Baron de Campagne, a Swiss philanthropist, who had contributed nearly $900 to Cornwall. The seventeen-year-old Elias proclaimed: "I am a Cherokee, from a nation of Indians living in the southern part of the United States. There are eight of us here from that nation. Six out of eight profess to be the followers of the meek and lowly Jesus. . . . I sometimes feel an ardent desire to return to my countrymen and to teach them the way of salvation."[5] And John had the honor of writing President Monroe to report on the condition of American Indians. Like Boudinot, he focused on how Christian benevolence had transformed and helped "civilize" the Cherokee people. "Indians," Ridge wrote, "who have missionaries among them, and who live on this side [of] the Mississippi, are coming up, with faster steps to civilization, than those who have been enticed to remove to the west."[6] The Cherokee people, he insisted, had set aside their ancient, primitive hunting ways and now amassed large farms, raising all manner of livestock, while women practiced the domestic arts of weaving and sewing. They were fast becoming "civilized."

———

Despite the dawn-to-dusk regimen of study and agricultural work—aimed at ingraining "habits of industry" in the Native American students—the boys had time to mix with the local folks in Cornwall. The school's principal, in fact, believed that the careful intermingling of the town's white women in particular with "the society of heathen" would only serve to further expose the Indian students to the values of a "civilized" people. As the principal noted, "The situation and character of females in Christian society, is one important point of distinction between that and the society of heathen."[7] Cornwall soon presented the spectacle of mostly Native American mission students and local girls riding horses and taking walks together all over town, "arm in arm, by night and by day," attending tea parties, conducting themselves like ordinary young people engaged in courtship.[8]

Boudinot and Ridge made good use of this multicultural intermingling: each soon struck up a relationship with a local Cornwall girl. Elias joined the First Congregational Church in Cornwall and there met Harriett Gold, the beautiful granddaughter of Hezekiah Gold, a Congregationalist minister with two Yale-educated uncles and two sisters married to prominent clergymen. They rather quickly fell for each other, but Boudinot became ill in 1822 and had to return home. If the Cornwall authorities hoped his departure from Cornwall would end the affair with Harriett, they were soon disappointed: their relationship, conducted strictly through epistolary means for two years between Cherokee country and Cornwall, only deepened the romance.[9]

Meanwhile, John Ridge suffered from a medical condition that turned into an opportunity for romance. Ridge's chronic scrofulous hip condition (he had been frail since infancy with a painful, tubercular infection of the skin and joints) was exacerbated by the cold and snow of New England. Despite the best efforts of Dr. Samuel Gold, the Cornwall physician, Ridge's disease worsened and he missed a lot of classes. Eventually, Dr.

Gold removed him to a special room in the Commons to be nursed by Mrs. John Northrup, wife of the steward who had joined the staff the year before. In spring of 1821, Ridge, now eighteen, was too ill to go home to recuperate, which prompted an emergency visit from his father, Major Ridge, who rode up to Cornwall in September. While tending to his son, Major Ridge, according to a Cornwall historian, impressed everybody with his resplendent coach-and-four and his remarkable, dignified appearance: "a large, tall man in white top boots" with a "coat trimmed with gold [braid]." Few Cornwall folks had ever seen such an impressive Indian chief, whose "tall and athletic form and noble bearing" made him "one of the princes of the forest."[10]

While recovering under Mrs. Northrup's care, John became enamored with the Northrups' sixteen-year-old daughter, Sarah, renowned for her beauty, who sometimes helped tend to Ridge in his sickroom. Her presence inspired John to rally, but even still, his doctor noted, John seemed deeply preoccupied. When finally Mrs. Northrup inquired what troubled him, he confided that he was in love with her daughter. Flustered, she left the room and asked Sarah when she came home from school if she loved John Ridge. Her answer was yes. The Northrups were dismayed at this news despite Ridge's graceful bearing and gentlemanly conduct.[11] But the Northrups spirited Sarah away to her grandparents in New Haven in hopes that she might forget Ridge and meet other boys. Exiled in New Haven, Sarah failed to meet anyone else and proceeded to lose weight and become ill. Within three months she returned to Cornwall.

Undaunted by the looming interracial furor, Ridge wrote home for permission to marry Sarah Northrup. His mother, Susanna, showed John's letter to a family friend, the missionary Reverend Daniel Butrick, who advised, "A white woman would be apt to feel above the common Cherokees, and that . . . her son would promise more usefulness to his people, were he connected with them in marriage." All of which made good sense to Susanna and Major Ridge, who all along wanted John to marry the daughter of some Indian chief—not a young white girl in Connecticut. So Susanna refused to consent. But Ridge would not be denied: he responded with an even more determined appeal, describing his love for Sarah. Sensing a lost cause, his mother relented.[12]

Armed with parental consent, Ridge pressed Sarah to marry him—and did so out of a strong sense of pride from being Cherokee, not one of racial inferiority. But now the Northrups were no longer so preoccupied with Ridge's Indian status; it was his physical disability that concerned them. So in 1822 Mrs. Northrup told Ridge he needed to go home and regain his health in the milder southern climate of Cherokee country. If he could return to Cornwall without crutches, Northrup promised, he could marry Sarah. At the time, Ridge was so "lame" that he could safely return to the Cherokee Nation only by boat. So after a sad parting with Sarah and with his commitment to get well, he boarded a schooner for Charleston, where he made a fundraising speech for missionary work and collected books for Cherokee students before heading back to Indian country.

In his address to the Charleston church audience, Ridge gave voice to the virtue and necessity of Indian advancement. "Will anyone believe," he asked the crowd, "that an Indian with his bow and quiver, who walks solitary in the mountains, exposed to cold and hunger, or the attacks of wild beasts, trembling at every unusual object, his fancy filled with agitating fears . . . actually possesses undisturbed contentment superior to a learned gentleman of this commercial city, who has every possible comfort at

Sarah Bird Northrup, wife of John Ridge
Courtesy of Oklahoma Historical Society

home?" Ridge, like Boudinot, stood as a perfect embodiment of all the uplift, piety, and self-improvement that the white civilization program had so longed to inculcate in Native Americans. Not surprisingly, when both Ridge and Boudinot returned to the Cherokee Nation by December 1822, they were treated like returning heroes. Each was viewed as a prominent figure in the Nation and much admired, especially by mixed-bloods.[13]

Ridge's focus, though, remained on healing and continuing his pursuit of Sarah. After a year convalescing at home, Ridge regained his health sufficiently to return to Cornwall and seek Sarah's hand. He still walked with a limp but was able to throw away the crutches. When he got back to Cornwall in December 1823, the locals erupted in anger, once they learned why. News about the romance, one friend of the couple reported, "spread like wildfire—the papers proclaimed it an outrage, and preachers denounced it in the pulpit—that an *Indian* should go into a civilized community of New England and marry and carry away one of the finest daughters of the land."[14]

Undaunted, Sarah and John were married in the Northrup home, January 27, 1824, with Reverend Walter Smith, pastor of the Second Congregational Church, presiding. After the ceremony, hostile mobs pursued Ridge, and the couple left Cornwall right away, along with the Northrups, out of fear for their safety. Angry crowds greeted them at every stop along the way, denouncing Ridge for stealing a white girl as his wife. At one stage station, Ridge's buried rage over the racist criticism to which he was subjected boiled over. When confronted with one crowd's angry, racially charged epithets, he denounced them all with an admission that he had trespassed in white country "and plucked one of its finest flowers." But in no way was he "her inferior in any respect."[15] They moved to New Echota, where they lived at first with Ridge's parents.

Even before the incident in Cornwall, Ridge had realized that racism was "the ruling passion of the age." In a published essay that was clearly stoked by the fury of bitter personal experience, he argued that "an Indian is almost considered accursed. He is frowned upon by the meanest peasant, and the scum of the earth are considered sacred in comparison to the son of nature." And he honed in on the hypocrisy in white culture that insisted, on the one hand, that Indians must become educated, but at heart found them irremediably inferior. "If an Indian is educated in the sciences," Ridge claimed, "has a good knowledge of the classics, astronomy, mathematics, moral and natural philosophy, and his conduct [is] equally modest and polite, yet he is an Indian, and the most stupid and illiterate white man will disdain and triumph over this worthy individual. It is disgusting to enter the house of a white man and be stared full in the face with inquisitive ignorance. I find that such prejudices are more prevalent among the ignorant than among the enlightened."[16]

He soon found that, whether enlightened or ignorant, the people of Cornwall, upon discovering the Northrup-Ridge marriage, fairly exploded with anger. Isaiah Bunce, editor of the *American Eagle* in neighboring Litchfield, published stinging, racist critiques of the union. In an editorial printed shortly after the news came out in January, Bunce argued that "to have her thus marry an Indian and taken into the wilderness among savages, must indeed be a heart rending pan[g] which none can realize except those called to feel it." Sarah Northrup, Bunce asserted, "has thus made herself a *squaw*, and connected her ancestors to a race of Indians."[17] The obvious culprit in this tragic union—that is, besides the misguided lovers—was the Cornwall school itself. In Bunce's no-holds-barred indictment: "The relatives of the girl, or the people of Cornwall, or the public at large, who feel indignant at the transaction, some of whom have said that the girl ought to be publicly whipped, the Indian hung, and the mother drown'd, will do well to trace the thing to its true cause, and see whether the men above named, or their system, are not the authors of the transaction as a new kind of *missionary machinery*." And to Bunce it was the school's missionaries themselves who presided over such an "unnatural connection." Racial intermarriages, Bunce insisted, were the "fruit of the missionary spirit, and caused by the conduct of the clergymen at that place and its vicinity." The school's agents were clearly "mediately or immediately the cause of the unnatural connection." To offended locals like Bunce, the victims of this sad business were the young white men of Cornwall. After all, he insisted, they had to witness Indians being viewed as if they were "the most favored gallants, and beaux, and the top-knot of gentry; while the young men of the town, poor white boys, were often cast into the shade by their colored and tawny rivals."[18]

Bunce's vitriolic reaction to the Ridge-Northrup marriage prompted other offended parties to issue their own angry responses. The young men of Cornwall, for one: the "Bachelors of Cornwall Valley" responded to Bunce's claim "that we have been cast into the shade, by our rivals, white or tawny." And Timothy Stone, local Congregationalist minister and agent of the Cornwall school, disputed the "malicious report" coming out in a number of newspapers that blamed the school, arguing that it "should be wholly exempted from blame. Also the people of this village," Stone insisted, "are to be entirely exonerated. Not a solitary instance is known of a female of Cornwall, who has been seen walking with a foreign scholar ('arm in arm') as it has been reported." Even Harriett Gold's father, Benjamin Gold, publicly denied Bunce's accusations, calling them a "*base fabrication.*"[19]

What could not be denied was that the young daughter of a prominent white Cornwall family had married a Cherokee man—and the very idea of a white woman marrying an Indian man conjured up some very troubling issues. White women in this era, after all, were generally viewed as pure and virtuous, often put on pedestals by white men. For a white woman to form a romantic union with an Indian man, universally seen as racially inferior, subverted every cultural expectation of the day. As a Cornwall woman suggested in her poem "The Indian Song, Sarah and John," published shortly after the controversial marriage, Sarah, once she began living among the Cherokees, would quickly realize that becoming an Indian's wife would "sink her pride—'twould raise her shame' when she realized her destiny would be to follow him on the hunt, carrying his game, while wearing a 'dirty blanket' and surrounded by 'a savage whooping throng.'"[20]

———

Whereas the interracial marriage of John Ridge and Sarah Northrup upset the racial and social order in Cornwall, Elias Boudinot's simultaneous courtship of Harriett Gold soon provoked a volcanic uproar. Early in the fall of 1824, nineteen-year-old Harriett confided to her parents that she wanted to marry Elias Boudinot. Dumbfounded, Benjamin and Eleanor Gold fought to change Harriett's mind. But she insisted that she so wanted to become a missionary to the Cherokees that marrying a leading Cherokee man offered a perfect path. The Golds adamantly opposed the marriage and sent Boudinot a letter saying so. Once again, though, illness conspired with love to force a dramatic change: Harriett became very sick that fall—so much so that her parents thought she might not survive. Eventually, then, they gave in to her marriage plans, believing they were "fighting against God" in opposing the marriage.[21]

Harriett's announcement in June 1825 of her engagement to Elias Boudinot—about one year after the Ridge-Northrup furor—prompted the school to issue an immediate condemnation of their relationship, labeling Harriett and Elias "criminal," their relationship "an insult to the known feelings of the christian community," and their upcoming marriage "as sporting with the sacred interests of this charitable institution." Jedediah Bunce again unleashed a torrent of editorial criticism against the young couple, focusing on how the engagement besmirched the respectability of the Gold family. Boston and Providence newspapers carried the story, one of them claiming: "It appears

Harriett Gold Boudinot
Courtesy of Oklahoma Historical Society

that the *orthodox fair ones*, at Cornwall, have an overweening attachment to the *Indian dandies*, educated at that Mission School. Their love-smitten hearts are probably overcome by the *celestial charms*, which their *spiritual eyes* discover in those tawny sons of the forest; and in a *divine hallucination*, they calculate on pure, unearthly joys, in the *sanctified objects* of their choice."[22]

A few days later, the anger and bigotry struck much closer to home, especially for Harriett. It had become unsafe for her to stay at home, and so she hid out in a neighbor's house. Her brother Stephen was deeply offended, confiding to family members on June 11, 1825, that "the dye is cast, Harriet is gone, we have reason to <u>fear</u> . . . she was engaged to that Indian E. and that she is determined to marry him. O!! dear !!! . . . Words cannot, no, let imagination <u>only express</u>, the feelings of my heart." Harriett tried hard to remain the steady young Christian woman (she had just turned twenty) amid the barrage of criticism from family and friends: "I still have the consolation of feeling that I have not acted contrary to duty & that what I have done as respects forming a connexion is not adverse to divine approbation. I know that I appear at present to stand alone, the publick, 'good people & bad,' are against me."[23] Many in Cornwall developed a conspiracy theory that Mrs. Northrup had secretly encouraged not only her daughter Sarah's marriage to the wealthy John Ridge but also the engagement of Harriett and Elias. This was an accusation that both Harriett and Sarah found cruel and unjust.

And then came even greater humiliation: on the evening of June 29, 1825, the church bell ominously began to toll—as if to signal a death. Then, according to Harriett, two men along with Harriett's own brother Stephen carried out enormous painted effigies of her and Elias Boudinot, "set fire to the barrel of Tar or rather the funeral pile—the flames rose high, & the smoke ascended—some said it reminded them of the smoke of their torment which they feared would ascend forever." Harriett, as it happened, was hiding out at the time in a neighbor's house for fear of community reprisals. From there she was forced to witness the whole spectacle. When Harriett tried to join the singing at church, she was told by her fellow choir members to leave so as not to "disgrace the rest of the girls." Reverend Timothy Stone's wife suggested that Harriett's fellow singers dress in white but wear black crepe on one arm. And Reverend Stone canceled communion. In reflecting on her brother Stephen's effigy-burning dramatics, Harriett insisted that while he may have sought to distance himself from his sister's controversial marriage, he had in fact brought "a real scandal upon himself." As Harriett noted sorrowfully, "Even among the most unprincipled

say, they never heard of anything so low even among the heathen as that of burning a Sister in effigy."[24] But Stephen pushed
Harriett's scandalous union even lower: he threatened Elias
with his life.

Some of Boudinot's missionary friends were outraged at the
hypocrisy and resentment of their New England brethren
against Boudinot. Reverend Daniel Butrick wrote an impas-
sioned letter to Jeremiah Evarts in March 1826.

> We understand that it is now stated in letters from the North,
> that if our dear br. Boudinot should appear in Cornwall, half
> the state would rise against him; and that his life would be in
> danger. Half the State Rise against him? That polished, that
> pious, that holy state? That state which gave birth, almost,
> to disinterested affection? . . . against the son of their own
> bowels? . . . whose learning, wisdom, virtue, & honour, deserv-
> edly place him in the first circle of civilized life? Half the state
> rise against our dear brother Boudinot? Even the heathen
> world blushes, and humanity sickens at the thought.[25]

How did Boudinot himself respond to the furor? Letters from
Boudinot for this period have not survived, so we can only imagine how he endured the humiliating controversy from Cherokee
country, where he was convalescing. We do know that he and
other Cherokees were sent lurid newspaper stories of the effigy
burning on the Cornwall green, complete with letters with pictures of a gallows.[26] David Brown, a Cherokee who had attended
Cornwall, proclaimed the whole episode "an expression of abhor-
rence to the Indian character" and wondered "whether our
friends in New England have always acted from love to us &

desire to do us good. If they loved us how could they treat us in this manner? They can not suppose it wicked for white people to marry Cherokees, because members of Baptists, Methodist & Presbeterian churches have married Cherokee ladies without censure. If white men may marry among us without offence, how can it be thought wicked for us to marry among them; especially if some of our white sisters are pleased with such con-nexions." Brown could only imagine that the answers to such questions about interracial marriages conjured up fears among "our beloved friends in Connecticut" of casting "an indelible stain on their characters & be a reproach to their state. . . . If our dear friends in New England loved us how could they treat us in this cold & unfeeling manner, especially at such a time as this when more than ever we need their prayers & increased exertions?"[27]

Although Boudinot's thoughts about the controversy in Cornwall are not recoverable, his missionary friends offer ample evidence that during the winter of 1825–26 he was a troubled soul. Daniel Butrick confided to Jeremiah Evarts on Christmas Day in 1825 that Boudinot, in an apparent moral lapse from his avowed Christian values, had broken the Sabbath to attend a ball play where nearly naked men performed in front of a largely female crowd.[28] Butrick tried to explain Boudinot's conduct as a desperate attempt to distract himself from "the shameless conduct of the citizens of Cornwall, & the cruel treatment he had received from those who would claim to be his spiritual fathers. . . . The smoke of his burning effigy, driven by the fierc-est northern blast, had, for a moment, darkened his eyes, & occasioned this fall from which he would arise as soon as he had time for deliberate reflection." After speaking with Boudi-not about the ball play incident, Jeremiah Evarts observed that

Boudinot "was very wretched, & did not care what became of him. It was just after he had heard of Cornwall himself, & had received anonymous letters, filled with the most [illegible] abuse, and threatening his life." Still a youthful twenty-year-old, Boudinot insisted his attendance at ball play was neither a "fall" nor a "temptation."[29]

We can only imagine the emotions racing through Boudinot as he contemplated his next step with Harriett. Having just witnessed the vitriolic uproar prompted by the marriage of John and Sarah, Elias could not have believed that if he and Harriett were to be married they would encounter anything less tumultuous. The attempt to shame them for their "unnatural" relationship doubtless sparked in Boudinot an unsettling combination of painful humiliation and fierce anger. Knowing that his marriage to Harriett would prompt widespread revulsion and repudiation in the community, how was he to maintain any sense of integrity and dignity? A young man who had come to see himself as a proud and gifted Cherokee rather than a "savage" Indian struggling to look "civilized," Boudinot believed that in Harriett, a lovely, educated white woman, he had found an equal, not a superior. He, like his people, was fully worthy of such an intimate connection with a white, Boudinot insisted, and having come this far, he was not about to withdraw as a defeated, lesser man.

Despite these conflicted feelings, Boudinot determined to go forward with Harriett. And so he returned to Cornwall early in the spring of 1826. He was forced to stop, though, during the last part of the trip to assume a disguise in case a lynching party awaited him.[30] While Boudinot's conduct was never actually treated as criminal, the controversy prompted revealing testimony about what was proper—and what was not—between whites and

Native Americans in this era. Two of Harriett's brothers-in-law, General Daniel Brinsmade and Reverend Cornelius Everest, offered up openly racist responses to the marriage. Brinsmade fairly bristled at the union, claiming that Harriett sought only to "gratify . . . the animal feeling of one—of its members" in the matter. "Shame on such love," Everest exclaimed, calling it "unnatural" for ignoring appropriate racial boundaries.[31] As for those more liberal missionaries and family members who saw "no evil results from Indian marriages . . . we don't see and feel how good and how pleasant a thing it is to be kissd by an Indian—to have black young ones & a train of evils."[32] To further underscore their moral certainty in the matter, both Brinsmade and Everest insisted that the entire community upheld such condemnation of interracial unions. Everest was careful to note that he and his family were not alone in their feelings. A full 95 percent of New England, he argued, saw the matter just as he did.[33] Brinsmade was equally confident: "The good people in this place do oppose such connections and all who have expressd an opinion favorable to them would revolt in a moment if it was brought home to their own firesides."[34] And, as Brinsmade concluded one handwringing letter, "so we go—White & black," a revealing reference to the commonly held assumption that, at bottom, Indians were no different, and no better, than blacks.[35]

Sympathetic observers read Harriett's decision to marry an Indian as a misguided and overzealous commitment to missionary outreach. "I know you have long had a desire to become a missionary helper in the cause of Christ among the heathen," her brother Herman Vaill noted. "But there is a wide difference between going among the heathen, by the call, & the leadings of Providence; & going among them merely because we will go. There is a wide difference between going, because we love the cause of Christ, & have a single eye to his glory; &, going because we love <u>another object</u>." And the Boudinot-Gold romance prompted another round of criticism that the school had betrayed its Christian, civilizing goals. Indeed, many believed that "the Indian Marriage" would not only weaken the missionary spirit but also reduce contributions to the school, ultimately sinking it. As Herman sadly noted, "And even now go where you will, the best friends of the cause, will quote the Indian Marriage, as evidence that <u>some thing</u> relative to the former management of that school, <u>must have been wrong</u>; or the marriage would not have taken place."[36]

Those who chastised the young couple, and especially Harriett, for such a flagrant disregard for racial lines usually cloaked their racially charged sentiments under the rhetoric of religious purity. Ever wary of being seen as a racist, Herman insisted that "sister H. should marry the man of her choice, be he white, or black, or even <u>red</u>, if that is the colour she prefers." But such a choice must be made "without endangering the interests of the Great Cause which she ought to love" and "as a professed Xtian, she is under obligations to maintain."[37] What truly troubled Harriett's closest critics, presumably, was that in marrying an Indian she was in fact harming her own Christian character.[38] Herman insisted that he knew Harriett had long made a commitment to marrying Boudinot. More than two years prior to the wedding, Herman contended, she had confided in her friend that her mind had been made up to marry Boudinot, even before "<u>the other marriage took place</u>." Once her circle of Christian friends declared that such an intermarriage would not harm the school, nothing was going to stop Harriett.[39]

When it became clear that neither Harriett nor Elias would bend to the attacks from family and friends—that their marriage would go forward despite accusations that they prized their "animal feeling" over their Christian duty—some of the community's withering criticism evolved into sad acceptance. Bennett Roberts, a close friend of Harriett, told Herman it was time to make the best of the "unpleasant situation." Cornwall and their circle of family and friends, he noted, "have gone beyond the bounds of decency. They have used H[arriett] in such a manner that instead of influencing her to give up the subject she would feel it a great relief to find shelter from their unnatural society, even among the <u>wild</u> men of the wood."[40] And by the early fall even brother Stephen Gold began to make peace with the inevitable. Despite feeling "strenuously opposed to Indian connections," Stephen gave up the fight against the marriage and was back to singing with Harriett in church. As for what he would do when Boudinot returned to Cornwall for the wedding, Stephen claimed he would steer clear of Boudinot and intended no violence toward him.[41] Harriett's sister Catherine grasped the essence of the matter better than anyone. In a terse defense of Harriett and Elias, she saw the inevitable and accepted it: "Strange that she can love an Indian but it is so. And she will get him if she can."[42]

Elias and Harriett took their vows on March 28, 1826, at a private ceremony at the Gold house with the new minister from Goshen presiding. Most family members had made their peace with the marriage. Stephen still couldn't bring himself to attend the wedding; he worked in the sawmill all afternoon to avoid the service.

Shortly after the wedding, Harriett joined Elias on a tour of speeches in cities such as New York, Philadelphia, Boston, and Charleston, where he raised funds for setting up a Cherokee newspaper. Meanwhile, the school at Cornwall closed that fall, mainly because the community support had evaporated over the controversy of the two high-profile interracial unions.[43] Rarely had marriages produced such powerful and opposing legacies: one dream—the missionary hopes at Cornwall—was extinguished, while another—Boudinot's and Ridge's determination to give Cherokees their own voice—caught fire.

———

John and Sarah's return to Indian country didn't end the bitter resentment over their union from the locals in Cornwall. Early in the marriage, vicious rumors followed them to the Cherokee Nation claiming that John abused his wife and pursued affairs with Indian "squaws" he allegedly brought into the home they were sharing with Major Ridge. According to these stories, Sarah became depressed and considered suicide—one rumor circulated that she had killed herself by jumping into the Oostanaula River. Missionary friends of the Ridges were quick to rebut these claims as little more than bogus, mean-spirited rumors. Jeremiah Evarts visited the Ridges, noting, "As to the inquiry whether young Mrs. Ridge is contented and happy, it is certain she often says she is; and surely she ought to know."[44] In a letter to the Northrups, Daniel Butrick likewise denounced the rumors while emphasizing the superior moral and living conditions that surrounded John and Sarah among the Cherokees. "Little did any of us think," Butrick observed, "that by this marriage [John Ridge] would expose himself to the hatred and slander of thousands who bear the Christian name, in a Christian land." Butrick pointed to the genteel household of Major Ridge the newlyweds were sharing. Major Ridge, after all, was "a gentleman" and John's mother, "a pious devoted Christian." "They live," Butrick insisted, "not like *common* white people in the southern country,

OUTRAGE IN CORNWALL 63

but rank among the first." And, Butrick told the Northrups, "your daughter dresses richer, and appears more like a lady, than when at Cornwall . . . she has universally appeared cheerful and contented, whenever I have seen her at their house."[45]

The Boudinot-Gold marriage was conceived in conviction and carried out with fierce independence. Although Harriett faced a barrage of resentment and criticism from family, friends, and the Cornwall community, her decision to marry Elias represented a major break from everything she knew and loved. Shortly after arriving with Elias in Cherokee country, Harriett acknowledged to her father that she missed her dear sisters, but there was no chance she would return to his family circle again. Confident and serene that Elias was the husband of her choice, Harriett could simply never go back, "unless providence made it as plainly" her duty "as it did to leave."[46]

Harriett firmly believed her marriage was genuinely rooted in love and thus posed none of the cultural or personal problems that so many of her family and friends imagined. In fact, she contended, Elias was nothing short of an ideal husband. Soon after getting married, Harriett told her mother, "He is all that I could wish him to be." She even went so far as to suggest that Boudinot was a better husband than any of the men her sisters had married. "My sisters need not think it is saying anything against their husbands to say I have excelled them all. I know they are all good <u>positively</u>, but mine <u>superlatively</u>."[47] Even six years after the wedding, Harriett remained convinced of her righteous choice. "I remember the trials I had to encounter," she told her parents in 1832, "the thorny path I had to tread, the bitter cup I had to drink—but a consciousness of <u>doing right— a kind affectionate devoted</u> Husband" made all the difference.

And in the wake of all the controversy and humiliation she confronted, "if any tears have been shed for me on that account," she wrote, "I can now pronounce them <u>useless tears.</u>"[48]

Initially, as a wife and mother in the Cherokee Nation, Harriett served as a model, "civilized" white woman displaying an abundance of domestic skills. She hosted quilting bees, sewed bonnets for Cherokee women, and taught Elias's sisters and missionary students housework. She supervised a household that included members of Boudinot's extended family, students attending missionary schools, and frequently as many as ten to fifteen political visitors to wait on.[49] She saw herself as a genuine part of the Christian missionary outreach among "heathens." As she told her parents early on, "I cannot but rejoice in prospect of spending my days among those despised people & as the time draws nearer I long to begin my work." Her entire focus, she claimed, rested on bringing "the greatest usefulness" to her adopted Cherokee people.[50] Despite all the labor-intensive domesticity, Harriett proclaimed herself quite happy: "I can truly say I am contented & never passed my days more pleasantly than while I have been in this Nation."[51]

After she lived for a few years among the Cherokees, Harriett's disciplined focus on Christian duty and benevolence lost some of its religious fervor and took on a clearly discernible political edge. "I am astonished at the apathy which prevails in the States in regard to the Cherokees," she wrote in 1831. Even their champions—missionaries and sympathetic politicians—had grown too passive while the Cherokee people suffered "beneath the oppressor's rod." "How are the American people," she charged, "ever to atone for the injuries done the original inhabitants of this Country?"[52]

The marriage and immersion in Cherokee country served only to deepen Harriett's self-identity as a Cherokee: "My Cherokee Father often reminds me of my own Father," she wrote her brother and sister, "by his cheerfulness & I think is remarkable for his amiable, kind, & affectionate disposition. . . . They must love me a <u>great deal</u> & both he & My Dear Cherokee Mother frequently say that I am like an own child to them."[53] Despite the very different environment among the Cherokees, Harriett felt totally accepted. "The country here differs much from Conn. Appears to me as I expected a new country would. Nothing appears strange, but as though I had always lived here." She ended several of her letters, "Your Cherokee Sister." And Harriett's convictions about the appropriateness and contentedness of living in the Cherokee Nation grew stronger over the years. She told her parents in November 1827: "I am much attached to this neighborhood. Almost all the people here are our relations. . . . I should like to visit you but is not likely we shall in several years if ever—am more attached to this than my native home. The place of my birth is dear to me but I do love this people & with them I wish to <u>live</u> and <u>die</u>. . . . Pray for the Cherokees that they may all be brought to the truth."[54]

For Boudinot, the marital uproar in Cornwall and his subsequent life with Harriett unleashed a host of more complicated emotions, ranging from buried anger and humiliation to overt outrage. For one thing, he clearly viewed the Cornwall incident as an opportunity to begin distancing himself from missionaries who had come to dominate much of his life. Samuel Worcester noted, "[Boudinot] will visit Cornwall and, I presume, does not intend to leave it without a wife."[55] Boudinot also fired off a letter to Reverend Timothy Stone—who, along with his wife, had humiliated Harriett in her own church—that "disclaimed any authority of the agents [of the Foreign Mission School] . . . insisted on a public recantation of the letter of the agents so far as it inculpated him, or that they should prove his conduct was criminal."[56]

Boudinot's marriage to Harriett may also have showcased his own conflicted self-identity as a Cherokee. After all, marrying the daughter of such a prominent white, northern Christian family offered Boudinot an exceptionally compelling opportunity to demonstrate his bonafides as a totally assimilated American. Indeed, Harriett's brother-in-law Herman Vaill gave voice to this speculation in a letter to Harriett just after learning of the engagement, arguing that "to become thus useful . . . & faithful to Christ, it is not necessary that he should marry a white woman."[57] Thus both Elias and Harriett may have been unconsciously bent on "proving" something with the marriage: for Harriett, the union with such a well-connected Cherokee offered a perfect way to become an even more effective missionary in Indian country; for Elias, marriage to a prominent white New England woman removed all doubt that he was anything but a worthy, fully "civilized" man.

If such a psychological strategy motivated Boudinot in his pursuit of Harriett, the marriage itself produced wildly different, and even more profound, results. Far from deepening his commitment to becoming a "civilized" Indian, the controversy in Cornwall in fact began to disillusion Boudinot about assimilation with white culture. Marrying Harriett Gold proved to be a life-changing moment for Boudinot: it is possible from this moment forward to see a new racial consciousness at work in him, one in which he began to imagine Cherokees developing their own separate, civilized institutions *apart* from white society. Boudinot's intensely personal and humiliating encounter with white racism at Cornwall made a mockery of the idea that the two cultures could peacefully and equitably commingle. And the very heart of what the school at Cornwall stood for—that education and Christianity would foster equality between Indians and whites—now rang hollow.[58] A few years earlier, in 1822, John Ridge had once pridefully noted in a letter to President Monroe, "My father and mother are both ignorant of the English language but it is astonishing to see them exert all their power to have their children educated, *like the whites!*"[59]

But the promise of Cornwall and the hopes of Boudinot and Ridge, like the effigies of John and Sarah on the town square, had now gone up in flames.

3

Removal

When newlyweds John and Sarah Ridge left Cornwall in 1824 and Elias and Harriett Boudinot followed them in 1826, they returned to a Cherokee Nation that had clearly made great strides forward and yet was also heading down an increasingly troubling path. No tribe had achieved as much of what the civilization program had called for as the Cherokees. Indeed, much of Cherokee country could also have passed for prosperous white southern plantation culture. By the mid-1820s the Cherokees, like the planters who surrounded them, raised abundant crops of cotton with black slaves, tended herds of cattle and horses, flocks of sheep, goats, and pigs, and not only traded profitably with the adjoining states but also exported cotton and woolen goods to New Orleans. The Cherokee population had more than doubled from around seven thousand in 1809 to nearly fifteen thousand in 1825. In addition, approximately five thousand Cherokees, anticipating an unhappy outcome with land-hungry whites in the East, had moved to the Arkan-

sas Territory by 1825. Public roads began to crisscross Cherokee country; schools and ferries dotted the landscape. Virtually
every family had a plow and spinning wheel, and one in four
owned a loom and a wagon. Which prompted the American
Board of Commissioners for Foreign Missions in 1820 to conclude: "The Cherokees are rapidly adopting the laws and manners of the whites. They appear to advance in civilization just
in proportion to their knowledge of the gospel."[1]

Amid these promising signs of economic and educational
progress—or perhaps in some cases *because* of them—massive
obstacles to the tribe's future loomed everywhere. White settlers
from northern Georgia who surrounded the Cherokee Nation
had for years made intrusions onto their land. Both the Creeks
and Cherokees in Georgia and Alabama faced continual encroachment on their territories from neighboring whites. Indian agents
and military officers made sincere efforts to enforce treaty laws
against the "licentiousness of daring and unprincipled men," but
land-hungry whites, even when removed, simply returned in full
force, placing increasing pressure on Indian country. Return J.
Meigs, a federal Cherokee agent, shrewdly assessed the difficult
situation as early as 1809.

> These intruders are always well armed, some of them shrewd &
> of desperate character, have nothing to lose & hold barbarous
> sentiments towards Indians. They see extensive tracts of for-
> rest exceedingly disproportioned to the present or expect pop-
> ulation of the tribes who hold them. They take hold of these
> lands, some of them in hopes the land will be purchased,
> when they will plead a right of preemption, making a merit of
> their crimes. With these people remonstrance has no effect,
> nothing but force can prevent their violation of Indian rights.[2]

The federal government genuinely wanted to prevent lawless encroachment on Indian lands, especially as a means of maintaining order in the region. But given the steady stream of whites angling for Cherokee lands and the limited military resources on the frontier, there was little the government could do.

At first, John and Sarah Ridge's return to Cherokee country in 1824 allowed them a measure of safety from this turmoil. They settled into the comfort and status of his father's home. The Ridges took up residence in an apartment in Major Ridge's elegant mansion, which John immediately began to fashion according to his own genteel sensibilities. Drawing on his New England knowledge, John helped design an addition to the mansion—Grecian-style columns supporting front and back porches. In the front Ridge had workers build an arched triple window that overlooked the river and ferry. Highly educated and committed to the same "civilizing" progress for the Cherokee people that his father for years had been championing, John quickly set himself up as a gentleman lawyer, one of the first in the Cherokee Nation, working in a partnership with Alexander McCoy—another mixed-blood descendant of a Scottish trader.[3]

An ambitious and prosperous lawyer, Ridge soon required more privacy and his own elegant home. John and Sarah moved out of Major Ridge's mansion and into a smaller version six miles away—a two-story home with large rooms, set on a high hill among the oak and hickory trees. Called Tanta-ta-rara, or Running Waters, John Ridge's estate included over four hundred acres and eighteen slaves his father gave him.[4]

His father's imprint lay everywhere in John's rising stature among his people. As one of the Cherokees' leading young men with uniquely expert language skills made possible by Major

Ridge's educational commitment to his children, John became a valuable negotiator for the nearby Creek Nation. Soon after John returned to Indian country, Major Ridge arranged for John and his friend David Vann to help the Creeks renegotiate a fraudulent treaty with the federal government. The Creeks, like the Cherokees, faced similar problems: intrusions from white squatters in Georgia along with state and federal pressure to remove. With no young men who possessed John and David's English-speaking and -writing skills, the Creeks were eager to hire such talented young Cherokees. Major Ridge was to receive $10,000 for hiring the young men; John and David were to be paid $15,000 each for their efforts. When they left for Washington in November 1825, their dual identities as exotic Indians and sophisticated leaders familiar with white culture were thrown into sharp relief: as the two young men, along with thirteen Creek chiefs, passed through the Georgia capital of Milledgeville, they arrived decked out in full Indian regalia. But to avoid anticipated conflict with resentful Georgians, they quickly changed into white men's clothes and avoided all contact with locals. When they arrived in Washington they took up quarters in the Indian Queen Hotel. While dealing with federal agents on behalf of the Creeks, Ridge had his portrait painted in Washington by the noted artist Charles Bird King (who had studied under the legendary portraitist Benjamin West in London). King's portrait of John Ridge captured a sensitive, intelligent young man who could have passed for a white man with a slightly dark complexion, dressed in a trim coat and vest of the latest fashion.[5]

It was Ridge's political savvy and skillful diplomacy that helped him find a respectable middle ground between a Creek faction that had swindled the tribe in a previous treaty and federal agents who were trying to exploit the Creeks. John and David's delegation proposed a unique, nonviolent position on the treaty with the federal government, which called for the Creeks to give up all their Georgia lands east of the Chatta-hoochee River in return for $217,600 and a perpetual annuity of $20,000. The government would also fund the removal westward of those evicted by the land cession. For their efforts, Major Ridge was paid his full amount, but John and David received only $5,000 each—one third what had been promised them. While federal officials charged that Ridge and Vann were "meddling" in Creek politics, the two young Cherokees nimbly negotiated a treaty on more successful terms for the Creeks than anyone would have imagined. But it signaled the removal of a neighboring southeastern tribe that could only have sent a chilling message of what lay ahead for the Cherokees in their struggle to remain on their tribal land.[6]

Earlier in the same year that his son was advising the Creeks, Major Ridge met with Andrew Jackson, an old acquaintance with whom Ridge had long maintained warm relations. Ridge had bravely fought for Jackson in the Creek War in 1814, prompting General Jackson to promote Ridge to the rank of major—he proudly kept the name Major the rest of his life. Although a quarrelsome and bitter Indian hater, Jackson displayed grudging respect for Ridge. And when they met in 1825, Major Ridge's greeting to Jackson (later translated and written down) conjured up the hope that two aging warriors would now set aside their differences in the interest of peace.

My heart is glad when I look upon you. Our heads have become white. They are blossomed with age. It is the course of nature. We ought to thank the Great Spirit who has taken care of our lives. When first we met we were taking the red path. We waded in blood until the murders of our women and children had ceased. In the land of our enemies we kindled our war fires. We sat by them until morning, when battle came with the yells of our enemies. We met them; they either fled or fell.

War is no more heard in our land. The mountains speak peace. Joy is in our valleys. The warrior is careless and smokes the pipe of peace. His arms lay idle; he points to them, and speaks to his children of his valiant deeds; his glory will not depart with him, but remain with his sons.[7]

If John Ridge's return to his people launched a promising political career closely linked to the unrivaled charisma and influence of his father, Major Ridge, Elias Boudinot's arrival back in Cherokee country in 1826 signaled the emergence of a powerful new voice in the Cherokee Nation. Although roundly disheartened by the uproar in Cornwall and now wary about the prospects of assimilation, Boudinot returned to the Cherokee Nation still fiercely committed to urging improvement in his people and to praising their successes to the broader world. Writing to the *Boston Recorder and Telegraph*, a Congregationalist magazine that spread news about religion, politics, education, agriculture, and temperance, Boudinot promoted subscriptions to the "Moral and Literary Society of the Cherokee Nation." Calling out to "the friends of Indian improvement," he urged readers to set aside the unfavorable public opinion about Indians, arguing that "it is nevertheless an acknowledged fact, that among the Cherokees, great and rapid improvement has been made, both in information and industry. Many who a short time since, bore the appellation of Savage, have bid a final adieu to the course and practices of their fathers." Boudinot's "Society" focused on moral improvement and education, insisting that "the Indians should become moral. For where is the nation that can exist without morality? And think ye a nation can be respected without knowledge?"[8]

In the spring of 1826 Boudinot took off on a lecture tour along the East Coast to make this case for Indian advancement, to raise funds for a national academy, and to establish a press and printing office. Drawing on Sequoyah's newly created syllabary, this new Cherokee newspaper would be printed in both English and Cherokee and would publish laws of the Cherokee Nation as well as spread news about its people's progress in education, religion, and the literary arts. Well publicized and attended, Boudinot's speeches in Charleston, Philadelphia, and Boston were aimed at encouraging prominent, wealthy whites to support Cherokee "civilization." A Boston newspaper pointed to Boudinot's education at Cornwall, which demonstrated "commendable progress in knowledge," and noted that in one week Boudinot had given speeches at Salem, two Boston churches, and by week's end would be in Philadelphia to give his "address to the Whites."[9]

Delivered in Philadelphia's First Presbyterian Church on May 26, 1826, Boudinot's address opened with the rhetorical question: "What is an Indian? Is he not formed of the same materials with yourself? For 'of one blood God created all the nations that dwell on the face of the earth.' Though it be true that he is ignorant, that he is a heathen, that he is a savage; yet he is not more than all the others have been under similar circumstances. Eighteen centuries ago what were the inhabitants of Great Britain?"[10]

If his listeners were unsure how to respond to such a question, Boudinot was ready with his own conviction: "You here behold an *Indian*, my kindred are *Indians*, and my fathers sleeping in the wilderness grave—they too were *Indians*. But I am not as my fathers were—broader means and nobler influences have fallen upon me." Given these "greater advantages than most of my race," Boudinot claimed he had earned the right to speak for his people and to press for fairness: "I now stand before you delegated by my native country" to insist on the worth, respectability and equality of the Cherokee Nation.[11]

The Cherokee people, Boudinot argued, were no longer "sons of the forest" who aimlessly wandered the land hunting game. The deerskin trade was a thing of the past, not the future. "In fact," he said, "there is not a single family in the nation that can be said to subsist on the slender support which the wilderness would afford." In truth, the Cherokee people had for generations raised crops along with hunting, but Boudinot chose to dramatize that his people were setting aside the deerskin trade in favor of more "civilized" agricultural pursuits.[12]

Equally significant to Boudinot was the growing receptivity in the Cherokee Nation to Christianity. Despite a conversion rate of less than 10 percent to the Christian message, Cherokees, he insisted, had embraced much of the moral vision in the Christian faith. And the growing awareness of the Bible among his people, he believed, testified to an increasingly religious and literate people—both important signs of "civilization." "In no ignorant country," Boudinot observed, "have the missionaries undergone less trouble and difficulty, in spreading a knowledge of the Bible, than in this."[13]

While Boudinot no longer looked toward an assimilated future, he did envision an independent, sovereign Cherokee Nation that would take its place alongside the United States. After all, the Cherokees had begun refashioning their laws, abolishing uncivilized practices such as polygamy and putting aged persons to death for witchcraft. New laws called for protecting female chastity and honor; the Sabbath was to be respected by the council in session.[14]

And now the crowning achievement lay in the effort to establish "a paper published in Indian country." Because "to obtain a correct and complete knowledge of these people [Indians], there must exist a vehicle of Indian intelligence." Such a press, he argued, "would go further to remove ignorance, and her offspring superstition and prejudice, than all other means." Thanks to the remarkable simplicity of Sequoyah's syllabary and his people's thirst for knowledge, Boudinot boasted, a huge proportion of the nation's young people was learning to read and write. In his own neighborhood, Boudinot claimed, "I do not recollect a male Cherokee, between the ages of fifteen and twenty five, who is ignorant of this mode of writing." Establishing a newspaper that would publish religious and political events, laws, and customs and showcase the "true character" of an improving people would "have a powerful influence on the advancement of the Indians themselves."[15]

All of which pointed to this moment as a pivotal one for the Cherokees. On the one hand, the evidence suggested a powerful rising up of his people. "Methinks I can view my native country, rising from the ashes of her degradation. . . . I can behold her sons bursting the fetters of ignorance and unshackling her from the vices of heathenism." But if the Cherokees should fail at this juncture, "then all hopes are blasted, and falls the fabric of Indian civilization. Their fathers were born in darkness, and have fled in darkness; without your assistance so will their sons." With all the pressures from white intruders, Indian haters, and exploitive federal officials, Boudinot could see but two outcomes for Cherokees and other tribes: "they must either become civilized and happy, or sharing the fate of many kindred nations, become extinct."[16]

Boudinot climaxed his speech with a clarion call that boldly contrasted a benighted past with a civilized future: "The Indian must rise like the Phoenix, after having wallowed for ages in ignorance and barbarity." If the U.S. government withdraws its help and the American people their aid, the Cherokees "will go the way that so many tribes have gone before them. . . . They will vanish like a vapour from the face of the earth, their very history will be lost in forgetfulness and the places that now know them will know them no more."

"I ask you," he concluded, "shall red men live, or shall they be swept from the earth? With you and this public at large, the decision chiefly rests. Must they perish? Must they all, like the unfortunate Creeks, (victims of the unchristian policy of certain persons) go down in sorrow to their grave? They hang upon your mercy as to a garment. Will you push them from you, or will you save them? Let humanity answer."[17]

It was a remarkable spectacle: a twenty-two-year-old Cherokee giving an eloquent, moving speech to an audience of highly sophisticated, white Philadelphians. And it worked. Boudinot's tour raised enough money to buy a $1,500 press and generated excitement about the national academy as well, even though sufficient funds did not materialize until after removal.[18]

Upon returning home from his fund-raising tour, Boudinot went to work as a clerk for the National Council and did some

Samuel Worcester
Courtesy of Houghton Library, Harvard University

teaching at the Hightower Mission school. And he also became
acquainted with a missionary who would prove pivotal to him
and the Cherokee Nation: Samuel Austin Worcester. A minister
and expert linguist from Vermont, Worcester was fully committed to missionary work—at first hoping that the American Board
would send him to India. Instead, he was assigned to the Cherokees. A tall, wiry, dark-haired man of unwavering religious commitment, Worcester and his wife, Ann, moved to Cherokee
country in the fall of 1825. Once he and Boudinot met, they
began a remarkable friendship grounded in a shared Christian
faith and an evangelical desire to improve the Cherokee people.
They immediately went to work translating religious literature
into Cherokee—producing a Cherokee edition of the Gospel of
St. Matthew, a Cherokee hymnal, and a moral tract, *Poor Sarah,
or the Indian Woman*. Despite his tireless devotion to transla-
tion, Worcester remained apologetic about his inability to speak
Cherokee. But he sometimes drew on his good friends Boudinot

and John Ridge at the Brainerd Mission school to translate his sermons into Cherokee.[19]

Making friends with Worcester was a critical development for Boudinot, but what happened shortly after their initial contact offered him an ideal vehicle to further "civilize" his people and spread the word about their progress as a nation: in October 1827 the National Council named Boudinot as editor of the new national newspaper to be published in English and Cherokee. At first, there was a stumbling block: the council was going to pay a white printer more than the editor, and Boudinot would not accept such an offer. But Samuel Worcester stepped in—as he would repeatedly—and coaxed the American Board into supplementing the council's funds. Boudinot then accepted the editorship. He came up with the name *Cherokee Phoenix* for the paper, meaning that the Cherokee people would rise like the phoenix from the ashes of the past. When Worcester, who soon befriended Major and John Ridge, showed the new paper to Major Ridge, Worcester pointed to three words on the masthead: *I will arise.*[20]

Major Ridge could not have been more thrilled with Worcester and Boudinot's newspaper endeavor. His own dream had been to fashion New Echota into a cosmopolitan capital of the Cherokee Nation—and by 1827 it too was "arising." Composed of tiny clusters of stores and frame houses surrounding a council house and courthouse, it offered a visual version of white culture fusing with Indian country. It could have passed for many Georgia crossroads settlements, except that during sessions of the General Council it teemed with Indians. White New Englanders visiting New Echota thought it was a "hansom spot of ground" and were much impressed by the "order &

Front page, *Cherokee Phoenix*
Courtesy of the Carol Vinson Institute of Government, University of Georgia

decorum" when they attended the National Council and superior court session. There were "quite a number of learned pol-
ished & well Qualified Gentlemen fit to appear in any place in
Connecticut"[21]

It was to this new cosmopolitan "civilized" Cherokee capital
of New Echota that Boudinot and Worcester moved their families in December 1827 and set up shop for the *Phoenix*. Boudinot and Worcester put together a prospectus for the *Phoenix*,
which would be published biweekly. The newspaper would
include laws and public documents of the Cherokee Nation,
along with news about religious, educational, and literary matters of interest to the Cherokees. Boudinot planned to publish
two hundred copies of each issue to circulate in the Nation;
agents in various states would accept subscriptions from whites
for the *Phoenix*. Boudinot sent his brother-in-law Herman Vaill

in Connecticut a short prospectus for the newspaper in November, claiming, "We have nothing to recommend our paper, but its novelty & our good intentions." In Vaill, Boudinot knew he had "a well wisher to all the Indians," who would "obtain as many Subscribers" as he possibly could, if any were to be had "in Connecticut, the land of *intermarriages*."[22] By July 1828 he had thirty to forty subscribers in Mobile, Alabama, and nearly as many in Troy, New York, along with scattered subscribers throughout the United States. In short order, some hundred newspapers throughout the country were exchanging papers with Boudinot, which allowed him to freely use these papers for national and world news—and they in turn sometimes reprinted editorials from the *Phoenix*.

The *Cherokee Phoenix* was indeed an historic publishing venture: it was the first newspaper ever published by or for Indians

The *Cherokee Phoenix* office
Courtesy of Georgia Department of Natural Resources

and printed (at least in part) in an Indian language. The first issue, February 28, 1828, contained excerpts in English and Cherokee from the newly crafted Cherokee Constitution; the Lord's Prayer; an article by Worcester praising and explaining Sequoyah's syllabary; and an editorial by Boudinot. And Boudinot wasted no time using his editorial position to advertise the accomplishments of his people and to refute the arguments of their opponents. Declaring the Cherokees were friends with all those "who are engaged for the good of the Indians of every tribe, and who pray that salvation, peace, and the comforts of civilized life may be extended to every Indian fire side on this continent," Boudinot pledged that he and the *Phoenix* would take issue with Georgians and federal officials who seemed bent on "removing and concentrating the Indians," and pursuing policies that would "prove pernicious" to them. Recognizing that most whites still viewed all Indians, including Cherokees, as little more than "savages" with no real future in the American nation, Boudinot focused on Indians' capacity for improvement as justification for a hopeful future. There was abundant evidence, he claimed, "that Indians can be reclaimed from a savage state, and that with proper advantages, they are as capable of improvement in mind as any other people."[23] "It is not a visionary thing," he insisted, "to attempt to civilize and Christianize all the Indians, but highly practicable."[24]

But Boudinot's optimism, even as he declared it from the pages of the *Phoenix*, would soon become suspect.

———

In January of 1827 the Cherokee Nation lost some critical leadership: its aged chief Pathkiller died, followed two weeks later by Assistant Chief Charles Hicks. The losses could not have come at a worse time: the Cherokee people were becoming increasingly unsettled in the growing fear that the white Georgians on their borders would soon extract Cherokee land through sale or theft. Shaken by the sudden death of their leaders, the Cherokee people turned to Major Ridge, Speaker of the council, and John Ross, president of the National Committee (the Cherokee legislature). Normally, Major Ridge, as a celebrated warrior and statesman, would have become the next principal chief, but, now in his midfifties and unable to communicate in English, Ridge understood better than most that in this difficult, tumultuous time his people needed someone adept in dealing with the white man. They needed a younger man, well versed in reading and writing English, and experienced in white culture. At the moment, few men fit this description better than John Ross.[25]

A well-to-do man, even by the white man's standards, Ross had been educated by whites and looked like a white man. (He was only one-eighth Indian.) Thoroughly devoted to his people, the thirty-eight-year-old Ross (in 1828) was highly popular in the Cherokee Nation. He was a small man, only five foot six inches tall, with a florid complexion and intense dark brown eyes; his appearance conjured up more a prosperous white planter and businessman than an exotic Indian. The grandson of John McDonald, a Scots Tory agent among the Chickamaugas during the American Revolution, and the son of Daniel Ross, a Scot of loyalist background, John Ross grew up in an Anglo-Indian world populated by white tutors and private academies. At first, his Cherokee friends mocked his "civilized" demeanor. When he was a young boy, his father bought him a good suit of fashionable "white" clothing, but his school mates ridiculed him so much he refused to wear them. On special occasions, his Cherokee mother dressed him up in Indian clothes, which may have prompted a certain pride in his Indian heritage. In the long run, though, it was his immersion in the white world that focused his vision on the need for enlightened, educated Cherokee leadership. Not only was Ross fluent in English and white ways; he actually had trouble speaking Cherokee. Indeed, he gave all his speeches to the Nation in English, thus requiring a Cherokee translator at all times. But perhaps to counter the possible resistance of full-bloods in the nation, Ross married a full-blood woman, Elizabeth Brown Henley (called "Quatie").[26]

Engaged in public life from an early age—he served as a clerk to Chiefs Pathkiller and Charles Hicks, a liaison to a federal Indian agent, a delegate to Washington in 1816, president of the National Committee, and one of the architects of the 1827 Cherokee Constitution—Ross had developed into one of the Cherokee Nation's most experienced and skillful politicians. He set up Ross's Landing (present-day Chattanooga), trading on the Tennessee River and tapping into very profitable government contracts with both Indians and soldiers. In the late spring of 1827 he moved his family to a new home, "Head of Coosa"—where the Oostanaula and Etowah rivers merged to form the Coosa—placing him firmly inside the Georgia border. At Coosa (present-day Rome, Georgia), Ross built a large two-story home on a 170-acre plantation that included smokehouses, workhouses, and quarters for his twenty slaves. "Mr Ross's House is a large & elegant white House," noted one New England visitor in 1829, "as handsomely furnished & handsomely situated as almost any house in Litchfield County [Connecticut].—he appears to be rich & no doubt he is so."[27] With his lucrative ferry business on the Coosa, warehouse, and trading establishment at Ross's

Landing, Ross had become one of the five wealthiest men in the Cherokee Nation.

Such wealth and political experience were put quickly to the test. At the Cherokee council meeting in New Echota in July 1827, enlivened by feasts and dances for the thousands who attended, John Ross, along with his mentor, Major Ridge, led deliberations over a new constitution. Drawing on the U.S. Constitution, the Cherokee leaders created a near-identical preamble except for inclusion of a reference to the deity whose "aid and direction in its accomplishment, do ordain and establish this Constitution for the Government of the Cherokee Nation." The inclusion of a divine being came from John Ridge, indicative of the significant impact the missionaries' Christian message had made on the young Cherokee. The new constitution strengthened the position of the principal chief, detailed the tribal boundaries, and forcefully proclaimed the sovereignty of the Cherokee Nation.[28]

When the council adopted the new constitution it alarmed both white Georgians and Cherokee full-bloods alike. Georgians were outraged that with the constitution and its language of being "sovereign and independent," the Cherokees were announcing to the world that they held constitutional rights to territory that Georgia (as well as the United States) had long claimed as its own. And the constitution's new laws about creating a national treasury, ownership of private property, money lending, prohibiting alcohol at ball games and all-night dances, and requiring Cherokees to take the new oath of office invoking "Almighty God"—all these changes violated traditional Cherokee values of community and harmony. Instead, they reflected individualistic free enterprise notions pushed by white leaders and Protestant missionaries. To traditionalist leaders like Whitepath, it was the acculturationists such as John Ross, Major Ridge, and Elias Boudinot—men who had been far too influenced by the white Christian missionaries—who were the real rebels trying to impose "white" values on the Cherokees while silencing forever traditional Cherokee beliefs and practices. Indeed a powerful faction of opponents to the constitution, led by Whitepath and other chiefs, along with shamans, began openly denouncing the new laws. Some of the more radical enemies of the new constitution talked of killing all the Christian Indians and closing the missions.[29]

Ross and Ridge chose to keep a low profile concerning this rebellion among the traditionalists. What little they did say was spun in more hopeful terms: finessing traditionalists by telling them the new laws were simply aimed at assuaging the concerns of the "outside" world and would rarely be strictly enforced. The Cherokee Nation might *appear* to be turning into a white Christian nation, the leaders suggested, but in fact traditional religious beliefs would remain in place. It was from this moment on that Ross began to publicly distance himself from the missionaries. Reverend Samuel Worcester, however, always an ally to this more "enlightened" progressive faction, privately offered hope to Ross and Ridge that the rebels did not truly intend to overthrow the government and in any event did not possess the leadership to pull off a rebellion. "Though perhaps the majority of the people are dissatisfied with some features of the laws," Worcester wrote in March 1827, "yet for want of system and energetic leaders, I presume the faction is not to be dreaded."[30] The policy of quietly waiting out the rebels proved to be wise. In a few months, with no spirited defense of the constitution by any of its mixed-blood advocates, the rebellion among the traditionalists lost focus and withered in force.

But other, more dangerous opponents of the Cherokees were watching these developments with grave concern. Thomas L. McKenney, director of the Office of Indian Affairs, sounded the alarm after the passage of the new Cherokee Constitution: "They seek to be a People." Cherokees, McKenney asserted, now had expectations to be included and fully integrated into the American republic. "It is much to be regretted," he reported to the secretary of war, "that the idea of Sovereignty should have taken such a deep hold of these people." Trying to remain balanced and humane toward the Cherokees, McKenney observed, "They deserve to be respected and to be helped but with the kindest regard to them [but] they ought not to be encouraged in forming a Constitution and Government within a State of the Republic to exist and operate independently of our laws."[31]

Georgia whites were outraged at the new Cherokee Constitution. Georgia's leaders pointed to their long-standing irritation over the unfulfilled 1802 compact with the United States that promised to extinguish Indian titles in exchange for the state's western land claims. Now the Cherokees were trying to erect their own sovereign nation on land they never truly owned. To the Georgia legislature, this was a matter of *Georgia's* sovereignty, not the Cherokees'. "The lands in question belong to Georgia" became the legislature's battle cry. "She *must* and she *will* have them."[32] Challenging the very idea of a Cherokee republic being established within the sovereign state of Georgia and declaring that it no longer respected tribal rights granted by treaties with the federal government, Georgia was laying down the gauntlet: the state of Georgia would not truck with an independent, sovereign Cherokee Nation.

For their part, the Cherokees, quite understandably, took a wildly different view of recent history and their destiny: All of the Cherokees' leading figures—from Ross and Major Ridge to John Ridge, Elias Boudinot, William Hicks, and George Lowrey—believed the new constitution, along with the recently established *Cherokee Phoenix*, stood as undeniable proof of Cherokee advancement. Surely by now, they insisted, white Americans could see that the Cherokees had achieved the same ability as white Americans to be "civilized," Christian, and successful farmers and entrepeneurs. The Cherokee Nation, they argued, clearly possessed the right to stand as an independent sovereign people within the United States—just like Georgia or Tennessee or North Carolina. All of which, they desperately hoped, would somehow derail the seemingly relentless efforts of Georgians and white leaders in Washington to take their land and remove them to the West.[33]

Such hope, though, crashed hard into the increasingly rabid racial separatism among Georgia's leaders regarding the nature of Indian people. As the U.S. congressman from Georgia George M. Troup asserted, Indians simply could not be assimilated: "The utmost of rights and privileges which public opinion would concede to Indians," he insisted, "would fix them in a middle station, between the negro and the white man." And if Indians stayed in the East, he argued, they would "gradually sink to the condition of the former—a point of degeneracy below which they could not fall."[34]

The Cherokees' tenacity in holding on to their homeland and independence—powerful though it was—had not fully confronted the Georgians' relentless land hunger or the equal and opposing force that was Andrew Jackson.

Andrew Jackson
Courtesy of Library of Congress, Prints of Photographs Division,
Detroit Publishing Company Collection

During the Creek War in 1813, as American soldiers were sur-
veying the gruesome Tallushatchee, Georgia, battlefield lit-
tered with the bloody bodies of scores of Indians, they came
across a dead Indian woman clutching a live ten-month-old
baby boy—the only survivor of a massacred Creek family. One
soldier snatched the baby from the dead mother's grip and carried him to the general. Deeply affected by the scene, the general took the baby into his arms and walked back into his tent

and fed him some sugar water. The boy's name, he was told, was Lyncoya. Moved by the moment, the general made an instinctive decision, rare at the time: he would adopt the boy into his own family.

The general was Andrew Jackson. Lyncoya was put in the care of Major William White, who was instructed to take him to the Hermitage, where he was nursed and clothed. Lyncoya was to be presented as a gift to General Jackson's adopted son, Andrew Jackson Jr: "Tell my dear little Andrew to treat him well," Jackson wrote his wife, Rachel. "Charity and Christianity says he ought to be taken care of." But Rachel was also clearly instructed on the boy's unique status: she was to "keep Lyncoya in the house" because he was a "Savage." Jackson wanted him carefully tended as "he may have been given" to the general "for some Valuable purpose."[35]

Although apparently loved and well cared for, Lyncoya was kept around the Hermitage as something of a novelty and pet. He would often dress up in Indian garb and war paint and yell wild war whoops at unsuspecting visitors to the mansion. A sickly child from infancy, he was bound out to a saddler in Nashville. But on June 1, 1828, he died from a pulmonary infection, at the age of sixteen.

Jackson mourned the loss of his adopted Indian boy. But Lyncoya's premature death offered a revealing glimpse into the mind and heart of Andrew Jackson on the subject of American Indians. The members of this "ill-fated race," as Jackson called them, were, in effect, children who could not mature, who could not grow up, while white Americans thrived all around them. Lyncoya, Jackson conceded, could never break away from the Indian inside him—the uncivilized, primitive savage who needed a wise father figure to save him from the sad destiny of all Indians who lived among whites. Lewis Cass, Jackson's secretary of war, bluntly pointed to the fatal character flaws he believed would forever prevent Indians from joining the ambitious, self-improving world of white America.

> Communities of men, as well as individuals, are stimulated by a desire to meliorate their condition. There is nothing stationery around us. We are all striving in the career of life to acquire riches, or honor, or power, or some other object, whose possession is to realize the day dreams of our imaginations; and the aggregate of these efforts constitutes the advance of society. But there is little of this in the constitution of our savages. . . . Want never teaches him to be provident, nor misery to be industrious.[36]

Under these circumstances, Jackson could almost sound humanitarian, promising to rescue his "red children" from the rising tide of land-hungry settlers that surrounded them by relocating them out West.

As a raw-boned, inveterate Indian fighter on the Tennessee frontier who had fought alongside valiant Cherokee and Creek allies against Creek enemies in the Red Stick War of 1814, Jackson sometimes showed respect for the bravery of individual Indians. But when it came to policy and strategy in dealing with tribal lands that whites coveted, he was uncompromising. From his earliest days as a general, he believed that only military options worked against an opponent he viewed as a disease. "[The Indians are] constantly infesting our frontier," Jackson observed to a federal agent in 1794, "their Peace Talks are only

Delusions. . . . Does not Experience teach us that Treaties answer no Purpose than opening an Easy door for the Indians to pass [through to] Butcher our Citizens?"[37] All of which prompted Jackson to dismiss the weak-kneed federal government approach to Indians. In the days of Washington and Knox when the nation's military force was feeble at best, this sort of management by treaty might have made some sense, Jackson reasoned, but after the War of 1812—with a much more effective American military presence and a strong, growing population—it was no longer necessary or appropriate to treat Indians as equals. As he noted to Secretary of War John C. Calhoun in 1820, "It appears to me that it is high time to do away with the farce of treating with Indian tribes."[38] Besides, in Jackson's view, Indians such as the Cherokees, if they had the means, would voluntarily relocate out West. It was only their dishonest leaders who were thwarting removal. So it was impossible to get a treaty, according to Jackson, "without corrupting their Chiefs. With the U.S. 'now sufficiently strong,' [it could] carry into effect every regulation which the wisdom, humanity and justice of its Government" might adopt with regard to "these unfortunate People." The Cherokees, he believed, were "ripe for emigration."[39]

For years federal agents and white politicians had circulated this idea in the Cherokee Nation that ordinary Cherokees wanted to relocate out West but had been prevented from doing so by "the fear of their chiefs." It was the "backward" Indians, the full-bloods ("the real Indians," in Jackson's view), who clung to the old ways as "nomadic" hunters and were therefore quite willing to trade depleted hunting grounds in the East for more productive ones in the West. Thwarting progress, then, for "these unfortunate people," according to Jackson, were the "half-breeds" or "White Indians," like Ross, Boudinot, and the Ridges, who were unwilling to give up their wealth and political power and remove to new land for their nation's good.[40] Jackson's take on the Cherokees was precisely opposite of the truth. As Evan Jones, a missionary familiar with some of the poorest Cherokees in the mountains of North Carolina, observed, the full-bloods were among the most strident opponents of removal and remained exceptionally committed to Ross. "For them," Jones noted, "every stream, cave, lake, spring mountain, and clearing had a special meaning; many of them were sacred places or spots where their ancestors were buried. Intermarried whites and mixed blood had far less feeling for the land—its spiritual power and its history."[41]

Sensing the approaching disaster with land-hungry southerners and a complicit federal government, roughly five thousand Cherokees had indeed left their homelands in the East as a result of land cessions in 1809 and again in 1817 and 1819 for territory west of the Mississippi. And in 1828, the federal agent Thomas McKenney completed a survey on what it would cost to remove the six thousand Chickasaw Indians in northern Mississippi: nearly $500,000. Scurrying to the Cherokees' defense, Elias Boudinot in the pages of the *Phoenix* estimated the cost of a possible Cherokee removal. Noting the larger population—more than twice that of the Chickasaws—and the purchase or replacement costs for all the livestock, fences, shops, grist- and sawmills, orchards, and barns, Boudinot arrived at a figure of $1,783,730—more than three times the cost of the Chickasaw removal. Boudinot's conclusion? "Cannot this sum be put to a better use?" he asked. The United States could establish schools and a college, could publish and distribute books and religious tracts in Cherokee and English. "If we fail to improve under such efforts," he argued, "we will then agree to remove."[42]

Boudinot challenged the common assumption of Jackson and other white politicians that, surrounded by a land-hungry white population, Indians could avoid inevitable extinction only by removing to the West. "Where have we an example in the whole history of man," Boudinot asked, "of a Nation or tribe, removing in a body, from a land of civil and religious means, to a perfect wilderness, *in order to be civilized*? We are fearful these men are building castles in the air, whose fall will crush those poor Indians who may be so blinded as to make the experiment."[43]

In the midst of such turmoil in the Cherokee Nation and mounting fear of Andrew Jackson's emergence as a prominent political leader during the 1828 presidential election, the Cherokees conducted their own elections for the new principal chief. The choice was between Assistant Principal Chief William Hicks and John Ross. With Hicks openly considering removal as a viable option, Major Ridge, himself a determined opponent of removal, threw his support to John Ross. Ross won easily, and Major Ridge was elected to a new post as adviser to the chief. Ross's rise to power in the Cherokee Nation was now complete. He had built himself a lucrative plantation on the Coosa River worked by a large slave force, and now as principal chief commanded great authority in New Echota.[44]

But it was a fragile, unsettling sense of command. Within a month of Ross's election, Andrew Jackson won election to the presidency over John Quincy Adams, a campaign riddled with mud-slinging and hateful rhetoric.[45] Boudinot and Ross had decided to remain silent and neutral during the presidential campaign for fear that any criticism of Jackson might push him, if elected, into even deeper antagonism to the Cherokee cause. They knew full well that Jackson's attitude toward Indians, coupled with the massive number of white southern planters who supported him and craved Indian lands, was a recipe for disaster for the Cherokees and other southeastern tribes.

Their fears would soon be realized. Indian policy was front and center on Jackson's mind after his election. In his inaugural address on March 4, 1829, he invoked some humane words about crafting "a just and liberal policy" in dealing with the Indians, but his intent was unmistakable: all remaining southern tribes must be removed beyond the Mississippi, where they would "always be free from the mercenary influence of White men, and undisturbed by the local authority of the states."[46]

Jackson's principal audience—or at least those listening most intently—were the white residents of the state of Georgia. They could only have been thrilled by Jackson's words. But not surprised: Jackson had already privately coached them on how to handle the Cherokees. As president-elect, he sent a message to a Georgia congressman about the Cherokees on their borders: "Build a fire under them. When it gets hot enough, they'll move."[47] The fire had already been set: within a month of Jackson's election, the Georgia legislature passed a law claiming that if Cherokees did not voluntarily leave for the West by January 1830, Georgia would assume jurisdiction over all their land inside Georgia's borders, invalidate Cherokee tribal law, and regard remaining Cherokees as the equivalent of free blacks— people who could not vote, become public officeholders, educate children in white schools, and testify in courts against white residents. Cherokees would be allowed to maintain their farms but they would now be taxed, and any Cherokee land not under cultivation would have to be surrendered to Georgians wanting to settle there. Georgia's irritation at not getting control of Cherokee lands stemmed from an agreement signed with the U.S. government a generation earlier. Since 1802 the federal government, in exchange for Georgia's western land claims, had promised it would extinguish Indian land titles within Georgia, but had never done so. To make matters worse for Georgians, the Cherokees just the year before had created a constitution that insisted on their own independence and sovereignty. But now, emboldened by Jackson's ascendancy to the presidency, Georgians knew they had a leader in Washington who understood and accepted their relentless ambition: to take over Cherokee land no matter what.

Soon a new song began circulating in the Cherokee Nation among watchful whites in the surrounding Georgia countryside.

> *All I ask in this creation*
> *Is a pretty little wife and a big plantation*
> *Way up yonder in the Cherokee Nation.*[48]

The greedy designs of Georgians for Cherokee land had stirred up tension for years in the Cherokee Nation. In the very first issue of the *Cherokee Phoenix*, Elias Boudinot gave voice to this growing anxiety. "The unpleasant controversy existing within the state of Georgia," he argued, "of which, many of our readers are aware, will frequently make our situation trying. . . . We pray God that we may be delivered from such spirit."[49] As someone who lived about one hundred miles from Athens, Georgia, Boudinot realized before Jackson's election that while "the Geor-

gians make us but little trouble at present . . . they are determined to have the land."[50] Aside from individual white Georgia
squatters on Cherokee territory, Boudinot and others did not
have to look far to see the basis for the blatant disregard for
Cherokee rights and property. As early as 1823, Georgia congressman Richard Wilde had made a point of excoriating Indians as a "conquered and degraded race." Like Jackson, Wilde
viewed native peoples as living on the wrong side of history—
doomed to extinction because of their inferior civilization. And
he was especially angry at missionaries and other "white gentlemen" who desperately tried to prop up such a failed race.

> When gentlemen talk of preserving the Indians, what is it that
> they mean to preserve? Is it their mode of life? No. You intend
> to convert them from hunters to agriculturalists or herdsmen.
> Is it their barbarous laws and customs? No. You promise to
> furnish them with a code, and prevail upon them to adopt
> habits like your own. Their language? No. You intend to super-
> sede their imperfect jargon by teaching them your own rich,
> copious, energetic tongue. Their religion? No. You intend to
> convert them from their miserable and horrible superstitions
> to the mild and cheering doctrines of Christianity.
>
> What is it, then, that constitutes Indian individuality—the
> identity of that race white gentlemen are so anxious to pre-
> serve? Is it the mere copper color of the skin, which marks
> them—according to your prejudices at least—an inferior—a
> conquered and degraded race?[51]

Boudinot's irritation over Georgia's new laws intruding into
Cherokee country boiled over into bitter anger at the betrayal

President Jackson and the federal government displayed toward the Cherokee people. It seemed obvious to Boudinot and other Cherokee leaders that neither Jackson nor the federal government intended to make good on previous agreements to protect Cherokees on their own lands. In fact, the veil had now been lifted, revealing that Jackson fully intended to allow Georgia whites to intrude at will: "The illustrious Washington, Jefferson, Madison and Monroe were only tantalizing us," Boudinot asserted, "when they encouraged us in the pursuit of agriculture and Government, and when they afforded us the protection of the United States, by which we have been preserved to this present time as a nation." For a generation or more, the Cherokee people, "as dutiful 'children' of the President," Boudinot argued, had done everything he had requested and created a new lawful government. But now, "when everything looks so promising around us, . . . a storm is raised by the extension of tyrannical and unchristian laws, which threatens to blast all our rising hopes and expectations."[52]

Even worse, the Cherokees had to fight vicious lies circulating in Georgia newspapers in the summer of 1829 claiming that the Cherokees were "making extensive preparations to remove to the west." Boudinot angrily protested such rumors, claiming that they were "without the least foundation." On the contrary, he pointed out, the Cherokees were still making all manner of improvements. "We see houses erecting wherever we go—they are enlarging their farms—the progress of education is encouraging and the improvement in morals has never been so flattering." "Coercion alone," he insisted, "will remove them to the western country allotted for the Indians."[53]

And then, in that very summer of 1829, "coercion" took a big step closer to reality: In July, a young Cherokee boy in northern Georgia stumbled across a shiny pebble on Cherokee land near Dahlonega. He sold it to a white trader who knew exactly what it was: gold. In no time, the deluge began. As one gold digger later testified, "Within a few days it would seem as if the world must have heard of it, for men came from every state. . . . They came afoot, on horseback, and in wagons, acting more like crazy men than anything else."[54] Lawless gold-hunting intruders soon flooded the territory. Chief John Ross, insisting that the United States should cover the costs of the intrusions of gold diggers, petitioned President Jackson for the money. But the Cherokee focus on the gold discovery seemed only to embolden the Georgia legislature to argue that the state was being unfairly deprived of great wealth. By the summer of 1830, Governor George Gilmer issued proclamations forbidding Indians or whites from digging gold in the Cherokee Nation and requiring whites living there to take an oath of allegiance to Georgia.[55]

Chief John Ross likewise lost no time challenging the illegal maneuvers of the Georgia legislature. In January 1829 he rode to Washington, D.C., to plead the Cherokee case. In a protest to Congress in February, Ross called the action by the Georgia legislature "a question upon which the salvation and happiness or the misery and destruction of a nation depends." And, obviously, since the Cherokee Nation was in no way a party to whatever "compact" the federal government had created with Georgia, he pointed out, it could not in any way be "held responsible for its fulfillment." "We cannot admit that Georgia has the right to extend her jurisdiction over our territory," he argued, "nor are we the Cherokee people prepared to submit to her persecuting edict."[56] Ross failed to persuade Jackson or his secretary of war, John H. Eaton, to invalidate the Georgia claims, but he had not given up on Congress—especially if his people would join him in holding firm to their sacred right to their land. In his address to the Cherokee Nation that summer, Ross positioned himself and the Cherokee people firmly against Jackson and Eaton: "Don't let the Talk of the President and Secretary of War that is going about scare you," he declared. "Their say so does not effect our rights to our soil. . . . The Georgians [are] threatening to extend their laws over us . . . to scare us and to make our minds easier to go off and give up our lands. . . . Friends, I have great hopes in your firmness and that you will hold fast to the place where you were raised."[57]

Elias Boudinot and family were holding fast to their homeland despite the dangerous winds of change swirling around them. When Harriett's Connecticut parents came to visit New Echota in the fall of 1829, they encountered a busy and prosperous people living comfortably in Cherokee country. Sixty-seven-year-old Benjamin and sixty-year-old Eleanor Gold drove their own buggy for the forty-seven-day trip from Cornwall to New Echota. Stopping off first at the home of Lewis Ross, the well-to-do brother of John Ross, the Golds also visited with neighbors John and Sarah Ridge, with Major Ridge riding up on horseback attended by a mounted slave. Boudinot's neighborhood also included Samuel and Ann Worcester, their house, along with the council house, easily visible from the Boudinots' back window.[58] Elias and Harriett oversaw a busy household that included two children—and one on the way—as well as various children attending missionary school, and frequent political visitors to the Cherokee Nation. "Mr. Boudinot has much good company," Gold wrote to relatives back in Connecticut, "and is as much respected as any man of his age. His paper is respected all over the United States, and is known in Europe." Gold was especially pleased to see that Harriett lived in a large, two-story frame house, "well done off and well furnished with the comforts of life."[59] Well supplied with clothes and food imported from Boston and Augusta, Georgia, Cherokee country, Gold concluded, was "as healthy a region as ever I was acquainted with. I traveled much & seen the people in various parts. I rarely see or hear of a sickly person."[60]

The Boudinots may have been living in comfort and good health, but when they looked toward Georgia or Washington, they saw nothing but trouble. Elias ardently took up the pen against lawless squatters streaming in from Georgia. "The intruders," he argued, "who to say the least have acted more like savages towards the Cherokees, than the Cherokees towards them, are still permitted to continue in their unlawful proceedings." All of which prompted an even more cynical take on President Jackson. With so much deception and thievery in the air, Boudinot wondered how to assess "the 'straight & good talk' of our father the President, & understand what he means when he says, 'your father loves his red children.'" When Jackson called out the military to deal with trumped-up Cherokee crimes against white Georgians, Boudinot claimed, he was, among other things, making a mockery of his "fatherly professions": Jackson acted on behalf of his white brethren in Georgia "merely because a malicious white child of his has told a falsehood," Boudinot asserted, "but will not raise his hand to protect us from encroachments and insults, under which we have been laboring for months? Is he not dealing out a 'forked' justice to us?"[61]

Boudinot also challenged the new Georgia laws, imploring

his readers to ponder "the effects of *civilized* legislation over poor *savages*." Declaring the laws explicitly drawn up as a prejudicial act against the Cherokees, he noted that the Georgian leaders had left them no legal recourse whatever to the predatory behavior of the people of Georgia: *"Full license to our oppressors, and every avenue of justice closed against us.* Yes, this is the bitter cup prepared for us by a *republican* and *religious* Government— we shall drink it to the very dregs."[62]

While Boudinot, like Chief Ross, now questioned the fairness and honesty of Andrew Jackson, the Jackson administration was beginning to take an equally unyielding position about the inevitability of removal for the Cherokees. Secretary of War John H. Eaton repeatedly quoted from treaties Cherokees made with the United States that clearly referred only to the Cherokees' "possessory rights" to their lands, as opposed to sovereignty, which, he insisted, remained with "those States within whose limits" the Cherokees were situated. For the Cherokees to demand that the federal government impose its will over an "independent state" such as Georgia was an unrealistic, unconstitutional request. "The arms of this country," Eaton told Ross, "can never be employed to stay any State of this Union from the exercise of those legitimate powers, which attach and belong to their sovereign character." Jackson himself had already made the same argument claiming that Indians had "only a possessory right to the soil, for the purpose of hunting and not the right of domain."[63] And so, the Cherokees' constitution was entirely unconstitutional, Jackson argued: the U.S. Constitution forbade the establishment of a new state within the territory of an existing state without that state's permission. The federal government, Jackson concluded, could not allow a "foreign and independent government" to establish itself there. Both Jackson and Eaton thus saw removal west of the Mississippi as the only appropriate and just course.[64]

All of which only emboldened land-hungry Georgians eyeing Cherokee territory. The intruders kept streaming onto Cherokee property, stealing horses and commandeering and settling into homes abandoned by Cherokees who had emigrated to the Arkansas Territory in 1819. In January 1830 Major Ridge, among others, had had enough. Angered at the lawless intruders and bent on revenge for their thievery, Major Ridge decided to take action. With authorization from Ross, Ridge, decked out in red war paint (made by his wife, Susanna, and some of his servants) and a horned buffalo headdress, along with thirty Cherokee warriors he assembled, rode through the snow- and sleet-covered countryside, yelling and shouting as they accosted a large group of white horse thieves at Beaver Dam and Cedar Creek near the Georgia-Alabama line. Some eighteen families of Georgia squatters had taken over the abandoned houses. When it became apparent that the only way to remove the intruders was to destroy the houses, Ridge and his raiding party set every building on fire and burned them to the ground.[65]

Ridge's war party returned home safely from its mission. But the incident did not end there. Four of his warriors got drunk from some whiskey they discovered at the home of one of the horse thieves. The four Indians were picked up by an avenging party of twenty-five whites who returned to the scene the next morning. They bound them all hand and foot and carted them off for the Carroll County jail. One especially intoxicated Indian, according to an eyewitness, "not being able to sit on [a horse] and falling off once or twice . . . was most barbarously beaten with guns &c in the head, face, breast and arms, and was then thrown across the pummel of a saddle on a horse, and carried by the rider in that situation about one mile and then thrown off." His "shockingly mangled" corpse was found on the road the next day.[66]

The incident ignited both Indian country and the halls of Congress. Bands of angry white Georgians roamed the Cherokee Nation claiming they were out to make arrests, but instead fired on Indians and threatened to lay siege to the houses of John Ross and Major Ridge. Trying to portray Georgia squatters as sympathetic victims of a vicious raid during a harsh winter day, Georgia governor George Gilmer accused Ridge's band of Cherokees of being controlled by "the most active and malignant enemy of Georgia" whose rampage took place "on a day when the earth was covered with snow and sleet. . . . A number of women, with infant children, were thus deprived of shelter from the severity of the coldest and most inclement weather."[67]

Newspapers throughout the North ran stories about "War in Georgia." Soon President Jackson felt sufficient pressure to send in troops to keep the peace. But as always, such a military show of force proved insufficient to deter white settlers bent on settling in Cherokee country. Indeed, Jackson withdrew the troops after Gilmer insisted on using the Georgia Guard, a special militia, to monitor Cherokee territory. The Georgia Guard would soon become well known for its passivity while whites moved onto Indian land, stole horses, pilfered gold mines, and harassed the Cherokee people.[68]

Major Ridge's retaliatory raid on unlawful intruders, Boudinot realized, had now opened up a new and especially dangerous situation for the Cherokee people. "[This is] a circumstance . . . we have for a long time dreaded," Boudinot observed. "It has been the desire of our enemies that the Cherokees may be urged

to some desperate act—thus far this desire has never been realized, and we hope, notwithstanding the great injury now sus-
tained, their wonted forbearance will be continued." Keenly
aware of the precarious moment in which his people were now
placed, Boudinot sounded a note of reconciliation: "If our word
will have any weight with our countrymen in this trying time,
we would say, Forbear, forbear—revenge not, but leave vengeance to him 'to whom vengeance belongeth.' "[69]

But reconciliation was not in the air. In fact, Boudinot's
attacks in the *Phoenix* on Georgia's intruders and their official
protectors soon landed him in trouble. Twice he was rounded
up by the commander of the Georgia Guard for printing libel-
ous articles about the Guard. Disprove a single incident reported
in the *Phoenix*, Boudinot demanded. Unable to do so, the commander released Boudinot without further punishment.[70]

And John Ridge, now a member of the Cherokee delegation
in Washington, must have wondered what dangers lay ahead as
he and his wife, Sarah, read editorials from Georgia newspapers
berating his buffalo-headed father. One writer wondered whose
houses Major Ridge and his war party had burned. Sure, they
may have formerly belonged to Cherokees, but how could it be
right to torch abandoned homes that could—should—belong
to someone else?[71]

Fear now clearly hung in the air in the Cherokee Nation,
including some self-imposed anxiety. Long worried that a small
tribal faction might one day give away the homeland through
an illegal treaty, the council in 1829 passed a law making the
sale of Cherokee land without official tribal approval a capital
offense. It was signed by Major and John Ridge. Such fears
were not ill-founded: twenty years before, the unscrupulous

chief Doublehead was killed for ceding land in 1809. Among his Cherokee executioners was Major Ridge. Ridge's nephew Elias Boudinot was likewise troubled by this fear. Referring to Cherokee chiefs in the Arkansas Territory making unlawful private land cessions in 1828, he wrote in the *Phoenix*: "We are sorry that there are self-interested men in all Indian tribes, who will not scruple to sacrifice the interest of their people, and that the United States, instead of discountenancing, will enter into treaties with them, contrary to the feelings of the rest of their brethren. If such a course is pursued, there is no hope for the Indians."[72]

Boudinot never dreamed that such a troubling concern would soon return to haunt him personally.

When Congress reconvened on December 7, 1829, a clerk in a flat monotone read aloud to the chamber a draft version of a bill that would decide the fate of several Indian nations: President Andrew Jackson's Indian removal bill.

According to the bill, because they were surrounded by a growing population of often hostile whites eager to take over their land and resources, southern tribes—principally the Cherokee, Choctaw, and Creek nations—were doomed to "weakness and decay" and eventual extinction. Thus "humanity and national honor demand that every effort should be made to avert so great a calamity." That effort called for exchanging Indian lands in the East for territory west of the Mississippi. Relocated tribes would presumably be placed on land where they could live and prosper beyond the intrusions of whites and acculturate at their own pace. Out West—far beyond the reach and hostility of white citizens—Indians would be free to be themselves, rather than assimilated red Americans. There, they could govern their own people without interference, learn the "arts of civilization," and maintain their tribal identity far into the future.[73]

This relocation, Jackson insisted, would be voluntary. It would be "as cruel as unjust," he claimed, "to compel the aborigines to abandon the graves of their fathers and seek a home in a distant land." Furthermore, there would be humane efforts to compensate Indians for the improvements to their land they would be leaving behind, as well as aid and assistance for all emigrants.[74] But any Indians refusing to leave their homeland faced a grim reality: they would have to submit to all the state laws established by their white enemies and anticipate a swift end to their tribal identity. They would "become merged in the mass of our population."[75] The president alone was empowered to manage relations with the relocated tribes, making sure that no violations of any existing treaties took place. Finally, Congress would pay $500,000 to cover the costs of removal. With solid support from southern Democrats in Congress totally committed to removal, Jackson's policy carried huge momentum.[76]

But it ignited a storm of protest in much of the nation. Voices of strong support for the plight of southern Indians could be heard in and out of Congress. Senator Theodore Frelinghuysen of New Jersey harangued the Senate for six hours, attacking the bill and those who crafted it. A deeply Christian man and former president of the American Board, Frelinghuysen, like many opponents of removal, was appalled at Jackson's executive intrusion into Congress in order to get his removal bill passed. Frelinghuysen lashed out at the neglect and mistreatment the American nation had imposed on its native "brothers" while stealing their land. Despite enormous Indian cessions of land over the years, "yet we crave more. We have crowded the tribes upon a few miserable acres of our Southern frontier: it is all that is left of them of their once boundless forests; and still, like the horse-leech, our insatiable cupidity cries, give!give!give!"[77]

Most supporters of the Indian cause came from New England. Massachusetts congressman Edward Everett called Indian removal "the greatest question that ever came before Congress, short of the question of peace and war."[78] And Peleg Sprague of Maine chided his colleagues lest they forget their "solemnly promised" duty to abide by the numerous treaties signed with Indian tribes. Honoring those treaties, he argued, would solve much of the difficulty in Indian country. Others lambasted the administration for planning to drop thousands of innocent people, including the elderly, sick, and children, into the "Great American Desert" that was ill-suited for agriculture, let alone a decent existence.[79]

No one poured more passion, insight, and commitment into advocating for the southern Indians, especially the Cherokees, than Jeremiah Evarts. A devout Vermonter who served as treasurer for the American Board, Evarts had traveled extensively through Indian nations and become friends with many Indian leaders. He was particularly knowledgeable about Indian legal rights and had become a staunch and articulate defender of the Cherokees. As an ardent leader in the Christian benevolence movement, Evarts saw the Cherokee cause as an inspiring moral crusade. For him it was this nation's godly mission to show goodness to a corrupt world—and that meant defending innocent Indians from greedy and conniving politicians. Godly Americans, he believed, worked to reform the world, rather than pursue their own grasping self-interest. In the summer of

1829, he composed twenty-four articles outlining in great detail why Jackson's removal plans demanded fervent, moral opposition. Written under the pseudonym William Penn, the articles appeared in a Washington newspaper, the *National Intelligencer*, between August 5 and December 19, 1829. The William Penn essays were widely circulated in more than forty newspapers and periodicals across the nation. Evarts also masterminded a powerful petition and memorial campaign in 1830 where he took on the pro-removal forces hammer and tong.[80]

While addressing removal in legal terms, Evarts compellingly placed his readers in the nation's courtroom alongside innocent Indians who faced an unfeeling country without a conscience.

> Let every intelligent reader consider himself a juryman in the case and let him resolve to bring in such a verdict, as he can hereafter regard with complacency. It is not a single man, who is on trial, and who may lose his life by the carelessness of the jury. Sixty thousand men, women, and children, in one part of the United States, are now in constant expectation of being driven away from their country, in such a manner as they apprehend will result in their present misery and speedy extermination.[81]

Calling Jackson's removal policy "a violation of the public faith," Evarts claimed that the relocation of southern Indians, if enacted, was "destined to bring upon our country the guilt and shame of oppressing the weak, robbing the poor, and violating the most solemn engagements which it is in the power of this government to make."[82]

Such words reverberated powerfully not only among white

benevolent Christians in the Northeast—where it was estimated that close to half a million people read the William Penn essays—but also in Cherokee country. Elias Boudinot was keenly aware of, and moved by, Evarts's effort. After reading the Penn essays, Boudinot wrote his in-laws in Connecticut, "Do write us soon, & let us know how the people about you feel respecting the Great Indian Question. William Penn is very popular amongst us."[83] Inspired by Evarts's words, Elias and Harriett early in 1830 named their newborn son William Penn.

Despite the efforts of Jeremiah Evarts and congressional friends of the Indians, the forces for removal—within both Congress and the nation at large—were simply too strong. Former Georgia governor John Forsyth led the pro-removal response by insisting that removal would not be done by force—and those Indian sympathizers who claimed otherwise were simply showcasing their anti-southern ideology. Besides, he claimed, northerners over the years had banished their Indian populations, but now they proposed to tell a southern state like Georgia simply trying to prosper that it could not do the same thing with its Indians. Echoing Jackson, Forsyth asserted that only in the West could Indians survive as a people.[84]

John Ridge and other Cherokee delegates sat in the gallery observing the often acrimonious oratory with growing concern. But finally the votes were taken in both houses. In late April the Senate passed the legislation by a vote of 28 to 19. After long, bitter debate in the House of Representatives, the House approved it by a close 102-to-97 margin. In both houses of Congress, the vote was mainly along party lines—Democrats standing firm behind Jackson and the bill; Republicans generally opposing it—and sectional. In the House, southerners voted three to one in favor of removal, with western states (except Ohio) also supporting it with strong margins. Twice as many eastern representatives opposed the measure as supported it. Jackson insisted that those opposing removal were simply engaged in party politics. Indeed, Wilson Lumpkin of Georgia claimed that there was not a single supporter of the Cherokees who was not mainly an enemy of Andrew Jackson on political grounds. On May 28, 1830, Andrew Jackson signed into law what became the Indian Removal Act of 1830.[85]

Indian removal, Jackson would later assert, was the "most arduous part of my duty, and I watched over it with great vigilance."[86] And those who defended the Indians heartily agreed. The distinguished Massachusetts congressman Edward Everett confided to Evarts the enormity of what had been transacted. "I cannot conceal from you the apprehension that nothing will be done, in behalf of the Indians. The President has sold them to the states, at the price of his own political support; & there is a bare majority in Congress, willing to ratify the bargain."[87] Evarts, always a sickly man, died at age fifty in 1831 and, perhaps fortunately, never had to witness what became of his moral crusade on behalf of the Indians.

For the Cherokees, despite Jackson's triumph with the removal bill, this was still no time for surrender. "The clouds may gather, thunders roar & lightening flash from the acts of Ga. Under the approvation of Genl. Jackson's neutrality," John Ross wrote to Evarts after the signing of the removal bill, "but the Cherokees with an honest patriotism & love of country will still remain peaceably and quietly in their own soil."[88] Boudinot likewise tried to sound a positive note, though it was clearly laced with worry. "I think the matter is coming to a crisis," he wrote his Connecticut relatives in January 1831, "and I am glad it is. Very soon the virtue of the Republic will be put to the test."[89] His wife, Harriett, offered a similar sentiment of fear mingled with hope: "Sometimes I fear the Cherokees will see evil days," she wrote, "but I think they will come off victorious in the end & that is all they want—they fear nothing; if but their country & freedom is spared them."[90]

Ironically, what the Boudinots—and no doubt the Ridges as well—feared most on the horizon was not only the continued mistreatment of the Cherokee people but also the growing jeopardy of their *white* friends and allies in the Cherokee Nation, especially the missionaries. For years Georgia's political leaders had been accusing the missionaries and other whites sympathetic to the Indians of meddling in the political affairs of the Cherokee Nation.[91] From the beginning of the *Cherokee Phoenix*, critics charged that the influential newspaper was in fact masterminded by sympathetic missionaries, in particular Boudinot's close friend Samuel Worcester. Georgia congressman Richard Wilde, like other white southerners, was intent on identifying and frightening missionaries and friends of the Cherokees; it was impossible for these watchful white critics to ignore that so many of the men sympathetic to the Cherokees came from religious and philanthropic circles of liberal New England—precisely the region that had always opposed Andrew Jackson.

Boudinot vehemently denied such accusations—as did Worcester—in the pages of the *Phoenix*. In a March 20, 1828, editorial, Boudinot insisted that the Cherokees "will not, by any means, permit them [missionaries] to have any thing to do with their public affairs" as their sole job is religious instruction and their religious societies that govern them explicitly forbid such political interference. "They have our hearty approbation for what they have done amongst us, and we hope those at a distance will reward them by their kind wishes and sympathies, instead of affixing to them the term of '*mercenary missionaries.*'" Boudinot pressed the matter in no uncertain terms: "to declare once and for all, that no white man has had any thing to do in framing our constitution, and all the public acts of the Nation. . . . We hope this practice of imputing the acts of Indians to white men will be done away."[92]

By 1830 such hopes were dashed. Georgia's laws extending state jurisdiction over the Cherokee people were targeted more at sympathetic whites living in the Cherokee Nation than at Cherokees themselves. Thus the laws criminalized those who tried to help Cherokees stay in the East or discouraged them from ceding their land. Those found guilty of aiding and abetting Cherokees who fought removal or the sale of tribal land faced imprisonment at hard labor for up to four years. Georgia's governor, George Gilmer, privately conceded the real purpose of the 1829 legislative acts: they were "calculated to induce [the Indians] to remove" and to frighten all their white sympathizers.[93]

At first Samuel Worcester remained largely unaware that Georgia's leaders considered him a "noxious presence" in the Cherokee Nation. But he was beginning to sense the increasingly dangerous position he was in. His first hint came when the American Board received a complaint from Colonel Thomas McKenney, chief of the Office of Indian Affairs. The offending letter, McKenney noted, contained "a charge against you" of "interfering with the press, & writing scurrilous articles, respecting officers of government & other public men." Worcester was told the American Board stood behind him: "Do what is right, & you need not fear."[94] Besides, Worcester recognized, he had his good friend Elias Boudinot speaking out in his defense.

Little did he—or his critics—realize that Worcester's growing jeopardy would soon become the Cherokees' best hope.

4

The "White Man's Weapon"

Since first arriving in Indian country in the early 1800s, missionaries mostly found favor, even admiration, among whites—and even many Indians—who watched their efforts to bring Christianity to Native Americans. Indeed, before 1828, they were generally viewed as heroic figures in the backcountry. With Jackson's election and the rising tension over removal, however, missionaries quickly became pawns in an increasingly volatile political climate. Trapped between Cherokees they wanted to protect and white settlers and politicians suspicious of their loyalties, missionaries were fast becoming an endangered people in Indian country.

Removal advocates in Washington by the late 1820s began publicly denouncing missionaries as enemies of removal. Peter B. Porter, secretary of war under John Quincy Adams, called missionaries "agents [who] are operating more secretly to be sure, but not with less zeal and effort, to prevent such emigration." Some fifty-six missionaries were living among the Cherokees in

1829–30, and no doubt all of them would have insisted they were simply servants of God. But they relied on the federal government to fund their work, which placed them squarely in the crosshairs of white leaders and settlers who demanded that missionaries remain politically neutral or, if anything, follow the lead of those who funded them in Washington. Instead, the Christian benevolence movement that drove much of the missionary effort—which aimed at wide-ranging reform in antebellum America—tended to push some preachers into advocacy for their Indian converts.[1]

Not that all missionaries agreed on the removal issue. Moravians, for example, successfully remained above the fray. Baptists, who saw the Indians as wards of the state, unanimously supported voluntary removal. A few of the circuit-riding Methodist missionaries gave strident anti-removal sermons claiming that removal would be "ruinous" to the Cherokees. The American Board, though, offered full-throated support for the Cherokees. Their partisanship angered Jackson and his followers, who saw these evangelicals as bleeding-heart political partisans funded by ill-advised philanthropists and dishonest Yankees. Georgia congressman (and soon-to-be governor) Wilson Lumpkin lashed out at the "wicked influence of designing men veiled in the garb of philanthropy and Christian benevolence who excited the Cherokees to a course [of resistance] which will end in their speedy destruction." For pro-removal leaders like Lumpkin, it was obvious who belonged to this "christian party" that was trying to undo Andrew Jackson: "the fanatics . . . from these philanthropic ranks, flocking in upon the poor Cherokees, like the caterpillar and locusts of Egypt."[2]

Early on, Elias Boudinot sensed that the battlefield over Cherokee rights was shifting to the precarious status of his missionary friends. In October 1830 he reprinted the Methodist resolves, originally published in New York City in the *Methodist Christian Advocate*, praising them for taking such a strong public stand for the Cherokees. "Why should not missionaries," Boudinot argued, "the true friends of the Indians, who toil day and night for their spiritual good, be permitted to exercise the sacred right of freemen—the liberty of free speech and freedom of inquiry?"[3]

With the missionary controversy deepening, Samuel Worcester could no longer hope to remain indifferent. After the passage of Jackson's removal bill and the growing chorus of white Georgians now focusing their anger on missionaries sympathetic to the Cherokees, Worcester realized he and his fellow ministers needed to make a public response. On December 22 Worcester called on missionaries from all four denominations to gather at his home in New Echota to draw up a public statement about their role in the thorny issue of removal. Thirteen attended the meeting and produced a manifesto, a draft statement (signed by all but one) aimed at clearing the air of untruths and rejecting unfair accusations that missionaries were attempting to trick Cherokees into defying Georgia's laws.

If Georgia officials were hoping for a statement of neutrality from Worcester and his colleagues, they were greatly disappointed. Worcester's manifesto offered unmistakable support for Cherokee resistance to removal and objected vehemently to the bogus claim of Jackson and Georgia's leaders that in truth the full-bloods sought removal but had been frightened into silence by their "half-breed chiefs." The issue facing missionaries and Cherokees alike, the manifesto forcefully argued, was nothing less than the transcendent cause of patriotism: "The people required patriotism of all whom they elect to office," insisted the manifesto, noting that "the very touchstone of patriotism is 'Will he sell his country?'" Removal, Worcester wrote, was "an event to be most earnestly deprecated. . . . The establishment of the jurisdiction of Georgia and other states over the Cherokee people, against their will, would be an immense and irreparable injury." Forced removal, Worcester insisted, would only "arrest [the Cherokees'] progress" in the civilization program.[4]

Not every missionary felt comfortable with this new, overtly political stance Worcester and his colleagues had crafted. In fact, Reverend Daniel Butrick believed that Worcester had stage-managed the meeting and resulting manifesto in a way that cornered missionaries to sign it, producing a dangerous political promise to the Cherokee people. "The Cherokees," Butrick argued, "should never have been taught to expect political aid from missionaries."[5]

The growing crisis over the political conscience of the missionaries no doubt weighed heavily on the Boudinot and Worcester families as they commemorated the new year in 1831 with fasting and prayer. But Worcester's manifesto only fueled Boudinot's growing commitment to his missionary friend and comrade in transforming the Cherokee people. A few days after New Year's, Elias Boudinot and Worcester published a special edition of the *Cherokee Phoenix* that included the full manifesto—as did numerous northern religious newspapers. In his editorial for the issue, Boudinot pointed to the new reality forced upon *every-one* living in Cherokee country, native or white: "We believe no one can now remain neutral—there is no halfway ground on this momentous question—each individual in America must either be for the Indians or against them." Boudinot challenged the assumption that missionaries somehow had to remain neutral. Such a presumption, he claimed, was itself partisan. Upon learning that a group of Methodists in the Tennessee conference had recently backed down from the public stand for Cherokee rights made by the national Methodist Church a few months earlier, Boudinot reacted angrily: "We sincerely regret that so respectable a body as the Tennessee conference should call the *Indian question* merely a political question. It is exactly the way the enemies to the Indians blind the people." Removal for Boudinot and others had become an inescapably moral question. Reverend Evan Jones, a Baptist, joined Boudinot in recognizing that amid the oppression of the Cherokees, silence now became a sin. "If we withheld our opinion when called for," Jones wrote, "we could not hold up our heads as preachers of righteousness among a people who would universally regard us as abettors of iniquity." If they caved in to removal, Jones concluded, they would be left "a broken hearted people."[6]

But the heartbreaking business had already begun. As Worcester, Boudinot, and their missionary friends fueled public anger against removal advocates, the Georgia legislature declared war on the missionaries: it passed a law stating that all white males living with the Cherokee Nation as of March 1, 1831, "without a license or permit" from the governor and without having taken an oath of allegiance to the state of Georgia would be arrested and, upon conviction, sentenced to four years of hard labor in the state prison. Since Georgia's governor, George Gilmer, never intended to authorize any missionary to continue residing in Georgia, this new law sent a harsh and obvious message: white missionary friends of the Cherokees were no longer welcome in Georgia, and those who remained in the state would be rendered common criminals.[7]

Georgia governor George R. Gilmer
Courtesy of Sterling Memorial Library, Yale University

Boudinot immediately attacked the law as "extremely unjust" and "oppressive," to both whites and Cherokees. The strategy behind such a law could not be missed: remove all the sympathetic whites and it would be easier to take over the Cherokees and their land. Any white person offering help to the Cherokees—from a minister or a schoolteacher to a blacksmith or carpenter—could be arrested. "If we introduce a minister of the Gospel to preach to us the way of life and salvation," Boudinot observed, "here is a law of Georgia, a Christian law too it is said, ready to seize him and send him to the Penitentiary, in violation of the constitution of the state itself." And it would be the same for any other white man trying to aid the Cherokee people: "If we bring a white man to teach our children, he is also arrested and suffers a similar punishment." The intended result for the Cherokee people would be "disastrous," destroying all their "improvements" over the past twenty years. It was also a disaster for the white man's freedom in Cherokee country. "What becomes of the liberty of conscience in this case?" Boudinot asked. "Here a white man cannot enjoy that liberty without going to the penitentiary."[8]

With such mounting legal and moral urgency swirling around the missionaries, the pressure on Samuel Worcester to act grew unbearable, both from within and beyond Cherokee country. Jeremiah Evarts, the treasurer for the American Board, wrote Worcester in early February 1831 suggesting that he consider suing Georgia over its new law. By following what was "clearly the path of duty," Evarts argued, and by "being willing to suffer for righteousness' sake, you will do much to encourage the Cherokees." Without ardent missionary support, Evarts reminded Worcester, the Cherokees' future would be hopeless. And, in a patronizing comment about the Cherokees—common enough among many northern benevolence leaders—Evarts stressed the heroic role Worcester's actions could play amid what missionaries viewed as the weak passivity of his Cherokee flock: "If you leave," he told Worcester, "I fear the Cherokees will make no stand whatever." But martyrdom in a Georgia prison would ignite a much more powerful spur to action: "If Georgia should carry some of you to prison, the fact would rouse this whole country in a manner unlike anything which has yet been experienced." Worcester's remarkable sacrifice, Evarts insisted, would generate petitions from all over the country; he would shake up the world. "You would do good to the poor and oppressed everywhere."[9]

Although at the time he was tending to his ailing wife, Ann, during a difficult delivery of their infant daughter, Jerusha, Worcester agreed to stay in New Echota without signing the oath of allegiance. Once the deadline passed, the Georgia Guard acted promptly and began seizing missionaries who defied the new law. On March 12, 1831, the Guard picked up the American Board missionary Isaac Proctor at his home. The next day, right after Worcester's church service, twenty-five armed Georgia Guards stormed into Worcester's home in New Echota and arrested him for residing inside the Cherokee Nation without state permission. The Guards also rounded up several other missionaries and teachers and marched them to jail at Camp Gilmer on the Chattahoochee River. But Worcester got a quick reprieve: because he also worked as a federal postmaster at New Echota, Worcester was an authorized agent of the federal government and, thus, exempt from prosecution. Judge Augustin S. Clayton reluctantly released Worcester. After Gilmer complained to Washington about the exemption, Secretary of War Eaton formally denied that any of the missionaries were agents of the United States. To further clarify the strategy, U.S. postmaster William T. Barry dismissed Worcester from his duties at New Echota. So on June 1, Gilmer announced that he would rearrest the missionaries if they did not leave the state within ten days. "Spare no exertions to arrest them," Gilmer instructed the colonel of the Guard. "If they are discharged by the Courts, or give bail, continue to arrest for each repeated act of continued residence in violation of the law."[10]

Three of the missionaries relented under the pressure and left the state. Although worried that "our ranks are broken," Worcester pledged to press on as he was "willing to bear the burden alone." Joining him as holdouts were nine other missionaries and his friend Dr. Elizur Butler, a physician working for the American Board at its mission school at Haweis, who had come to

Cherokee country around the same time as Worcester. Like the others, Worcester believed his legal challenge to the Georgia law would in the long run prove successful, but his overriding strategy was more ambitious: he asked his friends that, in the event he was imprisoned, to spread the word everywhere so that ultimately the country would see the need to defeat Andrew Jackson in his 1832 reelection bid. Worcester wisely recognized that Jackson was the central figure in the pro-removal cause.[11]

Angry that Worcester and his recalcitrant missionary friends had refused to leave the state, Governor Gilmer on July 7 once again sent the Guard after them. The Guard cursed and beat the prisoners throughout the eighty-five-mile forced march to the jail in Gwinnett County. They chained Butler to the neck of a horse, forcing him to walk the entire distance. Despite Ann's illness and infant daughter Jerusha's grave condition, the Guard forced Worcester to leave his family for prison. The missionaries were thrown into a dirty, foul county jail. A few days later Worcester was able to post the $500 bond to return home to see Ann and Jerusha.[12]

Wary of being arrested again, Worcester moved across the state line to work at the mission in Brainerd, Tennessee. Worcester wrote Gilmer claiming he had never intentionally tried to influence the Cherokee people, while observing, "the state of Georgia has no rightful jurisdiction over the territory where I reside." Such a statement did nothing to help Worcester's cause. And then tragedy struck. Six-month-old Jerusha died on August 14 while Worcester was living in Brainerd, and Worcester could not be notified in Brainerd in time for the funeral. His good friend Elias Boudinot conducted the service. Worcester returned to New Echota to rejoin his family just after the burial, only to be confronted by a Georgia Guardsman, who arrested him on his doorstep for entering Cherokee territory without a license. When he heard the sad news explaining why Worcester had returned to New Echota, the Guardsman released him but ordered him to leave the state until the trial in mid-September. The trial was brief and predictable. On September 16 the jury gave Judge Clayton a verdict after only fifteen minutes of deliberation: the men would get the maximum of four years of hard labor in the state penitentiary in Milledgeville.[13]

Worcester reported that the judge invoked the laws of God as well as those of Georgia in pronouncing the sentence: Judge Clayton "urged upon us those laws of God in regard to obedience to laws and to rulers which we have violated." But Governor Gilmer clearly did not want the public relations nightmare of sending Christian ministers to prison. He wanted them to officially recant or, better yet, to quietly leave the state. With the harsh alternative of four years of prison at hard labor, nine of the eleven missionaries caved in either by signing the oath or by departing the state. Only Worcester and Butler refused either alternative, insisting they were willing to serve out their sentence while hoping to challenge the constitutionality of Georgia's laws. Worcester and Butler were quickly marched off to Milledgeville to serve their terms.[14]

Gilmer was right to worry about public fallout over the imprisonment of white missionaries in Georgia. Newspapers throughout the nation, even in the South, ridiculed Georgia for jailing the preachers. Editors in the North depicted Worcester and Butler as heroes, sacrificial martyrs to the Cherokee cause, while religious spokesmen everywhere denounced the harsh treatment handed out to the missionaries. The *Vermont Telegraph*

castigated Georgia in unequivocal language: "Perhaps no event
has occurred in the country, which has excited greater surprise
and displeasure among good men, than the degrading manner
in which the missionaries of the cross have been arrested, conducted in chains to trial, and consigned to the penitentiary."
Gilmer himself would later concede, "No official act of mine
occasioned so much abuse at the time, or was so little understood as the punishment of the religious missionaries by imprisonment."[15]

When Worcester and Butler arrived at the Milledgeville
prison, a member of the Georgia Guard announced their fate:
"There is where all the enemies of Georgia have to land—there
and in hell." Nonetheless, the two men were decently fed and
sheltered but had to perform manual labor, working in a cabi-
netmaking shop. Worcester preached on Sundays to some two
dozen other prisoners; on other days he and Butler sang hymns
and taught Bible lessons. Likening himself to Old Testament
figures Nehemiah, Shadrach, and Daniel—imprisoned for defying the authorities—Worcester proclaimed he was committed
to serving his sentence: "I am led firmly to believe that any man
contending for the rights of conscience and the liberty of spreading the gospel, will always find strength given him from above."
And he came to prize his growing reputation as a troublemak-
ing Cherokee sympathizer: "It is a great happiness," he wrote
from prison to the American Board, "to be esteemed a deluded
good man, rather than an ill-designing hypocrite. Let my name
be sounded abroad as a weak, misguided enthusiast, yet a sincere
lover of Jesus."[16]

The Cherokee people were deeply moved by the sacrifice
the two men languishing in prison were making on their

behalf. Boudinot, John Ridge, and John Ross solicited contributions from their friends and sent the money to the wives of
the two prisoners so they could visit their husbands in Milledgeville. "Perhaps," Boudinot wrote Ann, "you will now have
enough to bear your expenses to Milledgeville and back and
to purchase for Mr. Worcester a couple of blankets. . . . Give
my *best, kindest* regards to him & tell him that the Cherokee
sympathize with him. He lives, and will live, in their affection &
remembrance."[17]

———

Such obvious sympathy for a marked man like Worcester placed
Boudinot in danger as well. Already under suspicion for his
anti-Georgia editorials, Boudinot once again became the target
for the Guard in the wake of the roundup of the missionaries.
Colonel Charles H. Nelson, commander of the Guard, attempted
to shut down the *Phoenix* in late summer of 1831, and he
approached his cause with all the personal vitriol he could mus-
ter. Georgia Guards summoned Boudinot from his house to a
meeting with Nelson. Having been frequently charged by Nelson with "abusive and slanderous" editorials in the *Phoenix*,
Boudinot at first refused to show up, not looking for an opportunity to be threatened with "personal chastisement." When
Boudinot failed to appear, Colonel Nelson became enraged,
declaring "he would whip" him "within an inch" of his life.
Actually, Nelson put it even more graphically: "I will mount
you," Nelson reportedly exclaimed. Boudinot explained to his
readers that Nelson did not mean "he would place me on a
horse and take me off as a prisoner. It is a Southern phrase,
meaning *he would fall upon and beat me*." When Boudinot

finally appeared before the Guard, Nelson insisted that he and the Guard were "well informed" that Samuel Worcester was in fact the real editor of the *Phoenix* and wrote all the incendiary editorials against the state of Georgia. Claiming that "there were not five lines of truth" in all the editorials about the Guard, Nelson charged that "their (Missionaries) character for falsehoods was so well established, and their motive so well understood, that *censure* from them was *praise to the Guard*." Boudinot dismissed the accusation that the missionaries were running the *Phoenix* as "too foolish to demand any attention." But he happily conceded that friendship and shared values brought him close to Worcester and others. "I entertain the highest regard for these persecuted men," Boudinot told Nelson. "I consider them to be men of the strictest integrity and veracity. Among them I have the honor to number some of my best and nearest friends, but they have as little desire to interfere with my duties as editor as to interfere with any other person."[18]

If Nelson had hoped his "personal chastisement" of Boudinot would serve as intimidation, he failed utterly, as he quickly discovered. A few weeks later, Boudinot again used the pages of the *Phoenix* to go on the attack against Georgia and its leaders. Governor Gilmer, Boudinot argued, charged missionaries "with crimes, such as *sedition*, *opposing* the HUMANE policy of the Government, *exciting* the Indians, &c." These charges, Boudinot claimed, were "utterly unfounded." "The Governor," he wrote, "is pleased to say that the rights of liberty, personal security and private property of the Indians are better protected under the laws of the state than heretofore. The Cherokees will laugh at this. They believe, and know by sad experience, the reverse to be the fact."[19]

While Worcester and Butler languished in prison, and Boudinot excoriated Georgia leaders from his perch at the *Phoenix*,
the American Board, in conjunction with Chief John Ross,
began preparing their legal case against Georgia. They hired the
prominent attorneys William Wirt and John Sergeant to handle
the appeal for the missionaries. Experienced in the constitutional
issues raised by Georgia's extension laws and well aware that the
fate of both the missionaries and the Cherokee Nation hung in
the balance, Wirt and Sergeant also brought national political
implications into the picture. In the upcoming 1832 presidential election to take on Andrew Jackson's bid for a second term,
Wirt stood as the Anti-Masonic Party presidential nominee,
and the Whigs chose Sergeant as the vice presidential nominee
to join their presidential hopeful Henry Clay. The Whigs and
Anti-Masons clearly dissented from Jackson's Indian policy—
and Georgia's treatment of the Cherokees and missionaries. So
with Wirt and Sergeant leading the Cherokees' legal battles all
the way to the Supreme Court, the fate of the missionaries as
well as the Cherokee Nation had now become inextricably
linked to the outcome of the 1832 presidential election.[20]

As Wirt and Sergeant prepared their case, Chief Ross prepared his people for the uncertain legal battles that lay ahead.
As if to underscore the growing danger that Georgia's new laws
imposed on him and other leaders, Ross was forced to meet
with his General Council in Chattanooga, Tennessee, rather
than in the capital, New Echota, to avoid a conflict with Georgia troops. In his annual address, Ross staunchly defended the
missionaries in their looming legal challenge against Georgia.
Worcester and Butler were missionaries, he claimed, "who have

met a welcome reception in this nation . . . have also been cru-
elly torn from their families" and thrown in prison "under the
charge merely of *residing* in this Nation and refusing to comply
with a law" that is clearly unconstitutional. Despite few positive
signs to point to out of Washington or Georgia, Ross boasted
to his people that Wirt and Sergeant would successfully take
the missionary case to the Supreme Court. "There can be no
doubt," Ross argued, "that a majority of the Judges of the
Supreme Court holds the law of Georgia extending jurisdiction
within our limits to be unconstitutional, and whenever a case
between proper parties can be brought before them, they will
so decide."[21]

Ross's public display of confidence, though, contrasted sharply
with the realities he faced in private. Governor Gilmer, in his
ongoing effort to sow dissent between various factions among
the Cherokee, sent Colonel John W. A. Sanford into the Cherokee Nation to dig up suspicious information on John Ross's
Cherokee heritage—in particular, to find out how much "Indian
blood" was in his background. Predictably, Sanford returned
with the conclusion Gilmer was seeking: that his claim to being
one-eighth Cherokee was not only entirely hollow but also a
source of betrayal to his people. "The native Indian has but little
part . . . in the administration of their government," Sanford's
inquiry observed, "but that its affairs are managed *exclusively* by
those who are so remotely related to the Indian, as gives them but
slender claims to be classed among that people." Such a claim,
of course, was common currency among Ross's white enemies,
who frequently asserted that he governed like a tyrant over his
people and that most "true" full-blood Cherokees secretly wanted
him out of office.[22]

Personal attacks on Ross reached a dangerous level when a

white Georgian, angry at Ross for taking on the state's intruders, accosted Ross riding home from a visit with Major Ridge on the night of November 30, 1831. "A tall, gaunt figure," a white man named Harris, rode up behind Ross and yelled, "Ross, I have been for a long time wanting to kill you, and I'll be d—d if I don't now do it." Shots rang out, but Ross managed to gallop away without being hit.[23]

With personal and political danger mounting from all quarters, Ross understandably felt increasing urgency to seek help for the Cherokees, the missionaries, and himself. A few weeks after the assassination attempt, Ross sent a delegation to Washington to lobby Congress and the Jackson administration. John Ridge was part of the delegation that arrived in D.C. on December 20. "Remind [President Jackson]," Ross instructed Ridge and his colleagues, "of the positive assurances of protection which he had made us, & respectfully ask the reasons why it has been so long withheld."[24]

At the same time, Elias Boudinot began a fund-raising tour of East Coast cities to keep the *Cherokee Phoenix* afloat and "to awaken American citizens to the crisis in Cherokee affairs." On one of his first stops, in Augusta, Georgia, Boudinot noted sadly that locals seemed strangely silent about the fate of Worcester and Butler as well as Indian affairs in general: "The people appear to be more indifferent than I expected to find them." After reading a story in the Milledgeville newspaper about the Georgia legislature passing a bill authorizing the immediate survey and occupancy of Cherokee country, Boudinot responded with alarm. "To take our lands by force," he wrote, "is a serious matter. . . . It would be robbery to all intent and purposes." A growing crisis for his people loomed unmistakably on the horizon:

"[The Cherokees] reside on the land which God gave them—they are surrounded with guarantees which this Republic has voluntarily made for their protection." But now those "guarantees" were being openly "violated." And who was to blame? "The sin will not be at our door, but at the door of our *oppressor* and our faithless *Guardian*."[25]

Just before taking off on his fund-raising tour, Boudinot had already voiced concern about how the Cherokees' white "fathers" had betrayed them. He admired the intentions of Washington and Jefferson and the benevolent associations that together had helped "civilize" the Cherokees from the early 1800s, but Boudinot could only lament that those "advancements" now everywhere confronted massive "obstacles" and "difficulties." In fact, "the 'Great Father' of the 'red man'" was now trying to block the Cherokee people. "The promises of Washington and Jefferson have not been fulfilled," he concluded.

> The policy of the United States on Indian affairs has taken a different direction, for no other reason than that the Cherokees have so far become civilized as to appreciate a regular form of Government. They are now deprived of rights they once enjoyed—A neighboring power is now permitted to extends its withering hand over them. . . . Ministers of the Gospel, who might have, at this day of trial, administered to them the consolations of Religion, have been arrested, chained, dragged away before their eyes, tried as felons, and finally immured in prison with thieves and robbers.

Sadly, the motive force for this betrayal was, for Boudinot, easy to see: "Cupidity and self-interest are at the bottom of all these difficulties—A desire to *possess* the Indian land is paramount to a desire to see him *established* on the soil as a *civilized* man."[26]

When he reached Washington, Boudinot joined Ridge and found pockets of support and hope. They paid a visit to Henry Clay, who assured his Cherokee friends of his commitment to their cause in the U.S. Senate. Ridge and Boudinot then traveled to New York City for a large meeting with sympathizers who would join them in writing a memorial to Congress. Six thousand people signed their petition in support of the Cherokees.[27]

Despite the mounting crisis, Ridge believed that Henry Clay's Whig Party within five years would "be irristable over the Union." But in the immediate term, he reported to Ross, with all the unchecked depredations from Georgia, and with various leaders traveling through Cherokee country trying to promote voluntary removal, "it is not good news." Still, the upcoming legal challenge mounted on behalf of the missionaries offered hope. "Onward in the path of duty is my motto," he insisted. A firm believer in the Cherokee people's need for unity under the guiding wisdom of their chiefs, Ridge sounded ever hopeful and determined: "Strongly opposed to surrender our National existence, I shall never give it up even unto death."[28]

While touring cities in the Northeast with Boudinot in February of 1832, Ridge lashed out at the hypocrisy of their "white fathers." As the Cherokee people awaited their case before the Supreme Court, Ridge pointed an accusing finger at the nation's political leaders, who had coaxed Indians into a "civilization" program only to withdraw their support at a critical moment.

You asked us to throw off the hunter and warrior state: We did so—you asked us to form a republican government:

We did so—adopting your own as a model. You asked us to cultivate the earth, and learn the mechanic arts: We did so. You asked us to learn to read: We did so. You asked us to cast away our idols, and worship your God: We did so.[29]

Ironically, sophisticated Cherokee leaders, well educated under the federal "civilization" effort, were now poised to use their legal knowledge against their white oppressors.

On February 20, 1832, William Wirt and John Sergeant stood before the United States Supreme Court to argue for Samuel Worcester and Elizur Butler in the case *Worcester v. Georgia*. No one was present on behalf of the state of Georgia, thanks to the Georgia legislature, which demanded no briefs be filed nor any representation be made in Washington. Wirt argued that Georgia's new law extending its jurisdiction into the Cherokee Nation was unconstitutional not only for ignoring Cherokee sovereignty but also for infringing on the federal government's exclusive power over Indian matters. Treaties and laws made with the Indians, Wirt and Sergeant insisted, stood as the supreme law of the land under the Constitution. The Court, then, must nullify any state law that violated federal jurisdiction.[30]

Wirt and Sergeant made an exhaustive case before the Court, their arguments lasting nearly three days. A New York reporter at the trial observed that Wirt spoke at such length and with such passion that he "was obliged, from fatigue, to ask for the Court to adjourn." Justice Joseph Story noted that Wirt's speeches were "uncommonly eloquent, forcible, and finished." The seventy-six-year-old chief justice, John Marshall, though recovering from a serious bladder operation, maintained strong interest in the case and was even reported to be moved to tears.[31]

Nearly two weeks later, the Supreme Court rendered its verdict: Marshall announced on March 3 that by a vote of 6 to 1, the Court overturned the missionaries' conviction. It was a stunning victory for the Cherokees and missionaries. Georgia's laws, Marshall held, were "repugnant to the Constitution, laws, and treaties of the United States." In unequivocal language, the Court had determined that the Cherokee Nation was indeed a separate, sovereign nation, that the federal government—not the states—maintained exclusive authority over its affairs, and that Georgia had no right to extend its laws over the Cherokee people. To support his decision, Marshall sketched an overview of American history and initial contact with native peoples that insisted Indians were *not* anarchic, wandering bands of "savages" but legitimate Indian nations with their own political, legal, and social institutions. Thus Marshall pointed to the numerous treaties over the years in which the United States dealt with Indians as equals, not inferiors.[32]

Elias Boudinot and John Ridge were in Boston on their speaking tour and were stopping by the American Board headquarters when the news from the Supreme Court came in. A friend from Washington burst into the missionary room, where Boudinot and Ridge were visiting. "Mr. John Tappan came in to see us," Boudinot reported. "He then told us the true story of the case, and produced a paper which contained an account, and tried to read to us, but he was so agitated with joy that he could hardly proceed." Some of the men danced a jig around the table in jubilation. The rejoicing was so contagious at the American Board that Boudinot could not contain his excitement. "It is a great triumph on the part of the Cherokees." John Ridge called it "glorious news." In Cherokee country John Ross claimed there were "rejoicings throughout the Nation on the decision of the supreme court upon the Cherokee case. Traitors and internal enemies are seeking places where to hide their heads." One army general told the secretary of war that "rejoicings, night dances, etc., were had in all parts" and there was "yelling and whooping in every direction."[33]

Georgia officials, predictably, responded to the news with bitter contempt. Labeling the decision a "usurpation" of state jurisdiction, Governor Lumpkin guaranteed that the ruling would encounter unyielding condemnation. Lumpkin claimed he would hang Worcester and Butler before he "submitted to this decision made by a few superannuated life estate judges." The editor of the *Macon Advertiser* was just as truculent: "[The missionaries] have been placed where they deserved to be, in the State Prison, and not all the eloquence of a Wirt, or a Sergeant, nor the decision or power of the Supreme Court can take them from it unless the State chooses to give them up." Worcester and Butler had been aided and abetted, Gilmer argued, "by religious fanatics everywhere," especially in the North where evangelicals had the luxury of sympathizing with Indians precisely because they did not exist in their region. The ultimate trump card, Georgia officials realized, came in their conviction that Andrew Jackson would never enforce Marshall's decision. "He will, if I mistake not," Congressman George Troup noted, "defend the sovereignty of the states, as he would the sovereignty of the union."[34]

Troup was right. Upon hearing of the *Worcester* decision,

Andrew Jackson reportedly commented, "John Marshall has made his decision, now let him enforce it." Whether or not he uttered those words, the sentiment accurately summed up his perspective. Jackson later wrote to a friend, "The decision of the supreme court has fell still born, and they find that they cannot coerce Georgia to yield to its mandate." Furthermore, Jackson pointed out, if a violent conflict arose between Georgia and the Cherokees, "the arm of the government is not sufficiently strong to preserve [the Cherokees] from destruction."[35]

The realization that Marshall's ruling, in the face of Georgia's intransigence on Indian affairs, carried no weight soon drained the hope from Boudinot, Ridge, and Ross. All of which made the Cherokees' celebration over the *Worcester* decision short-lived. By the time Boudinot and Ridge returned to join the rest of the Cherokee delegation in Washington in early April, the mood had shifted from jubilation to despair. While initially Ridge felt "greatly revived—a new man" after the Marshall ruling, he knew the contest was not over. "The Chicken Snake General Jackson," Ridge observed, "has time to crawl and hide in the luxuriant grass of his nefarious hypocracy."

Days later, Ridge had a private meeting with the "nefarious" Jackson to confront the president about whether he would stop the Georgia intruders. In that meeting Ridge no doubt emphasized the critical moment all parties had now reached over the "Cherokee question." The Marshall decision, Ridge argued, surely gave compelling force to the Cherokee cause. And there could be no doubt that Georgia had acted unconstitutionally and that the Cherokee people, as Jackson himself had on occasion observed, were an improving people with their own legitimate, independent government. Under these circumstances, Ridge insisted, the president had the obligation to step in and end Georgia's dangerous incursions into Indian country. To Ridge's astonishment, Jackson bluntly replied that he felt no such obligation. The Cherokees had been warned for years that this day was coming, Jackson pointed out, and his plan to relocate them out West offered them the best way to safeguard their future as a people. Wounded and pained at this complete rejection of the Cherokee cause, Ridge struggled to maintain his composure. Sensing Ridge's indignation, Jackson told him to go home and tell his people that "their only hope of relief was in abandoning their country and removing to the West." Jackson later confided to a friend that his message for Ridge plunged him into melancholy. "I believe Ridge has expressed despair," Jackson observed, "and that it is better for them to treat and move."[36]

Anguished over the turn of events, Ridge and Boudinot fell into a powerful soul-searching crisis over precisely how to protect the Cherokee Nation. And with Jackson poised to win reelection in the fall—a very plausible prospect even with his many detractors—the future look even grimmer. Ridge, perhaps owing to the rejection from his recent personal conversation with Jackson, had become so demoralized that he signaled to Boudinot his dramatic change of heart: the Cherokees future, he believed, no longer lay in resistance but in negotiating a treaty for removal. Boudinot was taken aback by Ridge's turnaround, but he reluctantly agreed. Yet both men instinctively knew two essential truths: that they were not empowered by the Nation to negotiate such a treaty in Washington and that they could not yet publicly acknowledge their new strategy. To do so, in the face of overwhelming tribal opposition to removal, would instantly destroy whatever power and influence they still possessed.[37] Not since their public embarrassments at Cornwall had Boudinot and

Ridge likely felt such a disconnect between their hopes and the crushing realities that lay before them.

And they must have felt increasingly alone. They still had friends in high places, but even those sympathetic to their cause were now pushing them toward acceptance of painful truths. David Greene of the American Board sent John a letter conceding that any further legal or financial defense of the Cherokees would be impossible. "It makes me weep to think of it," Greene wrote. "But if your friends in Congress think that all further effort in your behalf will be useless . . . then, for aught I can see, you must make the best terms you can, & go." Greene was right: the Cherokees' friends in Washington were losing heart for their cause. While the delegation was still in Washington, John McLean, a Supreme Court justice quite sympathetic to the Cherokees, offered to meet with them. McLean told them that with Jackson's unwillingness to enforce the ruling in *Worcester*, the Court stood powerless. So he advised that they try to craft a treaty on the best terms possible and offered to help the process along by serving as a commissioner at any treaty council that could be arranged.[38]

Even as he pondered what course to follow, Ridge felt compelled to play both sides against the middle. He became alarmed, for example, that two Cherokees, John Walker Jr. and James Starr, had come to Washington spreading the word to Cass and others in the Jackson administration that "many Cherokees were despondent and ready to emigrate." Like Ross, Ridge worried about such irresponsible conduct that would only divide the tribe. "Appearances," Ridge told Ross, "are everything with the multitude."[39]

Appearances quickly became troubling for Ridge and his

friends who now favored negotiating for removal. When word leaked of McLean's meeting with the Cherokee delegation, Georgia congressman Daniel Newnan excitedly pronounced it as news: "The Cherokee Delegation," Newnan boasted, "have at last consented to recommend to their people to make a treaty with the government upon the general basis that they shall acquire a patent for land over the Mississippi, and, at a proper time, be allowed a delegate in Congress." Newnan's letter was reprinted in the *Phoenix* by Stand Watie, Boudinot's brother, who was substituting for him as editor while Boudinot was away on tour. Boudinot knew the letter was going to be made public, but once it came out, Ridge and William Shorey Coodey, Ross's nephew, quickly denied the story.[40]

Warming to this moment of growing confusion in the Cherokee leadership, on April 16 Secretary of War Lewis Cass summoned Ridge and the other members of the Cherokee delegation to the War Department. He suggested terms of a treaty providing a large tract of fertile land west of the Arkansas Territory. He reminded them that if the Cherokees remained on their lands in the East, they would have to become citizens of the states in which they live—with no help or protection from the federal government.

The terms Cass offered were, in fact, rather liberal: The Cherokees could run their own government; white people would be prohibited from the territory; removal could take place via whatever mode of travel suited the Cherokees; the federal government would subsidize the Cherokees for the first year in their new land; the Cherokees would be compensated with an annuity equal to the value of their holdings left behind; the federal government would fund the building of schools, churches, council houses, and homes for the principal chiefs; families would be given blankets, axes, plows, hoes, wheels, and looms. And the U.S. government would protect the Cherokees from any hostile Indians out West.[41]

Despite Cass's relatively generous offer, Ridge clearly found dealing with the Jackson administration a disgusting proposition. How should one trust an administration that had trampled Cherokees' rights underfoot "to offer new pledges from their rotten hearts"? On the other hand, he and his colleagues John Martin and William Shorey Coodey confirmed that they were leaning toward cutting a deal for emigration out West. Therefore, Ridge's delegation told the secretary that personally they favored making a treaty, but they did not want to say so in public. And so they asked Cass to send the treaty terms to the Cherokee Council via his own emissary. Cass agreed, arranging for the tribe's missionary attorney, Elisha Chester, to deliver it.[42]

When John Ridge returned home in late spring, news about his dramatic change of heart on removal had already spread within the Nation—along with his own assorted retractions and denials. Ridge first had to face his parents, whose position on such a critical tribal matter loomed large in the Nation. Major Ridge had just returned from a tour of the Nation, and John was likely quite worried about how his father would respond to a strategy of removal. But he was relieved when Major Ridge reacted with joy at seeing him. And, upon hearing his son's explanation for his decision, Major Ridge concurred and promised total support for him and Boudinot. Major Ridge had always planned for his son to be a leader among the Cherokees; if leading his people to a new land offered the best hope for their survival, Major Ridge suggested, then so be it.[43]

Boudinot likewise had been forced to rethink his position on the Cherokees' dilemma. The Cherokee people, he wrote, had to face the "unpleasant" fact that the president of the United States would not enforce the decision of the Supreme Court. Worse yet, he realized, Jackson had informed the nation that not only was he "*not bound*" by the ruling, but he willfully intended to ignore it: "What sort of hope have we then from a President who feels himself under no obligation *to execute*, but has an inclination *to disregard* the laws and treaties?"[44]

Such candid truth-telling among leading Cherokees upset Chief John Ross's plans. He was angry at Ridge and Boudinot—both for their reversal on removal and for the confusion and dissent it would sow in the Nation. He was especially irritated about the Newnan letter that, thanks to its publication in the *Phoenix*, was circulating widely in the Nation. "Those statements [in Newnan's letter] are well calculated to mislead the public mind in regard to the subject on which they are made," Ross complained to Boudinot. "No power," he stressed, "has been given to our delegation to treat away this country during their visit at the seat of the General Government." Early on, Ross leveled most of his outrage at John Ridge's reversal as nothing short of treason: he claimed Ridge led "one of the most consummate acts of treachery towards his country that the annals of any nation affords."[45]

By the summer of 1832 a full-blown split emerged over what had become known as the "Cherokee question": not only how to respond to the obvious lack of support for the Cherokees from

the federal government as well as Georgia's continuing encroachments but also how to deal with growing divisions within the
Cherokee Nation itself. On one side stood Chief John Ross, who
insisted that the Cherokees must remain in their homeland at
all costs, that removal must be resisted, and that anyone who
endorsed, let alone participated in, negotiating a removal treaty
was, in effect, a traitor, an enemy to his people. The great majority of the Cherokees, intent on keeping their homeland, supported Ross's unrelenting stance of resistance to removal.

A smaller but highly vocal portion of the Cherokee people,
though, had come to believe that removal represented the only
alternative to the Nation's eventual degradation at the hands
of what Boudinot called "an overwhelming white population"
who, "in their sovereign pleasure . . . consider [the Cherokees]
as their inferiors."[46] Boudinot, John and Major Ridge, along
with David Vann and a few other acculturated Cherokee elites,
comprised the leadership of what became known as the Treaty
Party because of their willingness to negotiate a treaty to emigrate to new lands out West, where they believed the Cherokees
had the best chance to survive as a people.

By the summer of 1832 an escalating war of words, grounded
in the fierce convictions of both parties, swirled throughout
Cherokee Nation. Initially, the conflict pitted a wealthy, slave-
owning acculturated principal chief against an outspoken newspaper editor filled with missionary zeal. What they fought over
was nothing less than the destiny of the Cherokee people. And
much of that debate turned on the question, at this critical
moment, What should a good patriot do for his people?

Chief John Ross and Elias Boudinot answered that question
in wildly different, contradictory ways. Portraying himself as

the unrelenting protector of the homeland, Ross argued that members of the Treaty Party were a "small minority opposed to the will of the people" who were attempting to sell out their sacred homeland without the authority to do so and "against [the people's] expressed injunctions." Boudinot bitterly fought back against "the illusive appearance of having a vast majority opposed to us."[47] The only reason the Cherokee people sided with Ross, Boudinot insisted, was because their chief had not seen fit to speak honestly with them about the grave dangers that lay ahead if they resisted removal. "We charge Mr. Ross," Boudinot wrote, "with having deluded them with expectations incompatible with, and injurious to, their interest." According to Boudinot, Ross was preventing discussion and debate of this "vital" matter, leaving his people "ignorant of their true condition." Truthful information, Boudinot fiercely believed, would lead his people to a wise decision: he was "firmly of the opinion, that a large majority of the Cherokee people would prefer to remove, if the true state of their condition was properly made known to them."

> If one hundred persons are ignorant of their true situation, and are so completely blinded as not to see the destruction that awaits them, we can see strong reasons to justify the action of a minority of fifty persons—to do what the majority *would do* if they understood their condition—to save a *nation* from political thralldom and moral degradation.[48]

Boudinot also lashed out at Ross's claim that somehow the pro-removal forces were to blame for the internal divisions within the Cherokee Nation, arguing that in fact it was the Treaty Party that had "sounded the alarm . . . to save the nation by timely action." Boudinot and his allies had been the true friends of the Cherokee people, desperately seeking answers and a new strategy. "We asked, we entreated, we implored—But we were met at the very threshold as *enemies of our country*."[49]

Boudinot did not hesitate to use his position as editor of the *Phoenix* to openly debate the issue, but Ross, who viewed the newspaper as the official organ of the Cherokee Nation, would not tolerate such dissent. The *Phoenix*, Ross contended, should present only the positions voiced by the constituted authorities of the Cherokee people. "The toleration of *diversified views* to the columns of such a paper would not fail to create fermentation and confusion among our citizens," Ross declared, "and in the end prove injurious to the welfare of the nation. The love of our country and people demands *unity of sentiment and action* for the good of *all*." Clearly fearing that white political leaders might look upon such public quarreling as an expression of weakness in the struggle to resist removal, Ross instructed Boudinot in July to stop publishing dissenting opinions in the paper.[50]

Outraged at Ross's act of censorship on such a crucial matter, Boudinot resigned as editor of the *Phoenix* on August 1. To stay on as editor, Boudinot declared in his final editorial, would put him in an "as embarrassing as it would be peculiar and delicate" situation. Seeing his position as a moral imperative, he put the matter in the starkest terms: "I do conscientiously believe it to be the duty of every citizen to reflect upon the dangers with which we are surrounded—to view the darkness which seems to lie before our people—our prospects, and the evils with which we are threatened—to talk over all these matters." Only "a free and friendly discussion among ourselves" will lead to a clear sense of

THE "WHITE MAN'S WEAPON"

"the will of the people," Boudinot argued. "It is the presenting
the serious and momentous things to the people, what I mean by
telling them the truth. And I am inclined to believe that it is the
best, if not the only way to find out what the *will of the people*
is. . . . What are our *hopes* and *prospects*? What are our *dangers*
and *difficulties*?"[51]

When Boudinot departed the *Phoenix*, Ross still needed the
paper to spread his anti-removal message. So he replaced Boudinot with his brother-in-law, Elijah Hicks. Hicks wasted no time
vilifying his predecessor: he promptly announced that Boudinot's
resignation represented a loss that was "but a drop in the bucket."
After all, Hicks claimed, Boudinot had become "detached" from
the nation and "was now *no more* a patriot."[52]

By questioning Boudinot's patriotism, Hicks had deliberately
pushed a very hot button. "I am not *detached from* but *attached to*
the nation," Boudinot fired back. "There is nothing in my letter
of resignation, or in my explanations," he insisted, "which shows
a want of patriotic views and motives—my motives certainly
were of the most patriotic kind. In one word, I may say that my
patriotism consists in the *love of the country*, and *the love of the
People*. These are intimately connected, yet they are not alto-
gether inseparable." Which was precisely the case, he argued, in
the decision facing the Cherokees. "If the country is lost, or is
likely to be lost to all human appearance, and the people still
exist, may I not, with a patriotism true and commendable, make
a *question* for the safety of the remaining object of my affection?"[53]

Boudinot's position could not have been plainer: the Cherokee
people were facing a devastating loss; better to relocate where
they could survive as a people than stubbornly resist the inevitable and lose both their land and their soul. "Our lands, or a

large portion of them, are about to be seized and taken from us," he wrote. "Now, as a friend of my people, I cannot say *peace*, *peace*, when there is no peace. I cannot ease their minds with any expectation of a calm, when the vessel is already tossed to and fro, and threatened to be shattered to pieces by an approaching tempest." The way he saw it, the Cherokees now faced a grim existential decision that held out but three choices: stay and fight for their lands against overwhelming odds; submit to an oppressive white population and suffer a "moral death"; or "avoid the first two by a removal."[54]

Among the leading Cherokees joining Boudinot's Treaty Party were his brother, Stand Watie, William Coodey (a nephew of John Ross), Willliam Hicks, John Walker Jr., David Vann, John Fields, William Rogers, and James Starr. The Treaty Party probably never represented more than 10 percent of the people and their chiefs (and an even smaller fraction of the traditionalists). So with the majority of Cherokees remaining strongly attached to their homeland, Boudinot understood he was fighting an uphill battle. Such a battle, he reasoned, required facing a harsh reality. And for Boudinot that reality pointed to but one question left "to every Cherokee . . . whether it is more desirable to remain here, with all the embarrassments with which we must be surrounded, or to seek a country where we *may* enjoy our own laws, and live under our own vine and fig-tree." Patriotism was a noble thing, Boudinot conceded, but how was one to love one's country that was destined for destruction? "Although we *love the land* of our fathers," he argued, "we consider the lot of the *Exile* immeasurably more to be preferred than a submission" to oppressive laws and the inevitable "ruin and degradation of the Cherokee people."[55]

While Cherokee leaders openly clashed over their people's future, Samuel Worcester and Elizur Butler languished in their Milledgeville, Georgia, prison. And by November of 1832, when they had been confined for more than a year, several painful realities—all of them beyond their control—intervened to shape their destiny. First, Andrew Jackson, the Cherokees' most powerful opponent, won reelection for a second term. That grim fact virtually ensured an even darker reality: the *Worcester* decision, which earlier in the year had given Worcester, Butler, and their Cherokee friends so much hope, would never be enforced. And the mounting crisis over nullification—in which South Carolina in 1832 threatened to nullify a federal tariff law, thus endangering national sovereignty—forced the missionaries to wonder if their cause was only further dividing the nation.[56]

Indeed, Governor Lumpkin of Georgia sent emissaries to Worcester and Butler to suggest that their personal battle, far from succeeding, was serving only to push America closer to civil war. In truth, public anger continued to haunt Georgia officials over their harsh treatment of the missionaries, and Lumpkin was eager to find a quiet end to the missionaries'—and Georgia's—ordeal. Lumpkin even tried to enlist the help of the wives of Worcester and Butler. Lumpkin invited the women to a party at the governor's mansion, where he tried to coax them into persuading their imprisoned husbands to give up their cause for the good of the country. He promised he would release them, if only they would apologize and request a pardon. Ann Worcester responded that any such decision would be up to her husband.

The mounting pressure finally got to the missionaries. On

December 7, both men agreed to give up the fight. That judgment unleashed a series of key decisions. They wrote to the American Board, asking if surrendering at this point was acceptable. On Christmas Day, the board agreed that Worcester and Butler should drop the case. Two days later, the board wrote Chief Ross, asking him to end the Cherokee opposition to a removal treaty. He declined. On January 8, 1833, Worcester and Butler requested that their lawyers end the effort to enforce Marshall's ruling. Although they had a "perfect right to a legal discharge," the men insisted, they had been informed that "the further prosecution of the controversy, under existing circumstances, might be attended with consequences injurious" to their "beloved country." Lumpkin took offense at the tone of the letter, so Worcester and Butler composed a softer note the next day: "In the course we have now taken," the note read, "it has been our intention simply to forbear the prosecution of our case, and to leave the question of the continuance of our confinement to the magnanimity of the state." Placated by the more compliant tone, Governor Lumpkin pardoned the men, but not without offering his own condemnation of their cause: "Whatever may have been the errors of these individuals—whatever embarrassments and heart-burnings they may have been instrumental in creating—however mischievous they may have been in working evil to the State, to themselves, and the still more unfortunate Cherokees. . . . They shall go free."[57]

They had served sixteen months in prison. A few days after their release in mid-January, Worcester and Butler explained in a public letter why they had given up their cause and requested a pardon. Georgia had finally repealed the offending statute, they pointed out. And they now knew that the *Worcester* ruling would go unenforced. To continue their fight, they also had been persuaded, would only endanger the Union, possibly leading to violence between Georgia and the Cherokee Nation. They had entered prison knowing that "the faith and justice of our nation were at hazard," and they left their confinement realizing the nation's pledge to protect the Cherokees had been "broken, and an act of flagrant robbery . . . [was] committed upon a defenceless people, with the sanction of our national authorities." Ultimately, they conceded, "there was no longer any hope" that they could help the Cherokee people.[58]

Despite that dramatic surrender of hope, the "Cherokee question" remained unanswered. Neither Ross nor the Treaty Party had lost an ounce of faith in the righteousness of their markedly different solutions for their people. As Worcester and Butler rejoined their families in freedom, the Cherokee people they so clearly loved continued their internal war of words. In early February 1833 John Ridge wrote John Ross, warning him about a group of unauthorized men on their way to Washington to undercut the official delegation and discuss a removal treaty. Ridge could not help but remind Ross that "other Gentlemen with myself [have] despaired of the existence of our dear nation upon its present Location" and urged him to listen to the advice of those beyond his inner circle. The Cherokee people, Ridge said, are being "robbed & whipped by the whites almost every day." It was time for Ross to do something: "I know you are capable of acting the part of a statesman." But "we all know, upon our consultation in Council that we can't be a Nation here, [so] I hope we shall attempt to establish it somewhere else!"[59]

They had thoughtfully employed the legal "white man's

weapon" and, despite victory in the Supreme Court, watched their efforts come to nothing. It seemed increasingly clear, at least to the Treaty Party, that they could no longer "be a Nation here." But trying to establish their home "somewhere else" would trigger an even larger battle—one that threatened the very soul of the Cherokee people.

5

New Echota

When the Treaty Party, led by Elias Boudinot and John and Major Ridge, finally went public by the end of 1832 with their conviction that the Cherokees' only hope lay in relocation to the West, Chief John Ross stiffened his resolve as well to fight removal—and its proponents—at all costs. Ross instinctively grasped his people's deep attachment to the land and adroitly used that emotional connection to battle his increasingly outspoken opponents. But because Ross viewed the Ridge or Treaty Party as "an unpatriotic threat" rather than a loyal opposition, he inadvertently exacerbated the very divisions and tensions within the Cherokee Nation that he otherwise worked so hard to calm. Likewise, as Ross grew more entrenched in retaining the homeland, the Ridge faction became all the more committed to emigration as the only true path for saving the Cherokee people. As the private bickering in Cherokee country erupted into open factional warfare between 1833 and 1835, federal officials effectively seized on these internal divisions to pursue their own relentless objective: removal.

———

What Ross considered a supreme virtue—his stubborn fight to retain the homeland—only irritated his detractors, who had lost all patience with such an approach. Ross's own nephew, William Coodey, a member of the Cherokee delegation in Washington, grew so frustrated at Ross's inflexibility that he circulated a petition at the May 1833 council meeting protesting the strategy. Some twenty-five leading Cherokees signed the petition—among them Major Ridge, Elias Boudinot, and his brother Stand Watie—which called on Ross to explain his policy of delay. After the council debated the petition, Ross, characteristically, requested and received a postponement of his response until the October council. Major Ridge stood up and ominously observed that the Nation could not afford to look the other way much longer. The Cherokees would, he argued, very soon have to "submit always to the evils and difficulties every day increasing around them, or look for a new home, promising them freedom and national prosperity." Ever the statesman, Major Ridge strongly advised that facing painful realities must not lead to division. In fact, his people needed "to bury party animosity, and in case they should conclude to seek a new home, to go in the character of true friends and brothers."[1]

Ordinarily, such a statement would have been received as welcome words of harmony. But in the growing crisis the Cherokees faced, Ridge's peaceful admonition fell on deaf ears. Indeed, Ross's ongoing delays inspired even more frustration. Days later, John Walker, annoyed by Ross's tactics, joined up with an unofficial delegation of western Cherokees and headed to Washington. A dashing, charismatic man, Walker traveled with another independent-minded Cherokee, James Starr. They managed to get a meeting with Andrew Jackson to talk about a removal treaty. Although Jackson declined to formally treat with the two men, he was clearly charmed by Walker and invited him to return to Washington to discuss removal when he had more official support. Walker did return later in the year with David Vann—at the very time Ross was in Washington lobbying the Jackson administration.

Men like John Walker troubled John Ross. With good reason, Ross worried about growing numbers of his people who were critical of his leadership and willing to press for their own removal solutions. Even John Ridge, hardly a Ross ally at this point, had concerns about unofficial factions led by men such as Walker. The mere fact that Jackson met with Walker, Ridge observed, simply showed "the extent that Jackson will go to divide our nation."[2]

Yet another dissenter-turned-diplomat was Andrew Ross, John Ross's younger brother. Andrew Ross, who claimed to represent many leading Cherokees looking to emigrate, caught the attention of Secretary of War Lewis Cass. In June 1834, Cass began treaty talks with Andrew Ross, who appeared willing to trade all Cherokee lands in the East for very modest financial incentives. Insufficiently experienced in such negotiations, Andrew Ross returned home and talked Major Ridge and Elias Boudinot into returning with him to Washington to meet with President Jackson. At the same time John Walker and David Vann arrived in D.C. trying to deal with Cass and Jackson with their own removal strategy. Disturbed by the presence of his own brother and his pro-removal friends, as well as these other unofficial delegations, John Ross promptly launched into treaty discussions of his own with Secretary Cass. Perhaps feeling besieged by all the competitive factions lobbying the administration on removal, Ross for the first time trotted out the idea of giving up part of the Cherokees' land in the East. If they could retain a small portion to live on, Ross suggested, they could hope to assimilate with whites and become subject to state jurisdiction. Both Cass and Jackson turned Ross's proposal down flat. When Ross aired out the plan to Major Ridge, Ridge also rejected it, noting that it would only lead to their oppression, poverty, and moral degradation.[3]

The Cherokee Nation, riven by clashes over the removal question, was also falling quickly into bankruptcy. At the heart of its financial problem lay the issue of annuities—the yearly payments made to the Nation by the federal government for lands that had been ceded—and how to receive them. Since 1830 President Jackson had ordered that the annuity payment be divided and paid per capita to each individual Cherokee. Although Jackson argued that he changed the annuity payments because tribal leaders had embezzled the funds, thus depriving their people of their fair share, the president's real purpose was obvious: to weaken the Cherokee Nation and deny the Cherokee government the cash required to defend the rights of the people. The Ridge faction supported the Jackson rule to convert the annuity to individual payments as a way to keep funds—and the resulting power—out of the hands of the Ross Party. Ross strongly opposed the change in the annuity, insisting that individual payments deliberately deprived the Cherokee Nation of a critical part of its funding. More than a few times Ross had to ask for volunteer contributions just to pay attorney fees for the tribe.[4]

With such a growing chorus of opposition and a financially

strapped government, Ross furiously lobbied his supporters throughout Cherokee country. He used every opportunity to underline his populist commitment to the "will of the people." "I shall never deceive you," he wrote one friend, "and that so far as my feeble talent and ability will permit it shall be exerted solely with the view of promoting the welfare and happiness of the whole people." Addressing a Seneca delegation in Washington about the looming crisis, Ross opened up about the increasingly bitter taste that the removal controversy produced: "We have been made to drink of the bitter cup of humiliation; treated like dogs, our lives, our liberties, the sport of whitemen; our country and the graves of our Fathers torn from us, in cruel succession." And now he began to condemn his adversaries as unpatriotic enemies of the Cherokee people. Ross bristled especially at the outspoken views of John Ridge. "A man who shall forsake his country," Ross charged, ". . . in time of adversity and will coop-erate with those who oppose his own Kindred is no more than a traitor and should be viewed—and shunned as such."[5]

The shunning began at the July council meeting. During a tumultuous debate at the Red Clay Council Grounds Tom Fore-man, a zealous Ross advocate, launched into an angry speech chastising Major Ridge for advocating removal in Washington. Foreman reminded the gathering that Ridge had frequently preached that Cherokees should "love their land" and to empha-size the point "stamped the ground. The ground was yet sunk where he stamped," Foreman declared, "and now he was talking another way." Sensing the rising tension, Ridge supporters John Walker and Dick Jackson stalked off after Foreman's harangue, as did his kinsman, James Foreman.[6]

But Major and John Ridge stayed behind to respond to Fore-man's charges. Major Ridge stood up and defended himself against "slandering men" like Foreman. The problem was, he argued, that those who clung to the "fatal delusion" of remaining in the homeland would face a calamitous future. It was John Ridge, though, who offered the more direct and forceful defense of his father and the future they both believed in. "Major Ridge [has with] distinguished zeal and ability served his country," John insisted. But just because he points to the real dangers facing his people, Ridge wondered, why should he suffer personal attacks? "If a man [sees] a cloud charged with rain, thunder and storm . . . [and urges] the people to take care . . . is that man to be hated or . . . respected?" And now, to make matters worse, John observed, the Cherokee people were descending into bitter factionalism stirred up by the likes of Tom Foreman. "What would become of our Nation," Ridge asked the council, "if we were all like Tom Foreman? . . . We should now fall together and twist each others noses. Our eyes would not remain in their sockets, but in general we [would] gouge them out."[7]

The Ridges' appeal convinced few in the crowd. Indeed, Elijah Hicks, Ross's brother-in-law, introduced a petition with 144 Cherokee signatures calling for the impeachment of Major and John Ridge along with the Treaty Party ally David Vann because of their pro-removal activities. In a near-unanimous vote, the council found them guilty and impeached the three men. Ross, though, did not advocate such an extreme measure as impeachment, and the matter was set aside for a later meeting.

Ross might have hoped to calm the Nation, but in truth, threats of retaliation were coursing through the council. An angry Cherokee reportedly told Major Ridge that "if some men did not take care they would drop from their ponies." Ridge wondered if this sort of warning was simply a tactic by Ross to divert focus from his own failures and generate animosity against

the Treaty Party. If so, it worked. One man inspired by Foreman's tirade against Major Ridge whispered aloud, "Let's kill
him!" Indeed, removal supporters John Walker and Dick Jackson, who had left the meeting early to head home, were riding
near Muskrat Springs at nightfall when Walker was suddenly
struck by a bullet in his back, toppling him from his horse. He
and Jackson managed to fire a few shots against their fleeing
assailants, who, it was reported, resembled James Foreman and
his half brother Anderson Springston. Jackson managed to haul
Walker back home, but he had lost so much blood by then that
he collapsed on the floor and died days later.[8]

The news of John Walker's assassination reverberated throughout Cherokee country and well beyond. It prompted his father,
Major Walker, to point a finger at Ross and his rabid followers
for inciting the murder. And as far away as the Hermitage
Andrew Jackson responded with fury over the incident. Jackson
had liked Walker, and upon learning of his assassination, he
instructed federal agent Hugh Montgomery to inform Ross that
he would be held personally responsible "for every Murder committed by his people on the emigrants." Ross was deeply offended
by such a warning as it suggested to Ross that Jackson sought to
protect only the Treaty Party faction rather than the Cherokee
people as a whole.[9]

Ross had reason to feel endangered himself. With Major
Walker accusing Ross of assassinating his son, Ross soon became
the object of threats. Rumors and actual attempts on his life
grew to the point that Ross was surrounded by guards at night
and traveled home from General Council meetings via armed
escorts. By the fall of 1834 a rich irony pervaded Cherokee
country: nearly all the leading men of the Nation—the Ridges,
Boudinot, Stand Waite, the friends of John Walker, along with

John Ross and his advisers—now faced more danger from their fellow Cherokees than from whites. And with their government teetering on the edge of bankruptcy, a cloud of uncertainty hung over Cherokee country. All of which prompted John Ridge to sadly observe, "Our Nation is crumbling into ruin."[10]

In hopes of calming the growing incidence of threats and violence, Ross and Major Ridge sat down together in September to talk. Both had distinct complaints to air out. Ross was worried about rumors that the Treaty Party intended to assassinate him; Major Ridge wanted Ross to admit that some of his supporters had been threatening Major Ridge. While Ross denied such charges, claiming it was "high time all such mischievous tales should be silenced," he still tended to defer to the celebrated Major Ridge. And so they closed their meeting on a positive note, with Ross declaring to Ridge that "partyism should be discarded. Our country and our people—should be our motto."[11]

But the doubt and division both parties had sowed only deepened in the months that followed. And from the perspective of the Treaty Party, it was Ross's policy of caution and delay that was plunging the Cherokees into further jeopardy. Boudinot wasted no words making the case against Ross's misguided leadership. "Mr. Ross," he argued in November 1834, "has pursued a mysterious course manipulating a plain and unsophisticated people." With an overwhelming majority of the tribe confused about how a removal treaty might work—in no small part due to Ross's misrepresentation of it—"plain dealing," Boudinot insisted, was what his people needed: "Tell them the truth in a plain and simple language, and they will understand it. It is this that we have not been able yet to induce Mr. Ross and his friends to do."[12]

Exasperated by Ross's evasive leadership, members of the Ridge faction resigned from the General Council and called a meeting themselves to announce a new direction. Held at John Ridge's home and with Boudinot serving as chairman, the meeting lasted three days and represented the official formation of the Treaty Party. A very small portion of the tribe attended—only about eighty-three—and nearly all were well-educated, acculturated Cherokees. The meeting ended with a clear purpose: a delegation went to Washington to present the Treaty Party's case. John Ridge headed the delegation, which included Boudinot and six other men.

John Ridge authored the Treaty Party's memorial that was taken to Washington, now competing with Ross's delegation that was already there. On February 4, 1835, Henry Clay stood up in the Senate and solemnly read from Ridge's statement. "Sir, it is impossible to conceive of a community more miserable, more wretched," he said. "Even the lot of the African slave is preferable, far preferable to the condition of this unhappy nation. The interest of the master prompts him to protect his slave; but what mortal will care for, protect the suffering injured Indian, shut out from the family of man?" Ridge's delegation met with Secretary Cass and proposed a "preliminary treaty" they could sign and take to the Cherokee Nation for approval. Cass agreed to work with the Treaty Pary and appointed as negotiator a retired Dutch Reformed minister from New York, Reverend John F. Schermerhorn.[13]

With the rival Treaty Party making such dramatic inroads with the Jackson administration, Ross felt driven to make his most desperate proposition. Barely a week after the Ridge delegation had met with Cass, Ross walked into the secretary's office and made a strikingly new offer: for the very first time Ross proposed that the Cherokees would remove if the United States paid them $20 million for all their lands east of the Mississippi River. The gold mines in Cherokee country alone, he insisted, were worth that price. Furthermore, his plan called on the federal government to protect the tribe from intrusions for five years— thus allowing time for the tribe to safely resettle out West. The U.S. government, under Ross's last-minute offer, would reimburse the Nation for the land, the cost of emigration, and all improvements and belongings of the Cherokee people. Additionally, the U.S. government would make compensation for damages from illegal acts of neighboring states and make good on previous treaties with the Cherokees in 1817 and 1819 to provide school funds and pay annuities. Although Cass felt Ross's purchase price was wildly unacceptable, he asked Ross to commit the terms to paper and stepped out of the room. Ross and his delegation talked privately about the deal; when Cass returned, Ross announced that, as for the final purchase price, they would accept whatever the Senate deemed appropriate. Cass agreed, noting that Jackson would also "go as far as the Senate." But Ross's gambit failed; the Senate found Ross's purchase price excessive, the removal price remained at $5 million, and Cass and Jackson resumed talks with the Treaty Party.[14]

Dejected, Ross now began flailing about for some sort of alternative to forced removal—including the somewhat bizarre idea of relocating the Nation in another country. Through a mutual acquaintance, Ross finagled a letter of introduction to the Mexican chargé d'affaires in Philadelphia, J. M. de Castillo y Lanzas. In mid-March Ross and Lanzas met privately in Philadelphia, where Ross complained that the "caprice and whim of power" was compelling the Cherokees to consider removal. So Ross had come to propose a possible Cherokee migration to

Mexico. Ross wanted to ensure that the Cherokee people would arrive as full citizens and that there would be no white settlers surrounding them in Mexico. Ross's long-shot plan for the Nation to move to Mexico never got anywhere, but it certainly indicated the anguish and despair that informed Ross's decisions at the time.[15]

Just as Ross headed back home, once again empty-handed, John Ridge pointed directly to his disastrous leadership. "Ross has failed before the Senate," Ridge noted, "before the Secretary of War, & before the President. He tried hard to cheat you & his people, but he has been prevented. In a day or two he goes home no doubt to tell lies. But we will bring all his papers & the people shall see him as he is." It was the Ridge faction that had fashioned a treaty with Jackson that both parties found acceptable. It called for $5 million for Cherokee lands in the East with the promise of 13 million acres of good land in exchange out West. A perpetual annuity would be set up for schools, subsistence allowances, and the cost of travel.[16]

To help sell the deal, Ridge convinced Cass and Jackson that the president should publish an open letter of friendship to the Cherokees. In the spring of 1835 Jackson's letter "To the Cherokee Tribe of Indians East of the Mississippi River" was printed in various newspapers throughout the country. Its tone and substance suggest as much the personal imprint of John Ridge and his Treaty Party colleagues as that of Andrew Jackson. After claiming that he had warned them for years of the dangers of living "in the midst of a white population"—dangers that included abusive white settlers, immoral habits induced by "habits of intoxication," and the precariousness of the marketplace on a primitive agricultural economy—Jackson implored them to see that removal would change everything for the better. Once they moved, he observed, they would be living on "open and culti-vated" farms, in "comfortable houses," and with "abundant" resources, all governed by "[their] own customs and laws." "Where you now are," he stressed, "you are encompassed by evils, moral and physical, and these are fearfully increasing." Since removal would lead to prosperity and safety, Jackson reasoned, the choice was simple: "You have but one remedy within your reach. And that is, to remove to the West."

In a closing passage that seemed to echo the frustrations of the Treaty Party in dealing with the Ross faction, Jackson posed the "Cherokee question" in an ominous, existential tone: "The choice now is before you. May the Great Spirit teach you how to choose. The fate of your women and children, the fate of your people to the remotest generation, depend upon the issues. Deceive yourselves no longer. . . . Shut your ears to bad counsels. Look at your condition as it now is, and then consider what it will be if you follow the advice I give you. Your friend, Andrew Jackson."[17]

Depressed and disappointed at so much rejection, Ross returned home from Washington in the early spring and con-fronted yet another piece of humiliation: Arriving at his house in New Echota at 10:00 PM, he discovered the place nearly empty except for a stranger and his family sitting at his dinner table. The Georgia Guard had evicted Ross's family, and a white Geor-gian was now occupying the place. To make matters worse, Ross was compelled to pay the "arrogant occupant" of his own home to tend to Ross's horse as he headed off to look for his family. Ross found his wife and children living across the Ten-nessee border in a simple, two-room log house. There he would live until removal in 1838—the principal chief and his poor countrymen enduring the same modest living conditions.[18]

While Ross faced forced eviction from his home, members of the Treaty Party escaped similar harassment from their Georgia neighbors. Georgia governor Wilson Lumpkin made arrangements that no "fortunate drawers"—Georgia citizens given special lottery choices to Cherokee land and property— would claim or seize the lands and homes of Elias Boudinot and Major Ridge while treaty negotiations were under way in Washington.[19]

No such accommodations were made for the Cherokees' best friends, the missionaries. Samuel and Ann Worcester had to confront their own fast-diminishing prospects. With the mission at New Echota already taken over by a Georgia lottery claimant, and the press always under threat of seizure, the Worcesters, like many missionaries, looked westward for the next best place to provide help to the Cherokees. On April 8, 1835, the Worcesters said good-bye to their friends the Boudinots and Ridges and began the trek to the Cherokee Nation West. Their journey was accomplished without incident and in relative comfort—they traveled on horseback, not on foot—arriving on May 29, fifty-one days later, at the Dwight Mission in the Cherokee Nation West.

The precariousness of the Cherokees' situation was driven home even more forcefully in July as they watched their Creek neighbors endure a fate most Cherokees feared lay in their own future: on July 14, 1835, about 2,500 Creeks were ordered onto two riverboats for a voyage south to New Orleans, then north up the Mississippi River to Little Rock, on steamboats. Andrew Jackson's will to remove southern Indians, this sad spectacle clearly suggested, would be fully enforced. All of the southern tribes were now on their way west—except the Cherokees.

And the federal government was moving as quickly as it could to end that exception. The newly appointed commissioner,

Reverend John F. Schermerhorn, arrived in Cherokee country to make what he hoped would be a final treaty arrangement. An ardently religious man, Schermerhorn approached the treaty with missionary zeal. His anti-removal opponents among the Cherokees, though, referred to Schermerhorn as "the devil's horn," for his notorious womanizing. For the July council meeting, Ross helped round up Cherokees to meet at John Ridge's farm home, Running Waters. The meeting began on July 20 and was aimed at settling the annuity question, but Schermerhorn had a removal treaty on his mind.[20]

The setting suggested a multicultural spectacle with the widely diverse, sometimes contradictory intentions of the various power brokers on display. John Ridge opened his plantation home to some 4,000 Cherokees, who traveled on foot, in wagons, and by horseback to the meeting. They camped out in his house, barns, and along the river. Ridge offered Ross a bed, but Ross declined and instead slept out in the open "with his people." The day started with a prayer led by the native preacher John Huss. Hymns were sung in Cherokee amid bugle and drum music coming from Georgia Guards who were stationed ominously nearby, presumably to keep order. But they were also present to create mischief, if possible. The Guards sent women into the crowds with whiskey while mounted Guardsmen galloped around the perimeter yelling insults, hoping to cause trouble. The "idiot brother" of John Ridge—Ridge's slow-witted sibling—was encouraged to hurl insults at Ross to stir up resentment. The federal agent Benjamin Currey made a speech accusing Chief Ross of deception in how he explained the Ridge faction's treaty proposal to the people. Ross rose to defend himself and claimed he held "no enmity to Mr. Ridge" or any other pro-removal leader: "I am not a party man . . . [in] what I have done. . . . I have been actuated by a desire to promote the best interests of my people." Ridge likewise sounded the note of duty, not division, claiming he would acknowledge Ross as principal chief once a treaty was finalized.[21]

Amid the posturing over tribal harmony, Reverend Schermerhorn focused on delivering a persuasive speech about the need for a removal treaty. Indeed, he had workers build a pulpitlike podium for his talk. Near the end of the meeting, he gave a three-and-a-half-hour oration that dwelled on the virtues of Jackson's treaty. Schermerhorn told the crowd to accept the $5 million and the treaty: "Take the money for, if you do not, the bordering States will forthwith turn the screw upon you tighter & tighter, till you are ground to powder." It was clear that there was little support for the treaty, especially among the traditionalists, who mostly milled around half listening to the speech. Finally, the vote came on the annuity question, the real business, after all, of the council meeting: by a two-to-one margin the Cherokees voted against individual payments. Frustrated that he was so roundly ignored, Schermerhorn pointed a finger at Ross, who, he argued, held an "uncontrolled sway over the Indians." According to Schermerhorn, Ross had turned the Cherokee people into his own personal militia, "drilled equal to a Swiss guard, *to do only what they were bidden.*"[22]

The level of distrust and partisan sniping only increased in the fall of 1835. And the *Cherokee Phoenix* lay at the heart of it. In late August Ross sent a wagon and team to Stand Watie's house and packed up the types, papers, and books related to the press and placed them in the home of his brother-in-law (and now editor of the newspaper), Elijah Hicks. Watie insisted that the materials belonged to his brother Elias Boudinot, since he founded the newspaper. Under Ross's control, Watie argued, the newspaper had been "prostituted to party politics." So within a few hours, the Georgia Guard, under the command of Colonel William N. Bishop, marched up to Hicks's house and stood sentinel while Stand Watie seized the press and types and put them in wagons that carted them off. The press was returned to Watie and Boudinot under the assurance that the newspaper would remain free and open to all Cherokees. Ross angrily responded to the seizure of the *Phoenix*, calling it a "high-handed measure" that "could not have been sanctioned for any other purpose than to stifle the voice of the Cherokee people."[23]

The partisan tension turned into personal danger for growing numbers of Cherokees, especially friends of removal. Indian sentries wrapped in blankets up to their eyes were spotted silently keeping watch on Treaty Party members and their wives. Such menacing vigils sometimes spawned violent revenge. Several Ridge supporters were beaten to death by Ross men. One Ridge man named Crow spoke at the close of a dance about the perilous state of Cherokee society and the urgency for negotiating a removal treaty. He was attacked by a Ross supporter and, after being stabbed sixteen times, bled to death. Two other Treaty Party advocates were also knifed to death at a dance. Ross certainly faced threats made on his life, but most of the violence was focused on those who advocated removal.[24]

A rising tide of threats and violence was crashing through Cherokee country—and no one seemed able to calm the waters.

———

Late in the summer of 1835 a literary celebrity entered the Cherokee Nation. John Howard Payne, a New York essayist, poet, playwright, and composer—best known for his sentimental tune "Home, Sweet, Home"—traveled through Georgia as part of his

John Howard Payne
Courtesy of Schenectady County Public Library

tour of America promoting subscriptions to a planned literary magazine. Payne had met and liked the Ridge family but kept hearing a lot of controversial things about Chief John Ross and was eager to meet him. When the two men got together, Payne was pleasantly surprised and full of admiration. "I found Mr. Ross a different man," Payne observed, "in every respect from what I had heard him represented to be." He found Ross smallish, "mild, intelligent, and entirely unaffected." Ross apologized for the modest log cabin accommodations but invited Payne to stay with him long enough to attend the upcoming October General Council. Payne accepted, obviously moved by the story of "hard conduct which had driven the principal chief to one of the humblest dwellings in his nation." Intrigued by the Cherokees' oppressive story, Payne began transcribing the Cherokee papers and documents Ross gave him.[25]

While Ross's houseguest sorted through papers at his Red

Clay cabin, Ross arranged meetings with the Treaty Party in the desperate hope that a unifying agreement might be reached. At the October council Ross suggested that two groups with five members from each faction come together to work out a resolution. Ross headed up one group, while the Treaty Party included John Ridge, Elias Boudinot, and David Vann. The groups met for five days, stressing harmony and cooperation. Finally they produced a resolution to Congress they could all sign. Composed by Ross, the resolution contained the stipulation that they would not accept the $5 million voted by the Senate. The plan now was to send yet another delegation to Washington. President Jackson, however, did not want any more Cherokee delegations showing up in D.C. Impatient for a final resolution to the situation, Jackson insisted on a treaty being signed in the Cherokee Nation. But Ross sent the delegation anyway—which included John Ridge and Elias Boudinot. Meanwhile Reverend Schermerhorn, following orders from Jackson, stayed in Cherokee country working to get a final treaty negotiated.[26]

Ross and Schermerhorn had come to intensely dislike one another—Ross claimed that Schermerhorn would not recognize him as the leading figure of the Cherokee Nation; Schermerhorn was angry that Ross tried to prevent him from speaking before the council—and now, with each pursuing wildly different tracks of negotiation, they were at a standoff. From Red Clay, Schermerhorn informed Ross that he had been instructed "to treat ultimately with the Cherokees in open council," and proposed the third Monday in December, the twenty-first. Schermerhorn asked Ross to call the tribe together on that date. "If the Cherokees refuse his terms," Schermerhorn warned, "it will be the last overture" President Jackson will make. And the president will not receive any delegation in Washington,

Schermerhorn added. "If a treaty is made," he argued, "it must be done here in the nation."[27]

Upon learning that Ross insisted on the legitimacy of his delegation going to Washington, Schermerhorn became livid. Schermerhorn accused Ross and his delegation of creating "many unnecessary & imaginary difficulties." In a deliberately insulting tone, Schermerhorn charged that Ross simply could not be trusted since all he said on this subject was "a miserable subterfuge for a trip to Washington." In Schermerhorn's opinion, Ross's party had "usurped & deprived" the Cherokee people while bringing nothing but pain and difficulty on the tribe. He insisted that he had full authority to conclude a treaty at New Echota. For his part, Ross protested Schermerhorn's planned meeting in New Echota in late December, claiming that his people "[had] already made their election upon the course they wish pursued." Any such meeting, Ross warned, would be seen as but "an unnecessary agitation of the public mind" and would "never be recognized by the Cherokee Nation."[28]

If Ross was infuriated by Reverend Schermerhorn's attempts to take over the treaty negotiations, he was literally assaulted by another old enemy. Late in the night of November 7, 1835, in the middle of a driving rainstorm, John Howard Payne sat reading Cherokee documents in the Ross home. According to Payne, suddenly "there was a loud barking of dogs, then the quick tramp of galloping horses, then the march of many feet." Some twenty-five Georgia Guards pushed into the small cabin with bayonets fixed. When the sergeant Young began rummaging through his belongings, Payne protested. "Hold your damned tongue!" the sergeant angrily responded and struck him across the mouth. "You'll know that soon enough," the sergeant said, grabbing up all of Payne's papers. The Guards announced that

Payne and Ross were under arrest. The prisoners were taken outside, thrown onto horses, and rode in the freezing cold to the military camp at Springplace. In the primitive log cabin that doubled as a jail, Ross and Payne soon found two additional bodies occupying their "cell": the son of Cherokee chief Going Snake, Speaker of the council under Ross, was chained to a table, and a dead Cherokee was hanging from the rafters after an execution a few weeks before.[29]

The Guards began tearing through Ross's and Payne's papers, finally deciding they were written in some sort of code that looked faintly French. With no charges leveled but suspicion hanging in the air, Ross tried to clarify the confusion, noting that Payne came to Cherokee country well recommended "as a literary Gentleman . . . of high standing." At one point, Colonel Absalom Bishop, one of the arresting officers, was heard humming "Home, Sweet, Home." When Payne noted that he wrote the tune, Bishop replied, "Oh yeah?" Eventually, Colonel Bishop declared that the Guard believed Ross and Payne were abolitionists plotting a diabolical collaboration between slaves and Indians to rise up against the whites. Ross was also charged with impeding the census of Cherokees. John Ridge rode over to Springplace on November 14 and asked to visit with Ross. At first Bishop would not allow it, referring to the suspicious nature of his prisoners' intentions. Finally, Bishop relented, and Ridge successfully negotiated Ross's release. Because the Guards insisted that Payne was some sort of French spy, he remained jailed. But three days later he too was released and instructed to leave Georgia.[30] Both Ross and Payne were convinced that somehow Schermerhorn and Currey played a role in the plot to arrest them.[31]

Payne did as he was told: he left Georgia with a vengeance.

Payne returned to Ross's cabin across the Tennessee line and began composing blistering essays about his imprisonment and the oppressive treatment of the Cherokees. The articles appeared in the *Knoxville Register*. In one article, crafted as if it were a plea from the Cherokees to the American people, Payne claimed that the Cherokees wanted to stay in their homeland and become citizens of Tennessee and Alabama. But, according to Payne's account, a very small faction of Cherokees advocating removal was doing the bidding of the U.S. government and fomenting untruths about tribal officials. Payne's article appeared to embrace Ross's perspective so completely that John Ridge and Boudinot assumed it had been all but dictated by Ross. John Ridge read the article in early December while journeying to Washington with Ross and the delegation and bristled with anger. He confronted Ross about the article, and Ross conceded that he fully agreed with Payne's ideas. At which point Ridge resigned from the delegation, informing Ross that the article, clearly composed at "[your] request and suggestion," "unfolds to me your views of policy diametrically opposite to me and my friends, who will never consent to be citizens of the States." Ross pleaded with Ridge not to leave the group, claiming that Payne had written the article on his own and insisting that he, Ross, remained flexible on policy: "It is the good of the whole Cherokee people alone which I desire in whatever may be done therefore I must request you to pause and reconsider your intention of declining to go on with the delegation." Eventually, Ridge relented and continued on with the delegation to Washington. Days earlier, Boudinot, convinced that any Ross-led treaty negotiations offered no hope for success, had resigned from the delegation.[32]

The two sides of this momentous debate, then, were literally and figuratively moving in opposite directions in December

1835: as Ross and his divided delegation headed to Washington to press for one final solution to their "difficulties"—despite warnings in advance from Secretary Cass that coming to Washington was "utterly useless"—Reverend Schermerhorn stayed behind in Cherokee country preparing for a meeting he was calling—on behalf of Jackson and Cass—at New Echota to be held on December 21. Viewed by Ross's people as a zealot and a buffoon, Schermerhorn was nothing if not a tenacious envoy for President Jackson. His unflinching commitment to getting a removal treaty played out against a painfully divided Cherokee Nation and would lead to ominous consequences.

———

On December 19, a cold wintry day, the Cherokee people began to gather in New Echota. Schermerhorn had circulated handbills throughout the Nation, printed in Cherokee, announcing the meeting, while explaining—as if anticipating a small turnout—that those who did not attend would be viewed as accepting whatever was decided. The meeting drew perhaps as many as five hundred, but only eighty-six stayed to vote. Very few came from the Valley Towns in western North Carolina where Ross had successfully lobbied against the machinations of the Treaty Party. John Ridge and John Ross were in Washington, in the fruitless campaign to engage the Jackson administration one last time, but Boudinot and Major Ridge were present.[33]

As usual, the assembled Cherokees were in no hurry to make decisions. As one white visitor from Georgia observed:

The Indian men of the crowd sat around and smoked for hours, plunged into deep meditation and reflection. Occasionally one would say something in the Indian language, very little of which I understood, in reply to which a member would give a guttural grunt. That would be followed by another long silence. So the time wore on, nothing being done, and if the affairs of Europe had been under settlement, they could not have been more deliberate.[34]

After a few days of Cherokees straggling in and the election of officers, Reverend Schermerhorn finally launched into his planned speech extolling the virtue and necessity of the treaty crafted by the Ridge party. In the middle of his address, the roof of the council house suddenly caught fire. One anti-removal observer wondered if the "fearful blaze" suggested "the indignation of Heaven at the unlawful proceedings, or of the great fiery trial of our people."[35] After the blaze was put out, the meeting resumed with Benjamin Currey going over the proposed treaty line by line, translating and recording it for everyone, which the crowd greeted with occasional grunts.

The treaty hammered out by the Ridge faction and Schermerhorn called for the U.S. government to pay the Cherokees $5 million in exchange for the Cherokees' surrender of all their lands in the East and their removal to the territory, in excess of 7 million acres, set aside for them west of the Mississippi River. Furthermore, the Cherokees would receive compensation for all improvements they left behind, for funding schools, orphans, and to pay the cost of emigration and full subsistence out West for the first year. The Cherokees had two years from the date of treaty ratification to prepare for removal, during which time the federal government would protect them and their farms, homes, and businesses. The Cherokee Nation would be assured that the United States would respect its rights to self-government in the West, guaranteeing that the Nation would never be absorbed into any state or territory without its consent. Finally, the federal government would protect its borders, remove hostile white intruders, and defend Cherokees against unfriendly neighbors.[36]

After the provisions were read and explained, the meeting turned into emotion-filled personal appeals. Major Ridge rose to speak. "I am one of the native sons of these wild woods," he said. "I have hunted the deer and turkey here, more than fifty years. I have fought your battles, have defended your truth and honesty, and fair trading. I have always been the friend of honest white men." But then came the "grasping spirit" of white Georgians who had for years harassed the Cherokees with one unrelenting goal: to take their land. All this, despite the much longer and more powerful claim the Cherokees had to it. "We obtained the land from the living God above," Ridge solemnly declared. "They got their title from the British." But in what must have been difficult to articulate, Ridge tried to push his assembled countrymen to accept a painful truth about their destiny.

Yet they are strong and we are weak. We are few, they are many. We cannot remain here in safety and comfort. I know we love the graves of our fathers, who have gone before to the happy hunting grounds of the Great Spirit. . . . We can never forget these homes, I know, but an unbending, iron necessity tells us we must leave them. I would willingly die to preserve them, but any forcible effort to keep them will cost us our lands, our lives and the lives of our children. There is but one path of safety, one road to future existence as a Nation. That path is open before you. Make a treaty of cession. Give up these lands and go over beyond the great Father of Waters.[37]

Seizing on the drama of the moment, Elias Boudinot stood to declare a similar conviction—a hauntingly prescient one: "I know I take my life in my hand," Boudinot told his fellow Cherokees, "as our fathers have also done. We will make and sign this treaty. . . . We can die, but the great Cherokee Nation will be saved. They will not be annihilated; they can live. Oh, what is a man worth who will not dare to die for his people? Who is there here that would not perish, if this great nation may be saved?"[38]

First signature page of the Treaty of New Echota
Courtesy of the Horgrett Rare Book & Manuscript Library,
University of Georgia Libraries

Moved by these stirring sentiments, the assembled Cherokees appointed a twenty-person committee to deliberate on the
specific terms and conditions of the treaty. And then on Tues-
day evening, December 29, 1835, they met at Elias Boudinot's
house. The completed treaty with pen and inkwell sat on the
table, awaiting signatures. In the hushed silence of the room
illuminated by candles and the fireplace, no one came forward
at first. Then John Gunter picked up the pen, dipped it in the
ink, and scratched in his name. Andrew Ross stepped forward,
then the others, including Boudinot and Major Ridge, who
signed with his trademark *X*. All told, seventy-nine signed the
Treaty of New Echota, and seven opposed it. It is unknown
what every signer felt upon committing himself to such a dramatic document. But Major Ridge reportedly said as he made
his mark, "I have signed my death warrant." Schermerhorn later
noted that Boudinot, and several others who signed, likewise
understood that in affixing their names to the treaty they were
also offering up "their lives as a sacrifice, to save . . . their nation
from inevitable extermination and ruin." Later John Ridge predicted that his fateful decision on the treaty would guarantee
his own death: "The Ross party here already count my death as
certain." But he was ready for it: "If I can relieve my bleeding
countrymen . . . I am even prepared to be immolated to gratify
the ambitions of my enemies."[39]

Within days, Ross, cooling his heels in Washington, learned
about "the late *Christmas trick* at New Echota." A letter from "a
painful spectator" informed Ross that "not more than 100 warriors" attended the meeting. Another Ross supporter also down-
played the numbers present and hinted at the largely acculturated

pro-removal advocates, noting that of the seventy-nine people signing the New Echota treaty "most of the people in attendance were white people."[40]

The New Echota delegation, headed by Major Ridge and Boudinot, would soon be leaving for Washington with the treaty, leaving Ross to vent with his literary friend Payne about not receiving an apology from Jackson for their imprisonment. "Neither the Secretary of War nor the President has said a word to me on the subject of our arrest by the Georgia Guard."[41]

When the New Echota delegation arrived in early February, John Ridge and Stand Waite left the official Ross delegation and signed the treaty. Then the New Echota group tried to get Ross to join forces with them. But Ross would have nothing to do with them. Instead, he sent a note to Assistant Chief George Lowrey instructing him to put together a petition against the Treaty of New Echota. Lowrey quickly got a petition together with some fourteen thousand names on it. Meanwhile, Ross angrily referred to the New Echota gathering as a "self constituted . . . small faction" that in no way represented the will of the Cherokee people. In a letter to Payne, Ross bitterly lashed out against his enemies from Schermerhorn to the members of the Treaty Party. "These men profess to have been sent on by the nation," Ross complained, "in pursuance of the New Echota meeting to effect the ratification of Schermerhorn's Treaty. The Delegation duly appointed by the Nation, have been excessively annoyed by intriguers, owing to the conduct of these individuals, who are under the influence of the Revd. Commissioner [Schermerhorn] and the demonical agent of the Govt." Ross noted that John Ridge and Stand Watie had made abrupt switches in their allegiance, indicative, he insisted, of their traitorous hearts: "John Ridge & Stand Watie, some days since, very abruptly withdrew themselves from us, without even making their intention known to the delegation, or assigning any reasons for so doing—their motives however cannot be misunderstood—and from past indications, no one can be surprised at their conduct—and if it be their own choice to stain their reputation with indelible infamy, by acts of treachery—I can now do no more than, to pity them—for their folly and wickedness of heart."[42]

While Ross inveighed against the "treachery" of his opponents, Boudinot ridiculed Ross's contention that as chief he channeled the will of the Cherokee people. In truth, Boudinot charged, Ross's intransigence on removal prevented him from giving "relief to his suffering people." "He says he is doing the *will* of the people, and he holds their authority; they are opposed, and it is enough. The will of the people! The opposition of the people! This has been the cry for the last five years, until that people have become but a mere wreck of what they once were." Ross could have led his nation toward "a happy and prosperous community," Boudinot insisted, but instead "he has dragged an ignorant train, wrought upon by near-sighted prejudice and stupid obstinacy, to the last brink of destruction. . . . he stands surrounded by a hungry, naked and destitute people—surprised at his unwise course, and confounded at his near sighted policy."[43]

President Jackson submitted the Treaty of New Echota to the Senate for ratification, where opponents fought it tooth and nail. John Howard Payne contributed an essay that railed against Georgia and those pro-removal forces who would surrender Cherokee land to white intruders. Ross introduced the petition he had solicited protesting the treaty, now with sixteen thousand signatures (despite the fact that roughly half were children), and charged that the Treaty of New Echota, because it was endorsed neither by the principal leaders of the Cherokee government nor by the majority of the people, was entirely illegitimate. Meanwhile, Andrew Jackson worked his supporters in the Senate to back the treaty, which brought the festering sore of slavery into the discussion. Because southeastern Indians were sitting on valuable cotton land, the Senate vote on the treaty was as much about slavery and sectional interests as it was about the needs and rights of Cherokees. The Cherokees' relocation out West would free up more land for the expansion of slavery. When a few senators from free states decided to support the treaty, Jackson had the votes he needed. Senator Thomas Hart Benton of Missouri observed that the free states' vote guaranteed the South a deal that would convert "Indian soil to slave soil."[44]

On May 17, 1836, the Senate approved the Treaty of New Echota by one vote more than the two-thirds majority required. A week later, Jackson signed it into law. Under the terms of the Treaty of New Echota, the Cherokee Nation by May 1838 had to give up its lands in Alabama, Georgia, North Carolina, and Tennessee and leave for present-day Oklahoma. The Cherokees had two years to leave.

When John Ridge returned home from Washington to Cherokee country in June 1836, he witnessed a people in decline. To be sure, John's wife, Sarah, and their slaves had already planted crops and a garden. Likewise, Major Ridge had instructed Susanna to get crops in the ground using their "servants"—Susanna would not call them slaves. Everything else in their world, though, looked very different. John Ridge's ferry had been taken over by a white Alabaman, John H. Garrett, a major general in the Alabama militia. Alabama had followed Georgia in crafting its property laws in the wake of the upcoming Cherokee removal, so there was no legal recourse available for John and Sarah. While trying to be upbeat in a letter to President Jackson about the treaty's reception among his people, John Ridge was clearly disturbed about the "griefs and afflictions" white settlers were causing the Cherokee people in the wake of the treaty. "They have got our lands," Ridge reported, "and now they are preparing to fleece us of the money accruing from the treaty. We found our plantations taken in whole or in part by the Georgians." Ridge and others loudly protested such illegal conduct, but it soon got worse: poor white settlers craving Cherokee property launched violent attacks everywhere against them. According to Ridge, "the lowest classes of the white people are flogging the Cherokees with cowhides, hickories, and clubs. We are not safe in our houses—our people are assailed by day and night by the rabble. . . . This barbarous treatment is not confined to men but the women are stripped also and whipped without law or mercy." Ridge pleaded with Jackson to provide federal troops to safeguard the Cherokees from these "lawless assaults . . . and protect our people as they depart for the West. If it is not done, we shall carry off nothing but the scars of the lash on our backs, and our oppressors will get all the money."[45]

By the end of the summer of 1836 the depredations of white intruders had left many Cherokees without crops or means to feed their families. Even Major Ridge and Susanna were nearly out of food, and John and Sarah Ridge had to purchase beef in order to feed neighbors and families who flocked to their plantation for help. It was not uncommon to discover displaced families wandering about Cherokee country idle and hungry.[46]

This sort of "barbarous treatment" and "lawless assaults" on property and persons added moral urgency to the agonizing issue of removal that still raged inside Cherokee country. As the Chero-

kees now confronted forced removal, Elias Boudinot and John
Ross engaged in an increasingly vitriolic war of words that dra-
matically revealed both the intensity of their emotions and the
huge gulf separating their opposing perspectives on the Cherokees' fate.

Disheartened but undeterred by the ratification of the removal
treaty, Ross immediately launched an effort to overturn the
treaty. There was an abundance of villains for Ross to single
out, beginning with the betrayal of the federal government. The
Cherokee people, Ross argued, had lived for many years under
the "fostering hand" of the U.S. government, making "rapid
advances in civilization, morals, and in the arts and sciences." And
now, ironically, after learning how "to think and feel as the American citizen . . . they were to be *despoiled by their guardian*, to
become strangers and wanderers in the land of their fathers,
forced to return to the savage life, and to seek a new home in the
wilds of the far west, and that without their consent."[47]

Ross reserved his harshest words, of course, for the Treaty
Party faction, who, he believed, in crafting a treaty that sold the
Cherokee homeland had betrayed the Cherokee Nation: "It is a
fraud upon the Cherokee people." "The Cherokee people will
always hold themselves ready to respect a *real* treaty," Ross
argued. But they would never respect "the attempt of a very few
persons to sell the country for themselves . . . our sacred inheri-
tance from our fathers!"[48]

To Boudinot, such an attempt to contrast the Treaty Party's
alleged "fraud upon the Cherokee people" with Ross's fervent
protection of the "sacred" homeland was itself a pernicious piece
of deception. While the Treaty of New Echota, Boudinot argued,
"was made in the face of day and in the eye of the nation . . . you
resort to matters which are deceptive and fraudulent." Because of

Ross's "want of candor and plain dealing," many Cherokees opposed the New Echota treaty by clinging desperately to Ross's frequent invocation of their sacred homeland. With Ross constantly instructing the people simply to fight for their land, Boudinot claimed, Cherokees "never spent one moment's thought beyond that of *loving* and *securing* the land upon which they live. This is the whole secret of this much talked of opposition." If Ross would only be honest with his people, Boudinot believed, they would see that moving out West was the only solution: "Be candid with them—tell them that their country cannot be saved, and that you want their authority to sell, yes, *to sell* it—an authority which you have alleged to the Government you have received, and you will see to where this opposition against a removal will go." To the signers of the treaty, the signs were everywhere: being surrounded by oppressive whites, along with Georgia's refusal to accept the Supreme Court's decision, meant that removal was simply unavoidable. Impoverished and degraded where they were, the Cherokee people now had to look west for their best hope for survival. As Boudinot explained, "I take the treaty as the best that can be done for the Cherokees, under present circumstances—a treaty that will place them in a *better* condition than they *now* are."[49]

Boudinot's challenge to Ross ran deeper than simply speculating on the likely outcome of removal. The convictions of Boudinot, an ardent Christian, about the fate of his people were inextricably linked to his highly moral values—values planted and nurtured as a young man when he was under the influence of white evangelicals. Since leaving Cornwall, Boudinot had been consumed with the idea that the Cherokees' self-advancement hinged not simply on material progress but on spiritual and moral improvement as well. So he was especially irked that Ross seemed to suggest that prior to being "despoiled by their guardian," the Cherokees lived in prosperity and happiness—and that somehow the treaty advocates were now responsible for ruining that bucolic world: "Have we indeed been the instruments of despoiling our nation? Have we destroyed their happiness, checked their civilization, and corrupted their morals?" Ross's rosy view of the Cherokee people, Boudinot contended, especially as it involves "whites intermarried among us" and their descendants, might be accurate. But most Cherokees, he believed, were suffering from everything from alcoholism to poverty to spiritual and moral despair. If Ross and his supporters would honestly face the truth about the moral condition of the Cherokees, they would discover a people desperately in need of a new start: "Look at the mass—look at the entire population as it now is, and say, can you see any indication of a progressing improvement—anything that can encourage a philanthropist? You know that it is almost a dreary waste. I care not if I am accounted a slanderer of my country's reputation— every observing man in this nation knows that I speak the words of truth and soberness."[50]

Ross's "truth," from Boudinot's perspective, focused only on the economic condition of his people, rather than on the character and morals, the soul of the Nation. Thus Ross was preoccupied with the value of the lands, mountains, and forests they would be surrendering. Ross had lost sight of a powerful reality about his people, Boudinot charged: "you seem to have forgotten that your people are a community of moral beings, capable of an elevation to an equal standing with the most civilized and virtuous, or a deterioration to the level of the most degraded of our race." Ross's preoccupation with the physical assets of the Cherokee Nation blinded him to more important realities: "Perish your gold mines and your money, if, in the pursuit of them,

the moral credit of this people, their happiness and their existence are to be sacrificed!"[51]

To Boudinot and the Ridges, remaining on the homeland
not only denied their inevitable fate of forcible removal by the
U.S. military, but also flew in the face of a powerful moral
imperative: that the Cherokee people, left surrounded by the
debasing elements of white culture, confronted a future full of
degradation and immorality. Boudinot seized on "the spread of
intemperance and the wretchedness and misery" already in evidence: "You will find an argument in every tippling shop in the
country—you will find its cruel effects in the bloody tragedies
that are frequently occurring—in the frequent convictions and
executions for murders, and in the tears and groans of the widows and fatherless, rendered homeless, naked and hungry."[52]

A genuine patriot, claimed Boudinot, seeks to save his
people's soul, not simply their land. And so for him and the
Ridges that meant resettling out West, where the Cherokee
people could reconstitute themselves in peace as a virtuous and
prosperous nation: "Removal, then, is the only remedy—the
only *practicable* remedy. By it there *may be* finally a renovation—
our people *may* rise from their very ashes to become prosperous
and happy, and a credit to our race. . . . Fly for your lives. . . . I
would say to my countrymen, you among the rest, fly from the
moral pestilence that will finally destroy our nation."[53]

———

While Elias Boudinot fought hard to save the Cherokee Nation
he loved, he could not save his beloved wife. On August 15, 1836,
Harriett Gold Boudinot died after after a lengthy illness, likely
related to the difficult delivery of her last child, Franklin, born
three months earlier. Surrounded by friends and numerous fam-

ily and neighbors, Harriett spent her final days, Boudinot reported to his Connecticut in-laws, praying and reading Scripture. Near the end Harriett told Elias, "[I hope] I may do good to the Cherokees; but he knows best and will do all things right." Heartbroken, Boudinot called his loss "irreparable," left, as he was, "with six helpless children, at an age when they most need the care, the oversight, and instruction of a mother."[54]

Not only had Boudinot lost a loving wife; he had lost a rare, and deeply personal, example of a white person who devoted herself to the Indian world and emerged universally loved: "Perhaps no one in this Country has ever commanded such universal respect as she did," Boudinot noted. "Even the people of Georgia, not unfrequently carried away with overwrought passions and prejudices against our race, such as personally knew her, or had heard of her from report have testified to her worth and unsullied character. " An obituary printed in the *New York Observer* referred to Harriett as a woman whose ten years "in the bosom of the Cherokee Nation" made her "an eye witness of Indian wrongs. She was devoted heart and soul to the welfare of that race, into which she was adopted."[55]

Ever since joining hands with Boudinot in their controversial marriage in Cornwall, Harriett had talked with exuberance about living among and identifying with the Cherokees: "I wish you *could* see us in our family, in our neighbourhood, and our Nation. . . . I wish you to see how Indians can *live*—how families, & how a *nation* of Indians can live." And far from regretting her decision to marry a Cherokee and immerse herself in Indian culture, she viewed her life with Boudinot in Cherokee country with deep pride: "I now look back to that day with pleasure, & with gratitude."[56]

As Elias and friends gathered over Harriett Gold Boudinot's

grave, the scene was no doubt suffused with anguish and humiliation because of the very spot where they stood: having lost all his
land to Georgia intruders, Boudinot was reduced to begging a
white neighbor for a place to bury Harriett. "As I have not a foot
of ground that I can call my own," Boudinot had to ask the owner of a nearby spring for the "privilege of depositing her beloved
remains on his land." And we can only imagine how his loss only
deepened the grief and tragedy he felt for his entire people. As he
noted a few days later, "This affliction came . . . in a most deplorable time just . . . when we are calculating to break up & go to
the west. The Lord be my strength & my wisdom." Boudinot
now felt adrift, both for his personal loss and for his people's
uncertain destiny. "All my plans are now disconcerted," he said.
"I really do not know what to do. You cannot imagine the extent
of my bereavement. I cannot express it—it is beyond the power of
language to express. When I think of that dear individual—for
ten years my endeared companion—one who was willing in
youth to leave her paternal home & her friends <u>for me</u>—now no
more—whose face I am never to see in this world."[57]

Elias Boudinot and the other members of the Treaty Party, like
Ross and his supporters, had for years struggled to answer the
same heart-wrenching question: What was the proper course for
a patriot? How could the Cherokee people best endure—by
honoring their traditions and fighting to stay in their ancestral
homeland or removing out West to prevent further suffering of
their people?

They would soon find their own answers. And no matter what
their choice, the suffering had only just begun.

6

Roundup

Whatever doubts some Cherokees may have clung to that the U.S. government meant business about the necessity of removal began to dissipate early in the summer of 1836. In June Brigadier General John E. Wool and some two thousand federal troops arrived in the Valley Towns trying to persuade Cherokees to enroll for emigration to western Arkansas. General Wool and his troops had also come to prevent violence as removal readiness got under way. Step one was to confiscate Cherokee guns so that when the uprooting process became absolutely mandatory by June 1838, recalcitrant Cherokees would have little means to violently resist. To help collect Cherokee guns, General Wool took the Baptist minister and staunch Ross ally Reverend Evan Jones along with him and his troops. Jones was a familiar figure among this strongly anti-removal part of Cherokee country. And now Wool had put Jones in a tough spot: if he did not provide help to Wool, his soldiers would likely consider Jones an enemy to the federal government. But providing aid to

Wool would make Jones an accomplice in removal—a policy that most Valley Town residents, along with Jones, vehemently opposed. Indeed, Jones and Wool debated the problem at length. According to Jones, Wool "used many arguments to induce me to advise the Indians to submit to the treaty. I took the liberty respectfully to state to him the plain truth with regard to the injustice practiced on the Cherokees" and their rationale for opposing removal. "He agreed to the truth of all this," Jones noted, "but said the treaty was ratified and must be executed. I, however, declined taking any part in the business." Jones did talk to some Cherokee elders and suggested they voluntarily bring in their weapons. In a revealing pragmatic compromise, the Cherokees agreed to turn in some old, unusable guns and carefully hid those they valued for hunting. Wool accepted the compromise. But he failed in his larger goal: no Cherokees enrolled to move west. As for Jones, his resistance prompted a quick response: for refusing to help disarm the Indians, Jones was arrested and ordered to leave North Carolina.[1]

Wool discovered firsthand the fierceness with which Cherokees in the North Carolina mountains resisted removal. It was these traditional full-bloods who were the most ardent opponents of removal and strongest supporters of Ross. For them, every stream, cave, lake, spring, and mountain held special meaning. Many of them were sacred places or spots where their ancestors were buried. In contrast, intermarried whites and mixed-bloods, who tended to prevail among the Treaty Party, had less feeling for the land itself—its spiritual power and history. Wool encountered Cherokees in the mountains of North Carolina so determined to hang on to their homeland that they "preferred living upon the roots and sap of trees rather than receive provisions from the United States. . . . Many have said they will die before they will leave the country." "The whole scene since I have been in this country," Wool wrote to his superiors, "has been nothing but a heart-rending one and such a one as I would be glad to get rid of as soon as circumstances permit."[2]

If Ross and the Cherokees hoped that, confronted with such resistance, the federal government would reverse, or at least postpone, its decision, they were badly mistaken. The Choctaws had removed first out West, then Chickasaws—both victims of robbery and disease. And the U.S. government had already begun forcible removal of the Creeks and Seminoles. Portions of the Creeks who had resisted were subdued by force, and some 1,600 Creek men were dispatched to the West. Another 776 Creeks were coaxed into helping federal troops root out Seminole warriors in Florida swamps. Captured Seminoles were sent out by boats to the Arkansas Territory. Among the Indians of the Southeast, only the Cherokees remained where they were—and now, thanks to General Wool and his troops, that distinction was about to end.

Despite being a military man prepared to carry out whatever orders he was given, General Wool was actually quite sympathetic to the Cherokees' plight, especially considering how the whites in the area were eager to exploit and take over Indian property. Wool claimed he would remove "every Indian tomorrow beyond the reach of the white men." The whites, greedily awaiting the Cherokees' forced departure, conjured up haunting images in Wool: "White men . . . like vultures, are watching, ready to pounce upon their prey and strip them of everything they have." Wool, in fact, openly pleaded with the Cherokee population to understand that removal, while perhaps cruel, was nonetheless a certainty that demanded acceptance. And they should ignore, he insisted, anyone who gave them false hopes to the contrary.

> Cherokees, I have not come among you to oppress you, but to protect you and to see that justice is done you, as guaranteed by the treaty. Be advised, and turn a deaf ear to those who would induce you to believe that no treaty has been made with you, and that you will not be obliged to leave your country. They cannot be friends, but the worst of enemies. . . . And why not abandon a country no longer yours? Do you not see the white people daily coming into it, driving you from your homes, and possessing your houses, your cornfields, and your ferries?[3]

When he cautioned Cherokees about unreliable "friends," Wool was no doubt thinking of Chief John Ross, who was busy making a career out of stubbornness over removal. Despite the presence of Wool and federal troops and the ratification (justified or not) of the Treaty of New Echota, Ross continued his campaign of denial and delay—a desperate hope for overturning removal that he would not surrender until the bitter end in May 1838. In the summer of 1836 Ross wrote a pamphlet highly critical of the treaty and the invalid assembly of pro-removal people who had crafted it. Ross headed a delegation of treaty opponents and once again traveled to Washington in February 1837 just before Martin Van Buren, Jackson's successor, took office. Departing Jackson officials, wondering if Ross had now taken up permanent residence in Washington, showed no interest in Ross's eleventh-hour appeals. He then pressed Van Buren's secretary of war, Joel Poinsett, to negotiate a new treaty. His request was quickly denied.[4]

Back in Cherokee country, John Ross was under siege both by depredations of invading whites and by accusations of self-interested autocracy from some of his fellow Cherokees. In the summer of 1836 Ross, one of the wealthiest men in the Chero-kee Nation, claimed "his houses, farm, public ferries and other property" had "been seized and wrested from him." He also complained that his friend Joseph Vann, an extremely wealthy plantation owner, and Vann's family had been "driven out, unpre-pared, in the dead of winter, and snow upon the ground, through which they were compelled to wade, and to take shelter within the limits of Tennessee, in an open log cabin, upon a dirt floor." This was the same Joseph Vann, Ross was careful to observe, who when a young man volunteered as a private soldier in the Creek War, "in the service of the United States," where he risked his life in the Battle of Horseshoe Bend. "What has been his reward?"[5]

Ross had to battle the nagging accusation from many Treaty Party advocates that his own "reward" came from hoarding the funds of the Cherokee people. "*This is a monstrous misrepresenta-tion*," Ross explained to Congress in July 1836. "The funds of the nation never have been in my hands" but have been controlled by the council. Ross had other charges to confront, namely, that he had been acting more like a dictator than a responsible agent of the Cherokee people. "The Cherokee people are not 'my people,'" Ross insisted. "I am only one of their agents and their elected chief: It is I who serve under them, not they under me." To the accusation that he lived by the principles of white men, Ross responded with anger. Noting that his "enemies" charged that he was not really an Indian and thus "unworthy of a hearing in the Indian cause," Ross insisted that "it has been my pride, as Prin-cipal Chief of the Cherokees . . . to cherish . . . *the principles* of white men! It is to this fact that our white neighbours must ascribe their safety under the smart of the wrongs we have suffered from them."[6]

Amid these various charges of misconduct and misrepresentation, Ross focused most of his outrage at the "spurious Delegation" that had assembled at New Echota. Their "false and fraudulent" work, he argued, had left the Cherokees "despoiled" of their "private possessions, the indefeasible property of individuals." They had been "stripped of every attribute of freedom and eligibility for legal self-defence." Ross argued that despite valid treaties to protect them, Cherokees now faced blatant acts of plunder, violence, and disfranchisement: "We have neither land nor home, nor resting place that can be called our own. . . . We are overwhelmed!"[7]

Under siege and in desperate straits, Ross sometimes responded with eloquence. In one of his final pleas to Congress, he claimed that the Cherokees' cause belonged to them as well: "It is the cause of liberty and of justice; it is based upon your own principles, which we have learned from yourselves; for we have gloried to count your [George] Washington and your [Thomas] Jefferson our great teachers; we have read their communications to us with veneration; we have practiced their precepts with success." All anyone had to do, Ross claimed, was look around them and see that the Cherokees no longer lived in "the rudeness of the savage state"; they had learned the arts of industry, cultivated fields, and intellectual life. The Cherokee assimilation to white culture, Ross argued—somewhat dubiously—had even included religion: "We have read your Sacred books. Hundreds of our people have embraced their doctrines, practiced the virtues they teach, cherished the hopes they awaken, and rejoiced in the consolations they afford." But now under the burden of removal, he conceded, the Cherokees had become a "subdued," "afflicted people." So they turned to Congress, "the representatives of a Christian country; the friends of justice; the patrons of the oppressed. . . . Before your august assembly we present ourselves. . . . On your kindness, on your humanity, on your compassion, on your benevolence, we rest our hopes. . . . Spare our people! Spare the wreck of our prosperity! Let not our deserted homes become the monuments of our desolation!"[8]

If Ross knelt in desperation for help from Congress, he assumed a rather different posture among his own people in Cherokee country. Despite all signs pointing toward the looming crisis of forced removal, Ross could be seen riding the countryside on his big black horse telling Indians to keep planting corn, to maintain trust in him and their future in their homeland, and that all would be well. While many Cherokees continued to look to Ross for hope and guidance, conditions on the ground—the presence of troops, the spreading news that the treaty would definitely be enforced, and the worsening circumstances of most Indians—pointed to a more depressing conclusion. "There is nothing but confusion amongst us," Lewis Ross advised his brother John. "Our people are bleeding at every pore. . . . The patience of many I know is worn out and as for my own self you may guess." Meanwhile, federal agents routinely opened Ross's letters in hopes of uncovering his plans to obstruct their efforts. The War Department warned Ross about the "utter hopelessness" of trying "to evade the execution of the treaty." Western Superintendent William Armstrong ordered his men to arrest Ross if he tried to "incite opposition to the treaty." And his brother conveyed the same alarming news: "There is nothing more certain than you will be arrested if you remain a day at home." Despite all these warnings, Ross pressed on with his increasingly futile campaign against removal: "So

194 AN AMERICAN BETRAYAL

long as there remains a single spark in my bosom, to inspire the confidence that hope has not been misplaced upon the American character—I never can despair. No Sir never, at least not until it shall have been finally extinguished by any conclusive action of the Govt."[9]

While federal officials generally viewed Ross as a wily, stubborn politician, the "Master Spirit" of opposition to the treaty, they sometimes offered grudging respect for the Cherokees and the close connection Ross nurtured with his people. The federal emissary John Mason walked around the Red Clay Council Grounds in the summer of 1837 admiring the "picturesque" beauty of the region, especially the "unceasing current of Cherokee Indians . . . moving about in every direction, and in the greatest order. . . . their turbans, their dark coarse, lank hair, their listless savage gait, and their swarthy Tartar countenances" that reminded Mason of the Arabs from Barbary. He conceded that for many Cherokees "opposition to the treaty . . . is unanimous and sincere." So for Ross now to change course and accept removal "would at once forfeit their confidence, and probably his life."[10]

But for others, moving west offered the only genuine hope— for themselves and for the Cherokee Nation.

While Ross railed against removal, members of the Treaty Party quietly planned their journey west. Major Ridge, now sixty-six and in poor health, and his wife, Susanna, registered their daughter Sally along with the rest of the family and some sixteen slaves. Along with Joseph Vann and John Ross, Major Ridge was among the wealthiest Cherokees with more than $24,000 in property. The Ridges' party, which included John and Sarah, was to be part of a large company of some seven hundred Treaty Party members traveling together in the fall of 1836. But a family wedding halted everything for the Ridges: daughter Sally, who had been attending the Moravian-run school at Salem, North Carolina, announced just before the planned departure that she was getting married and wanted her family's blessing. Major and Susanna did not hesitate to postpone their journey. They unpacked their belongings so they could attend the wedding. Meanwhile, the Treaty Party group assembled in New Echota and departed for the West without them. Decked out in tribal garb, the chiefs rode at the head of the caravan. Carriages bore the women and children, with wagons loaded with household belongings, and herds of cattle followed behind.[11]

By early spring 1837 Major Ridge and his family were ready to head west. Rather than take the difficult overland path, they chose to go by water. (Meanwhile, John and Sarah stayed behind, opting to remove by land in the fall.) As part of a detachment of 466 Cherokees, half of them children, the Ridges boarded boats at Ross's Landing in present-day Chattanooga on March 3, 1837. Government-supplied provisions—150 bushels of cornmeal, 78 barrels of flour, 12,000 pounds of bacon—had been loaded onboard the boats. A missionary witnessed their departure: "It is mournful to see how reluctantly these people go away, even the stoutest hearts melt into tears when they turn their faces towards the setting sun—& I am sure that this land will be bedewed with a Nation's tears—if not with their blood. . . . Major Ridge is . . . said to be in a declining state, & it is doubted whether he will reach Arkansas."[12]

Watched over by the detachment's physician, Dr. C. Lillybridge, Major and Susanna were soon moved into one of the boat's private cabins. Except for a few miles aboard a new rail-road line (the Tuscumbia, Courtland and Decatur Railroad) that rumbled over land that Cherokees had once traded in return for bribes, the Ridges' entire journey west was over water. They floated down the Ohio River to the Mississippi. Along the way, Lillybridge noted in his journal, the "wind makes it diffi-cult for the Indians to cook, as their fires are on top of the Boats." After carefully navigating the muddy Arkansas River, they reached Little Rock on March 21 and boarded keelboats towed by a steamer. Despite suffering severe colds, Major and Susanna arrived safely on March 27 at their new western home, about two miles above Fort Smith, Arkansas. Major Ridge set-tled his family on Honey Creek, in the northeastern corner of the Arkansas Territory. Quite unlike what many of his fellow Cherokees would soon experience in journeying west, not a single soul died along the way.[13]

Like his uncle, Major Ridge, Elias Boudinot found his plans altered by important family developments. In the wake of his wife Harriett's death in August 1836, Boudinot began casting about to find ways to properly care for and educate his six chil-dren. He planned at first to send four of them to Connecticut while spending the winter in New Echota preparing property claims for the Cherokees as they began heading west. "This will give me full employment," Boudinot noted, "and may be some-what profitable." At the time Boudinot seemed to others very much adrift and saddened. Sophia Sawyer, a tutor who taught the Boudinot children and had lived with the family for nearly a year, observed, "[Boudinot] has lost one of the most lovely women in the world" with "six children hanging now solely on a father's care. . . . I fear for him amidst the wreck of his nation."[14]

But Boudinot, like his people, proved resilient. Even as he made arrangements to place a marble slab at Harriett's grave and have a miniature copy of her portrait sent to him, Boudinot moved beyond his grief over Harriett. By the spring of 1837 he found a new companion, Delight Sargent, a young woman from Vermont who had been working as a teacher at the Brainerd, Creek Path, and Red Clay missions. In May Boudinot married Delight and reported the news to his former father- and mother-in-law, Benjamin and Eleanor Gold, in a letter suffused with joy that connected Delight and Harriett. "The person who has now become the Mother of my dear Children," Boudinot reported, "is so exceptionable, so universally acknowledged to be like your dear daughter Harriett, I have ventured at the step before receiving any intimation of your opinions. I hope it will meet with your approbation, for I can assure you, and your friends in the Nation will assure you, your dear grand children could never expect a better friend, a better mother." Not only was "Miss D. Sargent" a near match for Harriett in virtue; "she was the favorite of all the Missionaries, and accounted the very best teacher that has been in this Nation." And in a phrase that gave voice to Boudinot's newfound sense of comfort and reassurance—not unlike perhaps what the Cherokee Nation was also desperately seeking—he observed that his children were loved by their new mother and felt that they had "a home once more."[15]

On October 11, 1837, Elias and Delight joined with their friends John and Sarah Ridge as part of a company traveling west. Ridge, who had received over $20,000 for his plantation and improvements, determined to make the trip by carriage and horseback. Most of his slaves and horses had left earlier with his former ferryman, William Childers. Three house slaves remained behind to help with the cooking and drive the carriage.

During their overland trip, they stopped in Nashville, where John decided to make a side trip to visit Andrew Jackson at the Hermitage. Though he was now nearly deaf and blind, Jackson reportedly was pleased by Ridge's visit. One can only imagine the emotions between the two men now that removal was not just a reality but, for John Ridge, a deeply personal one.

The Ridges and Boudinots followed an overland route through southwest Kentucky, crossing the Ohio River at Berry's Ferry. Then they journeyed through the northern Illinois Territory and finally across the Ozark plateau and prairies. Along the way, they would camp and rest in their tents. At one such moment we can glimpse the missionary-like hope that animated these families looking for rebirth out West. One night in camp, secure in their tent, Delight Boudinot read aloud to Elias and the children from the biography of William Carey, an English missionary working in India. From his family's nearby tent John Ridge overheard her reading and joined the Boudinots to ask about the book. Mrs. Boudinot told him about how Carey had gone from a shoemaker to a missionary to India and ultimately became a prominent Oriental scholar. "And since the days of the Apostle Paul, who has equaled him?" she asked. To John and Elias the answer was obvious: Samuel Worcester, whose missionary zeal, they hoped, would one day gain the appreciation it deserved. And, Ridge observed, thanks to the school funds carved out of the removal treaty, Worcester would soon be heading up the Cherokee college in the new territory.

They arrived at Honey Creek in late November, after seven

weeks of travel, where they found Major and Susanna Ridge already well settled on the land. Together John and Major built a store in Honey Creek. Elias and Delight settled close to the Worcesters, very near the new town of Park Hill. There Elias and Samuel would reforge their close relationship working on translations of the New Testament into Cherokee and begin plans to found a college for Indians.[16]

Whatever sense of displacement and sadness that the Ridges and Boudinots felt upon settling into their new life out West must be judged against the world they left behind in the East. What happened to their fellow Cherokees in the coming months would have only deepened their determination that removal was their only realistic choice.

By the end of 1837 more whites than Cherokees lived inside the Nation. Thanks to Georgia's land lottery, most of the Cherokee land in Georgia had been given away to—or forcibly taken by—white settlers. Federal agents kept encouraging Cherokees to remove, but with the approach of the deadline in the spring of 1838, only about two thousand had in fact voluntarily left for the West. The fact was, Cherokees continued to believe—to hope—that somehow Chief John Ross's resistance would prevail. So most Cherokees made no preparation for leaving their homes and farms. In fact, in the spring of 1838, Chief Ross instructed his overseers to plant crops, clearly signaling to his Nation that they were going nowhere.[17]

Although he constantly lamented the Cherokees' painful dilemma, Ross spent much of his time defending himself against criticism from federal officials. He was especially angry at the presence of U.S. troops when his own people had shown no violence. He wondered "why an army should be sent among us while we were at perfect peace, to enforce the stipulations of a treaty, which, if even obligatory, was not to be executed for two years." Ross told his brother Lewis that the Cherokees could not be blamed for "their present embarrassing & distressing situation, unless their weakness and incapacity for self defence can be construed into an offense." When Secretary of War Joel Poinsett ended all negotiations with Ross in December 1837, Ross momentarily seemed at a loss: "This cup of hope has been dashed from our lips," he conceded. Soon, though, he simply turned his attention to pressing Congress for help, telling one friend that he was "still sanguine" that if the Cherokee people continued to oppose the "spurious 'treaty,'" they would "succeed soon in negotiating a new arrangement." But he was hearing very different things from some of his Cherokee friends. George Lowrey wrote Ross a letter in January 1838 that was full of sadness and hopelessness. Noting that the Cherokees he knew once "had hopes" that Ross would save the land, now, he reported, "we have heard . . . that you have failed to do us any good. Now the Cherokees are very sorry and some have got no hope making a crop this coming spring and the white people are very glad."[18]

Ross also had to contend with an embarrassing pamphlet excoriating him for "bad faith" in resisting the treaty. Published in early 1838 in various newspapers and distributed to members of the U.S. Senate, the essay was authored by Elias Boudinot before he left for the West. Predictably, the pamphlet got under Ross's skin. He lashed out at Boudinot's "wicked and perfidious" attack, which Ross charged was aimed only at "alienating the confidence of the Cherokee people from their own friends, countrymen & representatives, by slander and falsehoods." An enraged Ross complained to the newspaper editors Francis P. Blair and John C. Rives that Elias Boudinot was nothing but "an unfriendly individual not employed in any public trust by our Indian nation." From Columbus, Tennessee, Evan Jones commiserated with Ross over the war of words and the growing tendency to criticize those who tried to thwart the treaty. "If a dog should bark [at] the treaty," Jones wrote, "he would no doubt be put in the guard-house for his temerity." As someone who was nearly confined to the guardhouse himself for opposing removal efforts, Jones was in a position to know.[19]

Before leaving for the West, John Ridge also added fuel to the growing firestorm of anger and recrimination over Chief Ross, removal, and the fate of the Cherokee Nation. In February 1838 Ridge penned a memorial to Congress, which claimed over fifteen thousand Cherokee signatures, attacking Ross for deceiving his people, enriching himself in office, and ignoring the sage advice of friendly U.S. senators to accept removal. Referring to the treaty as "the forgery palmed off upon the world by a knot of unauthorized individuals," Ross vehemently refuted the charges as "utterly unfounded" and "gotten up for political effect." In particular, Ross insisted that he never deceived his people or deserted their cause; otherwise, as he observed, "I should not so long have possessed the confidence with which they honor me, and which I prize beyond all wealth or praise."[20]

But real changes in Cherokee country soon swamped confidence in Ross. Few Cherokees felt sufficient certainty about the future even to make basic decisions about planting crops. In a frantic note in March Lewis Ross advised his brother to find some way to reassure an increasingly anxious people. "The season of the year," Lewis reminded his brother, "is now at hand when preparation should be making for farming and I know of many that are very much discouraged from making a commencement toward farming until they hear from you. We have nothing but troubles and vexations staring us [in] the face." Troops were pouring into the region, leaving Cherokees "more restless than ever." And then there was the swarm of "speculatars" [*sic*] conniving "to get hold of the Indian money." Given all the "perplexities" and uncertainties now facing the Cherokee people, Lewis observed, "I would not be compelled to live at this place . . . for all the money in the world." The final blow to Ross must have come from his brother's news that Georgia governor Wilson Lumpkin was successfully undermining Ross's reputation among the people and was prepared "to show the world . . . that those who made the Treaty were the True Patriots of the Nation."[21]

Ross, though, still clung to his eleventh-hour hope of wrangling a new treaty out of President Van Buren. As late as April 10, he boasted, "[The Cherokees] are reported to be planting Corn, and they have no desire for removing to the West—this troubles the mind of the President and his host of subordinate officers very much." Meanwhile, Lewis kept pointing to the harsh truth: "Our situation is truly a critical one. Our whole country is full of troops and fortifications. . . . There is no time to be lost. We are in a dreadful state of suspense and the agents of the Govmt. are using every exercise to discourage our people."[22]

But with the announcement in April that General Winfield Scott, veteran of the Black Hawk War of 1832, would be arriving in Cherokee country, Ross finally accepted the painful inevitability of forced removal. Ross conceded to his brother on April

5, "Finding it impossible to get justice extended to our Nation [for] a quiet, permanent, and happy Continuance upon the land of our Fathers—the Delegation are now satisfied that the only alternative left us, in the last resort for an adjustment of the affairs is to negotiate a Treaty on the basis of a Removal." General Scott, he acknowledged, "expects to be sent into our country to remove us after the 23rd of May." As that day drew nearer, Ross accepted that May 23 was "the fatal day decreed for the removal of our people by the armed power of the United States."[23]

Historians have generally praised John Ross for his intransigence over removal, correctly noting that a clear majority of his people wanted to stay on their ancient homeland. Ross's biographer claims he was "no unbending arbiter but a practical politician long accustomed to compromise." But when confronted with a treaty signed by a small faction of his opponents that he feared would be carried out by federal officials unhappy with

General Winfield Scott
Courtesy of the National Archives

his delaying tactics, "Ross set himself rigidly against removal."
The Cherokee historian Theda Perdue likewise defends Ross's
inflexibility over the treaty. Perdue concedes that Ross did
employ delay tactics, but, she claims, such a strategy grew out of
his hope that the U.S. government would one day tire of the
Cherokee controversy or that a new administration would be
more sympathetic to the Cherokees. Ross's hopes may have been
unreasonable, she argues, but they were "probably genuine and
they were certainly shared by the vast majority of Cherokees. In
the final analysis, the wealthy, acculturated principal chief and
not the editor filled with missionary zeal represented the sentiments of the Cherokee people."[24]

Such an assessment has its merits, but a strong leader must
do more than represent a majority sentiment; a leader must have
a vision that protects his people against inevitable annihilation
and offers them a future where they can survive as a people. Elias
Boudinot and John and Major Ridge, whatever their failings
in protecting tribal land, faithfully sought to safeguard the
Cherokee *people*.

———

By May 1838, two years after ratification of the Treaty of New
Echota, time was up for the Cherokees; after that point, they
faced forcible expulsion. But in those two years relatively few
Cherokees had removed. By early May, General Winfield Scott
moved into Cherokee country bringing some seven thousand
troops, militia, and volunteers charged with evicting the Cherokee people who failed to depart voluntarily by May 23, 1838—
at the end of the two-year mandatory removal period. On May
10, Scott ordered all Cherokees to leave their homeland within

the month. Scott distributed an address that day to the Cherokees notifying them that their two years to prepare for removal
were now up and removal must begin immediately. At first
about sixty Cherokees came forward for removal, but letters
from tribal delegates in Washington assuring everyone that a
two-year extension was still possible ended hope for quick and
easy removal.[25] Scott requested his troops to use civility and
kindness toward the Cherokees. In a proclamation to the Cherokees, he advised them that the troops were "as kind hearted as
brave" and were their "friends" who could be trusted. "Obey
them when they tell you that you can remain no longer in this
country," Scott said. The soldiers had invaded Cherokee country, according to Scott, only because the president, in carrying
out the treaty of 1835, had commanded them to execute their
"painful duty in mercy . . . such is also the wish of the whole
people of America."[26]

Scott divided Cherokee country into three sections—western,
central, and eastern—and had his troops construct huge collection camps and stockades in each section near water and shade
where Cherokees who had been rounded up would be brought.
Scott had his troops build thirty-one forts or stockades near
Cherokee towns. From there they would be taken to one of
three river ports: Ross's Landing and Gunter's Landing, both
on the Tennessee, and the Cherokee Agency on the Hiwassee.
Enormous keelboats, recently built by the U.S. government,
would then float them to the Mississippi, then down to the
Arkansas, and upstream to their new homes in the Arkansas
Territory. In carrying out the roundup, Scott commanded his
soldiers to do it with civility: "Every possible kindness, compat-
ible with the necessity of removal, must, therefore, be shown by

the troops." He promised to prosecute "to the severest penalty of the laws" any soldier insulting or injurying "any Cherokee man, woman, or child."[27]

Each "Indian prisoner" would be given a daily ration of one pound of flour or corn and a half pound of bacon. Scott worried about his soldiers' conduct around the Cherokees. While volunteers from Tennessee and North Carolina posed little threat, the Georgia state militia, which drew recruits from the very same people who had invaded Indian gold fields and lusted after Cherokee lands, was openly hostile to the Cherokees. To guard against unwelcome violence, Scott remained personally with the Georgian division of the roundup operation.[28]

On the first day of the roundup Scott watched as thousands were brought into the camps. At first there was no bloodshed, but it was cruel work, with troops rousting families out of homes and fields at gunpoint and white settlers cravenly lurking in the background like vultures to steal whatever was left behind. Indeed, knowing what could or should be left behind, with soldiers pointing guns and demanding instant obedience, must have been yet another indignity for Cherokees being forced from everything they knew and loved. After all, what were they to do or think about cherished items they could not easily bring but now had to suddenly leave behind—from pet dogs and cider barrels to smokehouses and favorite livestock?[29]

The roundup experience revealed deeply affecting moments of emotional upheaval and personal loss. "Squads of troops were sent to search out with rifle and bayonet every small cabin hidden away in the coves or by the sides of mountain streams," according to one observer. Daily life was interrupted with shocking immediacy: "Families at dinner were startled by the sudden gleam of bayonets in the doorway and rose up to be driven with blows and oaths. . . . Men were seized in their fields . . . women were taken from their wheels and children from their play." Snatched up from their homes and field and marched off at gunpoint for the stockades, many Cherokees turned for a final look: "They saw their homes in flames, fired by the lawless rabble that followed on the heels of the soldiers to loot and pillage." Soldiers also tore into Indian graves, hoping to steal silver pendants and other valuables that had been buried with the dead.[30]

In many cases, when the troops arrived at a home, Cherokees simply waited quietly and allowed the trespassing soldiers to arrest them and send them off to the stockades. Few had time to pack their goods or sell their livestock. And frequently, soldiers were ordered to come upon the Cherokees without warning, presumably to reduce resistance. James Mooney, the ethnographer who lived among the Cherokees in the late nineteenth century and interviewed some of the trail survivors, reported that "one old patriarch, when thus surprised, calmly called his children and grandchildren around him, and kneeling down, bid them pray with him in their own language, while the astonished soldiers looked on in silence. Then rising he led the way into exile." In their stoic silence, many Cherokees were making a powerful statement: any preparation to remove they viewed as obedience to unjust orders. Their behavior was a powerful example of passive resistance to tyranny. They were being driven from their rightful homes at gunpoint. It was as if to say, "Let the white men live with that memory—if they could." And some were indeed troubled with the memory. A Georgia volunteer, who later became a colonel in the Confederate service, confessed, "I fought through the civil war and have seen men shot to pieces and slaughtered by thousands, but the Cherokee removal was the cruelest work I ever knew."[31]

The horror of the roundup affected young and old alike. Rebecca Neugin, a small child at the time, remembered the moment: "When the soldiers came to our house my father wanted to fight, but my mother told him that the soldiers would kill him if he did and we surrendered without a fight. They drove us out of our house to join the other prisoners in a stockade." Neugin's family could not take provisions with them: "After they took us away my mother begged them to let her go back and get some bedding. So they let her go back and she brought what bedding and a few cooking utensils she could carry and had to leave behind all of our other household possessions." Frequently, corn was left in the fields and food on the table. Other families endured the terror of separation during roundup. The missionary Daniel Butrick observed two small children running off to the woods when they saw soldiers coming. Despite their mother's attempt to search for the children, the soldiers did not allow it. Much later a family friend managed to find the children and return them to their mother. A deaf man who did not obey a soldier's orders was shot dead.[32]

In Georgia the roundup turned especially brutal. The Baptist missionary Evan Jones bore witness to much of it. "The Cherokees are nearly all prisoners," he reported. "They have been dragged from their houses, and encamped at the forts." As Scott feared, Georgian troops gave their Cherokee prisoners "insulting treatment" and abusive language while forcibly moving them out of house and home. Many were evicted with nothing but the clothes they had on. Even the affluent paid the price: "Well furnished houses were left a prey to plunderers. . . . It is a painful sight . . . the soldiers standing with guns and bayonets."[33]

The mountains of western North Carolina offered some of the most tragic consequences of the Cherokee roundup. Soldiers trying to seize the last remnants were on their way home when they apprehended a man named Tsali, a sixty-year-old Cherokee living with his family on a few acres in the mountains. Tsali was seized along with his wife, his brother, three sons, and their families. Angered by the brutal way the soldiers treated his wife, Tsali attacked the soldiers and escaped. Two soldiers were killed in Tsali's dash for liberty, while the Indians fled to the mountains, including hundreds of others escaping various stockades.

The Tsali story highlighted a real problem for General Scott: he realized he could not round up these elusive fugitives hidden away in the recesses of the Smoky Mountains. So he cut a deal: if Tsali and his party would surrender, the rest of the Cherokees remaining in the mountains of western North Carolina could stay in the region. Tsali came out of hiding with his sons and offered himself as a sacrifice for his people. At which point General Scott ordered that Tsali, his brother, and the two elder sons be shot by a detachment of Cherokee prisoners—a clear message to the Indians about their powerless position. For the few hundred eastern Cherokees, Tsali's sacrifice was nothing short of heroic. They were able to avoid removal because of lands purchased for them by an adopted white man, William Holland Thomas, in accordance with a treaty negotiated in 1819 making them citizens of North Carolina rather than the Cherokee Nation. These four hundred Cherokees living in Oconaluftee in the western North Carolina mountains remained exempt from removal, as did another one hundred Cherokees as a reward for helping troops in the mountain roundup. And then there were several hundred additional Cherokees who successfully hid in the mountains, mostly full-bloods who farmed small plots of land, spoke little English, and practiced the traditional Cherokee religion. All told, perhaps fourteen hundred mountain

Cherokees, the Oconaluftees, remained in the East and are today recognized as the Eastern Band of Cherokee Indians.[34]

If the roundup was an exercise in humiliation, the camps were a clinic in the dangers of disease. The suffering in the camps that summer grew unbearable. Scott himself showed up in camp on the Hiwassee River at the first day of the roundup. Thousands were there. By all accounts, it was a moving sight, even for Scott. The heat was terrible and debilitating, with suffocating clouds of dust stirred up by oxen and wagons. There were on average three to four deaths a day. Still, Scott urged all able-bodied men to do a daily march of twelve to fifteen miles—to prepare themselves for what lay ahead. To avoid the worst of the heat, the marches were to start before sunrise and end at noon. As one soldier's journal revealed, the heat and sickness were overpowering: "Did not move this day, the party requiring rest and being more than one half sick; notwithstanding every effort used, it was impossible to prevent their eating quantities of green peaches and corn—consequently the flux raged among them and carried off some days as high as six and seven."[35]

Within a month after the roundup began, disease and death attacked the removing parties in epidemic proportions, killing hundreds of Indians. Only a few doctors were available in the camps, and many of the Cherokees preferred their own medicine men, believing that white doctors visiting the tents of dead and sick patients brought death with them. Contact with such unclean people, Cherokees believed, subverted the efforts of their medicine men. The two conflicting systems of medicine simply compounded the problems. As a result, the stockades and embarkation depots became worse death traps than the boats. "There is a repugnance of many of the Indians, especially the mountain Cherokees, to the use of medicine no matter how pressing the necessity," noted the army physician J. W. Lide. Cases of dysentery, measles, and whooping cough rose to epidemic proportions among the Cherokees in the camps about the first of June. "All these diseases are now rife among them," Lide observed. The best estimate is that 2,000 to 2,500 died in the camps before setting out for the West.[36]

To those who managed to escape the dangers of disease, general conditions in the forts were nothing short of appalling. No privacy was afforded except what little could be achieved by hanging a thin cloth partition in the tents. Whiskey sellers lurked everywhere, adding to the problem of alcohol-induced violence in the forts. While being moved to more permanent internment camps in western North Carolina just prior to the journey west, Daniel Butrick reported on the humiliating circumstances of the Indians: the Cherokees, he said, "were obliged at night to lie down on the naked ground, in the open air, exposed to wind and rain, and herd[ed] together, men and women and children, like droves of hogs, and in this way, many are hastening to a premature grave."[37]

Weakened by disease and humiliating treatment, removing parties had to contend with summer travel, which posed especially significant dangers. It was the "sickly season" for heading west. Cholera, smallpox, malaria, and dysentery were common afflictions in large traveling groups. And the rivers were low in the summer, making voyages by boat difficult; parties had to stop for weeks waiting on rain to raise the water level. All the while passengers remained crowded together without adequate food or water.

The dangers of summer detachments got so bad that a

hundred prominent Cherokees petitioned General Scott in early June to stop them.

> We your prisoners wish to speak to you. . . . We have been made prisoners by your men, but we do not fight against you. . . . We do not want to see our wives and children die. We do not want to die ourselves and leave them widows and orphans. . . . Sir, our hearts are very heavy. . . . we ask that you not send us down the river at this time of the year. If you do we shall die, our wives will die or our children will die. . . . if you send the whole nation, the whole nation will die.[38]

As a result, General Scott ordered forced removal suspended until September due to the heat and sickness of the season. He had planned for a fast and efficient military operation, but bad weather and independent-minded Cherokees who deserted and sometimes refused supplies dashed all his hopes. Scott assured Chief Ross that he wanted to prevent bloodshed and unnecessary suffering. Such assurances would soon come to nothing.

Besides, Ross had his own plans.

———

By the summer of 1838 John Ross had accepted removal, but as much as it was possible, he wanted it to happen on his terms, on his people's terms. The safest, most humane way to move his people, he argued, would be at their own direction: self-removal. In July 1838, in one of Ross's rare diplomatic triumphs, he coaxed Secretary of War Joel Poinsett into agreeing to allow the Cherokees to manage their own removal. Ross negotiated a contract that called for a cost of $65.88 per person for the entire journey—which came to sixteen cents a day per person for rations, and forty cents a day per horse or ox. He also argued for soap, coffee, and sugar as essentials, but the government said no, these were not necessities. Ross organized the tribe into thirteen detachments of approximately one thousand people each. About one tenth of the emigrants was black—slave and free. Each detachment had a conductor and assistant to supervise. Journeying with each detachment was a physician, an interpreter, a wagon master, and a commissary agent.

At first, General Scott balked at this plan, thinking it extravagant. Scott told Ross he had an offer from a white contractor who had been moving Creeks to the West—for <u>half</u> the Ross-estimated price. Ross's price assumed migrants could cover ten miles a day, and with a journey of roughly eight hundred miles removal could be accomplished over land in eighty days. But water was safer and better, Scott argued. What was safest, Ross insisted, was for the Cherokees to remove themselves.[39]

Self-removal might have been a bit safer, but it was definitely more profitable—at least to whoever was running it. John Ross put his brother Lewis Ross, a well-to-do merchant, in charge of provisioning Cherokees and handling contracts for wagons, horses, rations, and other supplies. Ross and a committee from the Cherokee Council would plan the routes, provide transportation, tolls for roads and ferries, blankets and clothing, get food and forage along the way. Lewis Ross was immediately inundated with white vendors willing to pay $40,000 to get the contract for Cherokee removal. Chief Ross's arrangement with his brother Lewis was made without General Scott's knowledge. When he found out, Scott exploded, claiming that Lewis would reap an "enormous profit." Scott and others pointed out that Lewis Ross stood to make a huge profit of around $150,000, so they insisted the contract be let out to the lowest bidder. Chief

Ross and members of the committee shot back that "they had
no wish to invite the competition of white contractors, not
responsible to themselves, nor answerable to their laws." Besides,
they argued, such contract letting would sacrifice the "health
and comfort" of the tribe just to save a few dollars. Those who
protested Lewis Ross's involvement may well have been disappointed white men greedy for contracts who wanted to embar-
rass the Ross party. Eventually, Scott agreed to the self-removal
arrangement. But his acquiescence only prompted another out-
burst: former president Andrew Jackson howled from the Hermitage that allowing Ross and the Cherokees to carry out their
own removal under their own contractual terms was "madness
and folly." "Why is it that the scamp Ross is not banished from
the notice of the administration?" Jackson thundered.[40]

The Treaty Party was also furious when it learned that the
government had cut a deal with Ross. They feared that funds
given to Ross would deplete money that would be made available
for distribution out West. And many members of the Treaty
Party resented the power bestowed on Ross in allowing him to
control removal, correctly fearing that the power would carry
over upon arrival in Oklahoma. For his part, Scott simply made
sure that the sale of Cherokee eastern lands would compensate for
whatever Ross's leadership would cost in the removal process.[41]

John Ross and his wife, Quatie, began packing their family
for the trip in late summer, determined to go by water from
nearby Ross's Landing in present-day Chattanooga. As Scott had
observed, water travel would be safer and quicker. While overland routes would take about eighty days, the trip by boat, with
good weather, had been done in around three weeks. The federal
government's specially constructed fleet of keelboats on the Tennessee River were waiting to be used. These were huge boats—130

feet long, each with a house 100 feet long, 20 feet wide, and two stories high. Each floor was broken up into rooms with windows and a stove. The fleet could carry more than one thousand people and, by returning for other people, the entire tribe, it was thought, could be moved over the winter.

But on the first voyage with the keelboats, only three hundred Indians showed up. Some fifty others deserted in fear after feeling the shifting of the keelboat's deck under their feet or hearing stories of shipwreck and cholera on the river. Traveling west by rivers also carried powerful meanings for Cherokees that white officials could not imagine. Cherokees believed that rivers had mystic powers that commanded their respect and fear: rivers, they believed, were waterways into the underworld. To take a river trip posed constant threats; it might disturb the spirits left behind and would definitely alert new ones with a possibility of danger and terror. Plus, west to native people conjured up the dark direction followed by the spirits of the dead.[42]

In the end, Cherokees traveled both by river and by land. The first detachments were set to leave by land at the end of August. On August 28, at an encampment twelve miles south of General Scott's New Echota headquarters, the first detachment, which had been holed up in a tent camp all summer, assembled for its long march west. Some 710 Cherokees by one army count stood ready to leave. The moving testimony of one witness, William Shorey Coodey, a nephew of John Ross, depicts an unforgettable spectacle: At noon on August 28, he noted, "the teams were stretched out in a line along the road through a heavy forest, groups of persons formed about each wagon, others shaking the hand of some sick friend or relative who would be left behind." It was a "bright and beautiful" day, Coodey observed, marred only by the "gloomy" mood he sensed in every face. "In all the bustle of preparation there was a silence and stillness of the voice that betrayed the sadness of the heart." When the command to "move on" was given, the aged chief Going Snake mounted his horse and led the way. And then Coodey recalled something "peculiarly impressive and singular": "At this very moment a low sound of distant thunder fell on my ear." Directly west on the horizon "a dark spiral cloud was rising" that prompted a "murmur" from the assembled crowd. "I almost fancied a voice of divine indignation for the wrongs of my poor and unhappy countrymen," Coodey noted, "driven by *brutal* power from all they loved and cherished in the land of their fathers, to gratify the cravings of avarice." And then, just as suddenly, the sunny sky reappeared, "the thunder rolled away and sounds hushed in the distance. The scene[s] around and before me [were] looked upon as omens of some future event in the west."[43]

All their fears of heading west toward the distant thunder and darkening clouds would soon reveal a tragedy of epic proportions.

7

The Trail of Tears

Elias Boudinot and John and Major Ridge likely knew very little about the elaborate plans or various routes for Cherokee removal. Boudinot, along with his new bride, Delight, was busy in his Park Hill neighborhood working with his neighbor and good friend Samuel Worcester on translations and publications of religious texts. And, according to John Ridge, they were making a positive imprint on the people in the new Indian territory. "I was pleased to find that religious tracts, in the Indian language," Ridge reported, "were on the shelves of full-blooded Cherokees, and everyone knew and seemed to love the Messenger, as they called Mr. Worcester." Ridge himself now wanted to steer clear of politics and concentrate his energies on his family and the large store he owned with Major Ridge. They were, however, mindful of the eventual arrival of large numbers of Indians, so while their fellow Cherokees were being rounded up, John Ridge was busy stocking the new store with tools and bridles, pans and skillets, and clothing and shoes. The Ridges decided to offer credit to Cherokees even if their customers had not received their federal allowance. John was also constructing a schoolhouse, to be completed by the time the removing parties arrived in their new western home.[1]

Whether by design or necessity, John Ridge expressed great optimism about the new world he and his fellow Cherokees encountered out West. "The country here is best adapted for agriculture & water privileges," Ridge proclaimed. "It is superior to any country I ever saw in the U.S." And not only was the entire region quickly expanding its population; it would also soon become, he predicted, "the garden spot of the United States. . . . Perfect friendship and contentedness prevail all over this land." As if to confirm the wisdom in the controversial choice he and his Treaty Party friends had made, Ridge frequently asked Cherokee settlers in their new home if they would "want to go back to homeland in the East, if they could have their same property and situation there?" Nearly everyone, he claimed, answered no. "God has thrown His favors here with a broad cast," Ridge said about their new western region.[2]

Prosperity and hope seemed to have returned to John and Sarah Ridge. In the spring of 1838—while Ross was still wrangling with federal officials trying to delay removal—the Ridges managed a trip to New York City, where they attended plays and concerts, and bought goods for the new store. John met with religious figures but could not avoid controversy over the treaty he had helped devise. Several essays of John Howard Payne were circulating in newspapers at the time, and they were all contemptuous of the Treaty Party. "Instead of receiving the late Treaty as a blessing to the Cherokees and as a measure of relief to them," Ridge observed, his supporters "considered it the source of all afflictions." Still, after explaining to his New York friends and acquaintances the errors in Ross's position, Ridge felt vindicated: "many of them are now convinced that the Treaty and its friends are in the right."[3]

Both Boudinot and the Ridges had found a promising new start for themselves and—they believed—for their people in what the U.S. government now called Indian Territory. And they doubtless looked forward to seeing the rest of the Cherokee Nation resettled alongside them.

Their journey west, though, changed everything.

———

On November 4, 1838, George Hicks wrote his friend John Ross from Mouse Creek in the Cherokee Nation that he and his family would soon leave their homeland: "[We are about] to take our final leave and kind farewell to our native land the country that the Great Spirit gave our Fathers" and "that gave us birth." Hicks was joining a detachment of nearly one thousand Cherokees to begin the eight-hundred-mile overland trek to their new land in Oklahoma. As with so many uprooted from their homes in the East, Hicks's tone suggested sadness mingled with inevitability. "It is with sorrow," he wrote, "that we are forced by the authority of the white man to quit the scenes of our childhood, but stern necessity says we must go." Well aware that they faced "a laborious undertaking," and angered that the property he was leaving behind had been "stolen and Robed" from them by white men, Hicks and his family nonetheless remained confident their forced removal would be successful, if the white citizens would permit them.[4]

Predictably, different pictures emerge of this powerful moment of departure depending on whether the source is a Cherokee or a white soldier. Soldiers tended to highlight the efficiency and safety of the operation; Cherokees, understandably, found heartache even when there were few if any casualties. According to Lieutenant H. L. Scott of the Fourth Infantry, for example, who followed the first emigrating parties for eighty miles, everything went smoothly: "The march of this party through the country was perfectly orderly . . . the greatest harmony & cheerfulness prevails in these two detachments, & with the exception of four deaths among the children, they have met with no mishaps & encountered no difficulties thus far on the route." William Shorey Coodey, John Ross's nephew, who witnessed the departure of the detachment, remembered a very different scene: Although it was a beautiful day, Coodey perceived "a gloomy thoughtfulness" etched "in the lineaments of every face," and a silence that "betrayed the sadness of the heart."[5]

The forced emigration of the Cherokee people beginning in the summer of 1838 was an experience that had been played out many times in the relocation of Indians from the American Southeast. Most of the Choctaws, Creeks, and Chickasaws, along with many Seminoles, had already endured their own forced removal to Oklahoma. The Cherokees suffered no more pain than these other tribes in the Southeast, but over the years the Cherokees' Trail of Tears has taken on an epic level of drama and sacrifice that, in effect, has placed our nation on trial for its treatment of Indian peoples.

The Cherokee removal did not happen all at once; it occurred over many years. As early as 1794 a few Cherokees voluntarily moved west. After land cessions in 1810–11 and again in 1819, roughly three thousand Cherokees journeyed to present-day

Arkansas—among them the brilliant inventor Sequoyah. But these people made a voluntary choice to move, and many, like Sequoyah, frequently traveled back and forth to visit family and friends. Meanwhile, the U.S. government offered inducements— rifles, blankets, cooking utensils, transportation, and a year's support in their new land—for any Indians willing to enroll for removal. Such incentives prompted fewer than a dozen families to sign up. But in the spring of 1834 some nine hundred Cherokees, sensing the inevitable expulsion from their homeland, did move west on flatboats provided by the federal government. Stories of great hardship, including outbreaks of measles and cholera, on the migrants' journey served only to alarm Cherokees in the East about the grave dangers of westward travel.[6]

Of the seventeen detachments under forced removal, four left under military conductors: the first three embarked from Ross's Landing in June 1838; the fourth under military control was the Bell detachment that departed from the Cherokee Agency near Calhoun on October 11. The other thirteen removing parties journeyed under John Ross's supervision with Cherokee conductors. All but one of these traveled by land.[7]

On June 6 at noon on a hot summer day, some eight hundred Cherokees boarded six flatboats lashed to a steamboat, three on each side, for the trip down the Tennessee River. This first detachment faced an ominous start: amid the stifling heat in a drought-stricken summer, the people on board were "literally crammed into the boat [which] . . . was so filled that the timbers began to crack and give way, and the boat itself was on the point of sinking." Three days later the group made it to Decatur, Alabama, where, due to the summer drought, the river proved too shallow to navigate. So the conductor in charge of the detachment, Lieutenant Edward Deas, loaded all eight hundred onto railroad cars to make their way across land to the next navigable waters at Tuscumbia. While transferring one group of Cherokees to the railroad cars, another group, primed with whiskey and angry at their circumstance, rebelled, with more than a hundred deserting. The other Cherokees continued by boat traveling down the Tennessee, Ohio, and Mississippi rivers, then finally journeying up the Arkansas River to Indian Territory. Amazingly, the detachment, stopping only for wood to fuel the steamboat, managed the entire trip to Arkansas by water and train without any fatalities.[8]

A second detachment embarked out of Ross's Landing a week later. Angered at being rounded up at gunpoint, then corralled in hot, sickly camps, many of the 875 Cherokees in this group also rebelled, refusing to give their names or accept government-provided clothing or food. Before being loaded onto the steamer *George Guess* (named after the Cherokee inventor Sequoyah), some twenty-five Cherokees deserted. Like most Indians, passengers in this group had never seen a train; one man, trying to retrieve his hat from under the train, was run over and killed. Five children died during the journey. When the boats could not navigate the shallow waters past Little Rock, the detachment was forced to walk the last hundred miles through Arkansas. Amid the heat and "suffocating clouds of dust stirred up by oxen and wagons," hundreds became ill. According to one witness, when the detachment rested, half sick, they ate enormous quantities of green peaches and corn, which produced a "flux" that "raged among them and carried off some days as high as six and seven." Some seventy Cherokees died from this episode of the flux. A total of 602 out of the original 875 survived the trip to Oklahoma, but more than one in four either died or deserted during the trek.[9]

With the oppressive heat and sickly conditions in the camps, combined with severe drought rendering the Tennessee River nearly impassable, General Scott decided to suspend further departures until September. This meant that Indians endured degrading conditions holed up in camps. Scott, like most soldiers, tried to focus on the positive here, referring to the camps as "healthful and convenient" and using them to conduct his daily "exercise" regimen of twelve- to fifteen-mile forced marches to prepare for the journey to the West. Meanwhile, Secretary of War Joel Poinsett officially agreed to John Ross's self-removal plan. So beginning in late August, removal followed Ross's scheme that divided the remaining thirteen thousand Cherokees into thirteen detachments of roughly one thousand each. They would now travel by land, an eight-hundred-mile trek that, with Ross's estimated ten miles a day, would take roughly three months. For

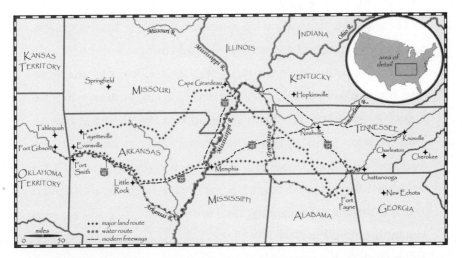

Trail of Tears Routes
Map by Rebecca L. Wrenn

most Cherokees, it would be the most perilous months of their lives.[10]

———

The land route west took most detachments across the Tennessee River at Blythe's Ferry, then on to Pikeville, McMinnville, and Nashville. In Nashville Lewis Ross met removing parties with clothes (to help them survive the approaching winter): cloaks, bearskins, blankets, overcoats, and thick boots and socks. From Nashville, parties proceeded across the Cumberland River toward Hopkinsville, Kentucky, and west over the Ohio River at Golconda, Illinois, then trekked over southern Illinois crossing the Mississippi River near Jonesboro, Illinois, to Cape Girardeau, Missouri. The last few detachments followed a northern route across central Missouri since previous parties had nearly wiped out the game supply along the southern route. These groups traveled through Farmington, Rolla, and Lebanon. When they reached Arkansas, they turned west around Fayetteville and headed into Indian Territory.[11]

Despite the depressing circumstances of the forced march, some of the travelers occasionally found unexpected pleasure in the majesty and novelty of what they saw along the way. One missionary arriving at the Mississippi River in January 1839 set aside his otherwise lugubrious mood to take in the moment: "We find our tent on the bank of this great river, one of the wonders of Creation." Shortly after they arrived, he noted, "Our attention was arrested by the passing of a large, beautiful and grand steamboat. Neither my dear wife nor myself had ever seen one before."[12]

Each detachment tended to develop its own sense of community, but there was considerable movement in and out of various removing parties. Some Cherokees—while searching for friends and relatives, scavenging for better food, or returning home—left one detachment to join another. Others, tired of the daily bland diet of salt pork and cornmeal, abandoned the march to hunt deer along the trail. Conductors tried to keep order and reduce the incidence of those giving up the march and attempting to return home. Ross reported only about 182 desertions among the thirteen detachments, but in a few groups desertion rates ran as high as 18 percent. Those too weak or ill to keep up the pace or who simply wandered off from their detachment usually found an unhappy fate. An elderly Cherokee who fell ill and was left behind in Illinois was discovered dead by some local whites, who proceeded to bury him only to sue the conductor of the next detachment to recoup the burial expenses.[13]

Organizing and provisioning such a venture proved to be a daunting enterprise. With so many Cherokees left destitute after a summer confined to camps, many desperately needed shoes, clothing, and blankets. Several conductors wrote Ross, pleading with him to send additional clothes or funds to buy them along the way. And one detachment had only eighty-three tents—far too few for the nearly one thousand people in the party. It took some 645 wagons (one for every eighteen to twenty people), each pulled by a double team of oxen or mules, and five thousand horses to transport thirteen thousand Indians and blacks. But many of the removing parties were plagued by insufficient wagons to carry the people and forage necessary for the journey. Wagons were filled with a family's entire belongings (from clothes to farming equipment). Given the significant number of sick and aged, conductors grew concerned about having enough wagons both to carry the weak and to haul food and other items. Writing from Sequatchie Valley, Tennessee, Jesse Bushyhead, who headed up a contingent of 968 Cherokees, put it simply to Ross: "We have a large number of sick, and very many extremely aged, and infirm persons in our detachment, that must of necessity be conveyed in the waggons. . . . There is forty nine waggons—so that you will see the impractibility of hawling forage from place to place to serve the convenience of the contracters. Aside from the subsistence rations, it will require twelve waggons to hawl the three days forage rations between this and McMinnville [Tennessee]." Bushyhead suggested buying a wagon and team strictly for the "very old and infirm."[14]

Sometimes, of course, the best-laid plans could not overcome the sheer difficulty in overland western travel. Journeying by land over Arkansas in this era was a slow-going enterprise at best, and sometimes nearly impossible. The *Arkansas Gazette* reported in 1825 that while the direct route from Memphis to Little Rock was 128 miles, the nearly nonexistent roads that the mail followed required a circuitous three hundred miles of travel and the water route covered at least two hundred miles. "Neither of these routes," the paper observed, "is passable when the waters are high; and at no time can they [the primitive roads] be traveled by carriages of any description."[15]

Despite such obstacles, Ross and his conductors believed they had done their best to organize and supply the removal enterprise. But General Scott criticized the effort for being slow and inefficient. Scott reminded Ross that several of the rolls revealed that far from averaging 1,000 people, as originally planned, many of the detachments contained as few as 559. If the detachment size did not quickly increase, Scott warned, Ross would have to pay for extra conductors as well as more physicians nec-

essary to make additional trips out West. In trying to fathom
what lay behind the sluggish removal process, Scott wondered if
the problem lay "in the want of sufficient moral influence &
official authority to enforce the execution of orders & arrangements." In a sharp response, Ross insisted that the removal effort
required a complicated and simultaneous preparation for emigration both by land and by water, as well as dealing with the
sick and aged, who were "unable to bear the fatigues of the journey by land." He defended himself by pointing to "causes beyond
human control"—large numbers of sick, with one detachment
losing its original conductor, and others who were "unavoidably
left behind." And he blamed some of the slowdown on Treaty
Party conductors John Bell and William Boling "& their associ-
ates" who had been "practicing a course of interference" aimed
at slowing down emigration and subverting Ross's well-laid
plans. At one point, Ross took comfort in regaling Scott with the
highly successful experiences of Peter Hildebrand's detachment:
while "quietly encamped" on the southern bank of the Tennessee River, this detachment had managed, thanks to a dawn-to-
dusk regimen of river crossing, to safely transport some sixty-one
wagons and all the people across the river. "Nothing but good
management, perserverence and energy," Ross insisted, "could
have accomplished it so sattisfactorily." Despite Ross's explanations, the trip out West in fact took much longer and proved
more costly than he had estimated; instead of 80 days, the journey averaged 125 days, and instead of a per-person cost of $65.88,
individual expenses came to roughly $103.25.[16]

The issue of money—whether it was assets left behind or
profits made along the trail—also plagued the removal effort.
Many Cherokees complained openly about having to leave

home with none of their property claims properly settled. After a detachment council held a meeting along the trail near McMinnville, Tennessee, its conductor reported to Ross that many Cherokees expressed anger over having to remove "under very unfavorable, as well as embarrassed circumstances" and feared they had no guarantee of fair and proper compensation for their property. Indeed, because they had been torn from their own homes, "the corrupt and designing man can make out fraudulent demands against them."[17]

Profiting from removal proved to be an even greater problem out on the trail. From the beginning Lewis Ross was accused of using his position for personal profit. T. Hartley Crawford, the commissioner of Indian Affairs under President Martin Van Buren, insisted that Lewis stood to make close to $150,000 off the contract to conduct the removal. Ross had no monopoly on the profit motive as greed ran nearly as epidemic as disease out on the trail. Nashville merchants charged exorbitant prices for goods; ferry operators and toll road keepers jacked up their fees as well. "On the Cumberland mountains," one missionary observed, "they fleeced us, 73 cents a wagon and 12½ cents a horse without the least abatement or thanks." Even the conductors, one man complained, were "too easily enticed" by craven food contractors, "those *vultures* of Indian money." And Lewis Ross had a keen eye for profit even after removal was accomplished. Early on he calculated that clearing and planting the fields out West would require a large market for black slaves. So he bought a big supply of slaves in Georgia and sent them out on a chartered boat. It is hard to know how much of these profits that Lewis Ross enjoyed found their way to his brother John. Ross took no salary as chief in the 1830s, and the funds cannot be easily traced back to him, but the suspicion both

among some of the trail survivors and among historians that he
participated in the profits has lingered over the years.[18]

———

Western travel, especially with so many people, horses, and wagons, required significant planning, if only to anticipate the most
basic needs of the people and their belongings. Advance scouts
or agents, for example, tried to plan appropriate stopping points
every ten to fifteen miles along the way (a day's march) by identifying campsites near water, wood for fires, and grazing grass for
livestock. But the weather and road conditions invariably subverted their best efforts. The mostly dirt roads they followed, once
pelted with rain, became muddy and sometimes impassable. To
pull heavy wagons over the hilly country that prevailed in much
of the trip, Cherokees had to use a double-span of horses. The mud
and wagon ruts that resulted created a jarring, mud-splattered
ride. In the winter, ice floes on the Mississippi and Ohio rivers
halted detachments up to a month. Even in good conditions,
river crossings could sometimes take several days. Peter Hildebrand's detachment, which Ross proudly cited in his letter to
General Scott, required nearly three days in mid-November for
the 1,766 people, 88 wagons, and 881 horses and oxen to cross
the Tennessee River. And sometimes the problem could never be
anticipated. Jesse Bushyhead's detachment was delayed for several days in McMinnville, Tennessee, due to oxen sickened from
eating poison ivy.[19]

While some Cherokees rode in wagons and on horseback,
most walked. Rebecca Neugin was only three years old when
she and her family were rounded up. Neugin's family consisted
of eleven people, including her eight brothers and sisters; two or
three widows traveled with them. "My father had a wagon

pulled by two spans of oxen to haul us in," Neugin remembered. Her older brother Dick "walked along with a long whip which he popped over the backs of the oxen and drove them all the way. My mother and father walked all the way also."[20]

The march west stretched out like a long, unbroken ribbon of people and wagons and horses. White observers along the way were often struck by the dignity and composure of the Cherokees. Although he was aware that the detachment had suffered an average of four deaths a day, a Batesville, Missouri, lawyer focused on the mainly admirable traits he saw in the procession of roughly twelve hundred Indians passing through his area in late December: "The whole company appeared to be well clothed, and comfortably fixed for traveling. . . . they are very peaceable, and have committed no depredations upon any property where they pass." One man noted in the *Nashville Whig* that the Cherokees "exhibited the utmost quiet and good

The Trail of Tears by Robert Lindneux
Courtesy of Woolaroc Museum, Bartlesville, Oklahoma

order" with no evidence of intoxication. As further evidence of their sober, well-mannered disposition, he pointed out that in one detachment "from three to four hundred" were "Christian communicants." And an observer in Yellville, Arkansas, seemed struck that so many of the Cherokees who came through the area in early 1839 were well dressed ("fine looking men"), if thinly clad. "Some of the women," he noted, "ha[d] only blankets wrapped around them, several carrying papooses wrapped in a blanket or some kind of cloth and fastened to the back of their mothers. Seeing so many, I wondered that I did not hear a scream from a single papoose."[21]

But the discomfort and pain of the journey were inevitable and spared neither the weak nor the elderly. A witness from Maine who watched several detachments trek through southern Kentucky in early December offered a vivid description of the trail: "We found the road literally filled with the procession for about three miles in length. . . . The sick and feeble were carried in wagons—about as comfortable for traveling as a New England ox cart with a covering over it." While many rode on horseback, "multitudes [went] on foot," the Maine bystander noted, "even aged females, apparently nearly ready to drop into the grave, were traveling with heavy burdens attached to the back— on the sometimes frozen ground, and sometimes muddy streets, with no covering for the feet except what nature had given them."[22]

In these circumstances, fatigue became the Cherokees' most dangerous enemy on the trail. It weakened their bodies, opening them up to sickness and disease. During the summer months before Scott suspended emigration, the oppressive heat ravaged Lieutenant R. H. K. Whiteley's detachment. "The weather was extremely hot," Whiteley reported, "and the rough and rocky roads, made the condition of the sick occupants of the wagons miserable indeed. Three, four, and five deaths occurred each day." Despite starting the "marches" before sunrise and ending at noon to avoid the worst heat of the day, within a month between 200 and 300 became ill.[23]

Daniel Butrick, one of the few missionaries who joined the Cherokees on the trail west, vividly testified to the sickness and death that plagued Cherokees on the road. During the heat and drought of the summer months, Butrick met a wagoner who told him about the large numbers of ailing Cherokees he had conveyed to Waterloo, Alabama. The wagoner said "he could not but pitty them though they were Indians," and described a detachment suffering "under a burning sun, scorching with fever, parching with thirst, rendered more intolerable by the air being darkened with heat dust." According to Butrick, the Indians were not allowed to stop or rest when they became sick: "They were driven on along as they could walk, and then thrown into waggons." Even when their condition approached "the agonies of death" and the wagon master was notified, "his order was, Drive on, Drive on." Butrick painted a desperate picture of a woman, "languishing, and almost ready to drop to the ground every step, and yet clinging to her friends, choosing rather to die in their arms, than be torn from them, and thrown into a heated waggon to be separated forever from all she held dear on earth. See her last despairing look toward her dear husband, as she sinks at his feet."[24]

Weakened by fatigue and exposed to the elements, Cherokees on the trail fell victim to diseases ranging from measles and whooping cough to dysentery and various respiratory infections. And unclean cooking utensils—often wiped by a rag full of grease and contaminated raw pork—also spread disease quickly. Sickness and death especially afflicted children and the aged. As Rebecca Neugin recalled, "There was much sickness and a great many little children died of whooping cough." Ignorant about the herbal medicine Indians relied on, the army doctors who accompanied the detachments proved unable to care for the sick and dying. In their sorrow and frustration, some Cherokees turned to whiskey brought along by white peddlers—a temptation that all too often produced drunken outbreaks of violence.[25]

Trail deaths often became a defining element of a detachment's journey. Elijah Hicks lost most of his petty officers due to deadly illness on the trail. His first wagon master died in Woodberry, Cannon County, Tennessee. The distinguished Cherokee chief White Path grew fatally ill "in the last stages of sickness," reported Hicks, was helpless, had to be "halled," and couldn't "last but a few days." Another Cherokee leader in the detachment, Hicks noted, "has given himself up to the bane of death and I have all together lost his services." Hicks maintained hope the detachment could reach its destination by December, but he was clearly concerned about provisions: "I do not like the prospects from Hopkinsville to the Missi. in the way of meat."[26]

The Baptist missionary Evan Jones, a loyal supporter of John Ross, accompanied his congregation to the stockades and on the trek out West. He was one of only three white missionaries who actually walked the Trail of Tears with the Cherokees. His detachment of 1,250 left in October and three and a half months later arrived in Indian Territory. En route, 71 died and 5 babies were born. "It will be a miracle of mercy," Jones observed, "if one fourth escapes the exposure to that sickly climate at this most unfavorable season." Jones depicted Cherokees who looked "exceedingly depressed, almost in the agonies of despair." And in the end, he felt the suffering he witnessed jolted him into silent anguish: "I have no language to express the emotions which rend our hearts to witness their season of cruel and unnecessary oppression."[27]

For Butrick, the danger of the trail only worsened in the winter. When his detachment was forced to stop at the Ohio River due to ice floes, Butrick noted that there were two other groups nearby, both crippled by sickness and death. "In all these detachments," he observed, "comprising about 8,000 souls, there is now a vast amount of sickness, and many deaths. Six have died within a short time in Maj. [James] Brown's company, and in this detachment of Mr. [Richard] Taylor's there are more or less affected with sickness in almost every tent; and yet all are houseless & homeless in a strange land, and in a cold region exposed to weather almost unknown in their native country." Butrick witnessed extreme heartbreak along the trail. A woman who had given birth to a child a few days earlier was found dead the next morning with the infant in her arms. The white man living nearby refused to have her buried on his property, and so "the corpse was carried all day in the wagon."[28]

A rare recorded remembrance from one Cherokee offers simple eloquence to the tragedy of the trail: "Long time we travel on way to new land. People feel bad when they leave Old Nation. Women cry and make sad wails. Children cry and many men cry, and all look sad like when friends die, but they say nothing and just put heads down and keep on go towards West. Many days pass and people die very much."[29]

While so many of his people were ailing and dying, John Ross remained behind to supervise the initial departures. With Ross's own removal looming, his friend Thomas N. Clark, writing initially from Nashville, warned the Ross family against traveling by land if the weather turned rainy. "I would advise you to put your family on a comfortable Boat," Clark suggested, "& let them go by water for you may rest assured that if you send them by land they will have a rugged time of it for the Detachments will put the roads in shocking order." Weeks later, Clark wrote again recommending that Ross leave as quickly as possible and join Clark at the Mississippi River; if Ross waited any longer he and his family risked "the severity of the winter & 2dly the scarcity of supplies." Ross took part of Clark's advice; he, his wife, Quatie, and their children left by boat once water levels had risen. But they did not depart until mid-December in the very last detachment—one that included 230 Cherokees too old and sick to go by land.[30]

Despite John Ross's best-laid plans and more comfortable traveling arrangements, he too endured personal sorrow along the trail. As Clark had feared, Ross's family encountered a cold and snowy winter as they began their final march out of Little Rock, Arkansas, in early February 1839. According to a story from an army private who accompanied the Ross detachment, Quatie Ross, after hearing the repeated cries of a sick child, gave the baby her coat for warmth "while she rode thinly clad through a blinding sleet and snow storm." The baby survived, but days later Quatie died from pneumonia "in the still Hours of a bleak winter night."[31] Like so many others who died on the trail, Quatie was buried in a shallow grave on the road.

———————

Just how many died on the Trail of Tears? It is hard to be precise. Hundreds died holed up in the camps waiting to leave.

Ross's own figures suggest about sixteen hundred perished on the trail itself. Then there were thousands more who died after arrival due to exposure and disease from the trek. Most scholars estimate that a grand total of at least four thousand died as the direct result of removal—one fourth of the entire Cherokee Nation at the time. And some historical demographers argue that when one considers the number of children that Trail of Tears passengers would have produced if they had survived the removal process, the total number lost to the Nation would be closer to eight thousand Cherokees.[32]

Such devastating mortality exceeded even the tragic experiences of most other tribes forcibly removed during this era. While the Chickasaw removal produced relatively few deaths, the Choctaws lost about 15 percent (six thousand out of forty thousand). The Creeks and Seminoles claimed much higher death totals—about 50 percent—but for the Creeks this seems to have been caused by an epidemic of "bilious fevers" after arrival out West rather than from the removal itself. Much of the Seminole mortality apparently stemmed from a horrific war of attrition that had prompted removal rather than from the trail experience. The ethnographer, James Mooney, may have put it best: the Trail of Tears "may well exceed in weight of grief and pathos any other passage in American history."[33]

———

Even as detachments made their way toward their final destination out West, both the painful past and uncertain future doubtless darkened the mood. Loss of life and the sadness of the trail conspired to sap the strength and spirit of many Cherokees. Writing from Port Royal near the Kentucky line, Elijah Hicks told John Ross his detachment would soon cross the Ohio

River, but he was deeply concerned about morale. "The detachment of the people are very loth to go on," he noted, "and unusually slow in preparing for starting each morning. I am not surprised at this because they are moving not from choice to an unknown region not desired by them. I am disposed to make full allowance for their unhappy movement." Hicks could not help but close his letter to Ross on an angry note: "Tell our friends that we are on the journey west, arising from the acts of wicked men & from our unfortunate fate." And to one white observer watching the solemn procession walking through Kentucky, a glance at the faces of hundreds of Cherokees spoke volumes: "The Indians as a whole carry in their countenances every thing but the appearance of happiness. Some carry a downcast dejected look bordering upon the appearance of despair; others a wild frantic appearance as if about to burst the chains of nature and pounce like a tiger upon their enemies."[34]

Amid the suffering, several missionaries who accompanied some of the detachments on the trek offered solace and ministered to the Cherokees. The Baptist missionary Evan Jones followed the fourth detachment and reported from Little Prairie, Missouri, in late December that, after traveling 592 miles, thanks to "the kind hand of providence of our heavenly father," the people suffered relatively few problems. "We have met with no serious accident and have been detained only two days by bad weather," he wrote. But the increasingly bitter winter weather and "thinly clad" people forced them to "make fires along the road at short intervals" to protect themselves from the cold. When they had to stop for ice floes on the Mississippi, another detachment joined them in the delay, offering the opportunity for their "native preachers" to help tend to the people. Despite the relative good fortune of his detachment, Jones was well aware of what lay ahead for most Cherokees on the trail: "There will be an immense amount of suffering and loss of life attending the removal. Great numbers of the old, the young, and the infirm will inevitably be sacrificed. And the fact that the removal is effected by coercion makes it the more galling to the feelings of the survivors."[35]

Not only did the misery and disease on the trail drive Cherokees to an early grave; the immense suffering took its toll as well on the human spirit. Butrick, who had seen such agony back in the camps—he had been so overwhelmed by what he saw in Brainerd, Tennessee, he claimed, that "it seemed a luxury to groan and weep"—took off with Richard Taylor's detachment that left Ross's Landing in September. Arriving in Arkansas after considerable delays on the trail six months later, Butrick's party suffered fifty-five deaths, one of highest death tolls among the detachments. During a delay due to ice floes the last few days of December at the Mississippi, Butrick paused to reflect on the pain and trauma he and the Cherokees had witnessed. "O what a year it has been," he wrote in his journal on New Year's Eve. "O what a sweeping wind has gone over, and carried its thousands into the grave; while thousands of others have been tortured and scarcely survive, and the whole nation comparatively thrown out of house & home during this most dreary winter."[36]

All of which plunged the Cherokee people into a desperate and lonely place, at least from the perspective of their missionary friends. "The year past has been a year of spiritual darkness," Butrick lamented from the trail. It had been a season of "awful profanements," filled with "scenes of wickedness." And it left him—doubtless like most Indians—wondering, pleading to understand why the Cherokee people had to endure such torment. "For what crime," Butrick asked, "was this whole nation doomed to this perpetual death? This almost unheard of suffering?"[37]

For Butrick and other Ross supporters, the only "crime" at issue, of course, was the Treaty of New Echota. Thanks to "a few unauthorized individuals," the Cherokee homeland had illegally been sold, leaving the Cherokee Nation "houseless & homeless." So even as detachments walked their final painful steps into Indian Territory, the battles with the Treaty Party resurfaced, especially since everyone knew that Elias Boudinot and the Ridges were already safely settled in their new western homeland. "I have no pleasing anticipation about arriving at the Arkansas," Butrick wrote toward the end of his trek. He was angry about the presence there of not only the Treaty Party but also some of their friendly confidants, such as Samuel Worcester. "Mr. Worcester will doubtless wish to sustain, or at least, excuse Mr. [Elias] Boudinot in the course he has taken," Butrick bitterly observed, just as the American Board had already accepted Boudinot as an "assistant missionary" in Oklahoma. While such forgiveness might be laudable, Butrick argued, those working in the mission churches could not overlook Boudinot's "conduct in making the treaty." Richard Taylor, who led Butrick's detachment, had already announced that "he could not commune with Mr. Boudinot," while other leading elders proclaimed they would not attend communion if held at John Ridge's home, due to lingering anger over "the measures adopted by the treaty party."[38]

After years of internal disputes culminating in devastating loss on the trail, an entire people had removed themselves to a strange and distant land. With Cherokees still fiercely at odds with one another over removal, emotions ran high and common ground remained elusive. And difficult questions persisted: Had the Cherokees, by removing west, saved their people and their nation from certain destruction in the East? Or had they shamefully surrendered their ancient homeland—and all the personal and tribal identity that was connected to it? In the agonizing circumstances that had led to the Trail of Tears, what was the more patriotic duty—saving a people or a homeland? And what would all the suffering of removal now mean to the Cherokee people? As Boudinot and the Ridges—the leading men who had orchestrated the relocation—learned all too quickly, the trail would leave a harsh and bitter taste.

8

Blood Revenge

The Cherokees' new home, some 7 million acres in what is now northeast Oklahoma, appeared to its new settlers at once depressing and abundant. Major Ridge's wife, Susanna, thought of it as "an entire wilderness," a country full of outlaws squatting in abandoned cabins eager to sell whiskey to dispirited Indians. To others, it was a veritable land of milk and honey, rich with "noble groves and forests which skirt and intersect the prairies, and extend along the alluvial bottoms of the rivers." It was a country offering hilly forests thick with hickory, oak, and ash, bottomlands replete with elm, willow, sycamore, and pecan trees, and plenty of rich prairie pastureland well suited for raising livestock. Upon arriving in early April 1839, the missionary Daniel Butrick, despite his anger over removal, could not suppress his joy: "The country is beautiful. In descending the road toward Fort Smith, at once a green meadow, almost without bounds, opened to our view. This was sprinkled here and there with beautiful shade trees, and sometimes with delightful groves,

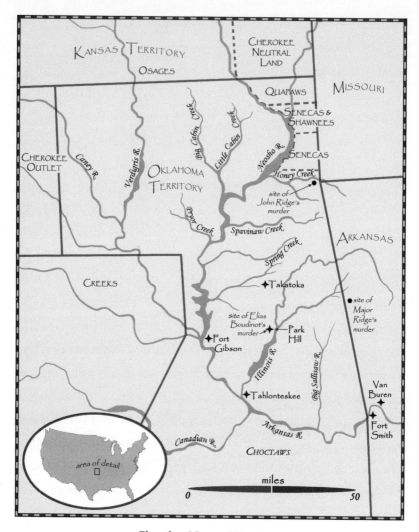

Cherokee Nation West, 1839
Map by Rebecca L. Wrenn

waving in the breeze." But as Butrick and his weary travelers
ventured closer a different sensation overcame the group: "We
were met by a nauseous, sickly breeze, which told us the dead
were there, and that we were drawing near the chambers of
death." Amid the beauty of their new land, they soon found

themselves haunted by the "pensive and gloomy" memories of the pain and suffering they had witnessed in being forced from their homes in the East.[1]

No such inner torment afflicted Elias and Delight Boudinot in their new home near Park Hill. Since his arrival in the fall of 1838, Boudinot had rejoined his friend and kindred spirit Samuel Worcester in their task of translating and publishing the Bible in Cherokee and English. Elias and Delight attended church with Worcester in the tiny congregation in Park Hill. By day, Boudinot divided his time between the work of the press and construction of his house; in the evenings, he worked on translations. Overjoyed to be reunited with his partner in mission work, Worcester said of Boudinot, "He is my right hand." Early on, Worcester had made a success of establishing the mission station as the focal point of the Park Hill community. The mission served as an informal center that disbursed information, money, and medicine.[2]

Winning souls to Christ had not been easy for Worcester and other missionaries in the West—the white man's religion the missionaries peddled had lost favor ever since forced removal— but their devotion to the Cherokees continued unabated. "I do not know," Worcester conceded, "that the cause of religion has made much sensible progress among the Cherokees since we crossed the Mississippi." But he was hopeful in his new moral crusade: battling the growing problem of liquor among the Indians. "There are immense quantities of whiskey in the country," one federal report concluded in 1837, and the Cherokees were more "disposed to traffic in ardent spirits" than the other tribes. Unless laws prohibiting liquor sales to Indians were rigidly enforced, many observers believed, "the evil of intemperance will spread its wide reign, and its effect will be ruinous to the morals of the natives, and dangerous to the peace of the country." Worcester set up a temperance society that required total abstinence. He found "encouraging success" in the society with about four hundred members, "the greater part Cherokees."[3]

Although focused on faith and temperance, Worcester could not avoid the painful tensions left by the Trail of Tears. With the arrival of the rest of the Cherokee people in 1838–39, harmony, even among the missionaries, remained difficult to preserve. Dr. Elizur Butler and Reverends Daniel Butrick and Evan Jones arrived full of anger at the removal party and its friends, such as Worcester. The American Board wrote Worcester urging him to search for peaceful common ground with fellow missionaries despite the antagonism of Butler and others and their painful struggle in working through "the anxiety & toil of removal." What was needed was "a softening, cooling, healing influence in the sore & troubled minds of the Cherokees" rather than missionaries vengefully airing out "what bad things one or the other party may have said or done."[4]

And much of what they were bickering about involved the very man Worcester had hired as his translator, Elias Boudinot. Worcester admitted that his partnership with Boudinot was "the greatest trial we have at present." Boudinot's "extreme anxiety to save his people," Worcester acknowledged, led him to make a treaty with the United States, "an act, in my view, entirely unjustifiable, yet in his case, dictated by good motives." Boudinot's pro-removal conduct "rendered him so unpopular in the nation" that his many critics were hounding Worcester to fire him. What was more, one of Boudinot's chief antagonists was a "distinguished member" of Worcester's church, a man who found Worcester's friendship with Boudinot such "an occasion of great sin" that he quit attending church. But despite Worcester's view that Boudinot had acted wrongly in the removal controversy, he fiercely supported his friend, both because Boudinot possessed unparalleled translating skills and because he faithfully shared Worcester's commitment to uplifting the Cherokee people. In the end, the Cherokee people accepted Worcester's decision to continue his religious work with Boudinot.[5]

Boudinot's Treaty Party friends the Ridges likewise sought to carve out a nonpolitical new life for themselves. John and Sarah Ridge, along with Major and Susanna, had settled on small plantations in Honey Creek, in the northeastern corner of this new Cherokee Nation, not far from the border with Missouri and Arkansas. They had arrived in time to see the bottomlands aglow with redbuds blooming from pink to purple and dogwoods flowering in white and pink. Fashioning logs drawn from forty acres of timbered land that Ridge's slaves had cleared, John built a spacious log house. An additional 150 acres of prairie land John fenced and planted in timothy, clover, and corn. Most of his attention, though, focused on the general store he opened with his father. John and Sarah, along with their children, John Rollin, Herman, Aeneas, Susan, Andrew Jackson, and Flora, lived in their new log house. They brought their devoted teacher, Sophia Sawyer, from New Echota, to help care for and tutor the children. A daughter, Clarinda (referred to as "feebleminded"), however, remained in the care of her grandparents, Major and Susanna, their son, Walter, and their eighteen slaves.

Despite her family's relative wealth, Susanna saw hardship as well as hope in the new land: "We had to undergo many privations in [the] new Country. But we bore [them] all under the belief that we had found a comfortable home for our children and grandchildren. We expended much money and labor on building houses and clearing land."[6]

The new western Cherokee world that Boudinot and the Ridges now inhabited, while less contentious than the crisis-filled one back East, still simmered with discord and suspicion over removal. When John and Sarah made their trip east in 1838 to buy supplies for their new store and visit friends, false rumors circulated in Cherokee country that Ridge was secretly planning to sell off some western lands to the U.S. government. Once Ridge's true purpose for his eastern trip was made clear, the matter was quickly dropped. But suspicion about his political motives lingered. And Ridge knew that in the eyes of Ross supporters he remained a marked man. Indeed, while on a subsequent trip to New York and Washington in the spring of 1839, Ridge said as much while commiserating with former federal negotiator Reverend John Schermerhorn over their unhappy struggles on behalf of the Cherokees. "My brother," Ridge reportedly told his friend, "we have been laboring long together in a good cause—the salvation and happiness of the Cherokees. You for what you have done, have been abused, misrepresented and slandered by your countrymen." And then Ridge, as other leading Treaty Party members had occasionally done since signing the New Echota treaty, gave prophetic voice to the dark personal fate he knew might await him: "I might yet someday die by the hand of some poor infatuated Indian, deluded by the counsels of Ross and his minions." And if that happened, he insisted, he would find comfort in knowing he had "suffered and died in a good cause": "My people are now free and happy in their new homes, and I am resigned to my fate, whatever it might be."[7]

John Ross's detachment, the smallest and last to depart from the homeland, arrived in Indian Territory in the spring of 1839. Only 231 individuals began the journey, which mostly followed a water route using the Ross-owned steamboat *Victoria* but ended on a forty-mile trek overland. Like most who had preceded them on the trail, Ross and the 211 other passengers in his detachment arrived dispirited and exhausted. And like so many others, they faced inadequate rations on which to survive. The U.S. government was to provide basic food supplies for a year, which amounted to a daily provision of three-fourths pound of salt pork or fresh beef, a pound of wheat flour or three-fourths quart of corn, and four quarts of salt for every hundred pounds of beef. But private contractors handled the rationing, and many of these contractors cheated the Cherokees out of what was owed them, sometimes giving them little more than rotting meat and moldy corn and flour. Many Cherokees asked for salt pork instead of the unhealthy fresh beef that could not be preserved in the warm season. George Hicks complained to Ross about the food given to people in his detachment: "[We have] some shelled corn & some very poor beef for our Subsistence which is unfit for use—& from the promises made to us in the Nation East we did not Expect such Treatment." Many of the contractors refused to supply the emigrants with the salt pork, claiming "they were only bound to furnish Beef rations." What provisions that did exist were often made available at places too remote for Cherokees to pick up. Ross's detachment, for example, received fifteen days of beef rations and forty-five days of corn upon arrival, with the assurance that a depot would be set up near their Illinois camp meeting ground. Within two weeks, though, the emigrants were out of food with no arrangement to supply them. Ross wrote the commanding officer of Fort Gibson, General Matthew Arbuckle, "Many complaints . . . are daily made to me by Cherokees who have been recently removed into this country, of their sufferings, from the want of being properly subsisted with provisions." The price for food skyrocketed in Indian Territory, forcing some Cherokees to sell their ration tickets for a penny per pound simply to raise cash so they could purchase higher-quality food. Liquor, though, remained cheap and readily available, despite Cherokee and federal laws preventing its sale. Given the exorbitant prices for meat and other foodstuff, Ross concluded that the Cherokees "will soon be found in a starving condition—instead of being provided with subsistence as was anticipated and promised them." As a result of the fraud and insufficient rationing, the sick and malnourished trail survivors only grew weaker upon arrival.[8]

Even as these provisioning problems mounted in Indian Territory, tension over who would govern the new Cherokee Nation loomed ever larger. When Ross's detachment arrived that spring, they confronted challenges by two political groups that preceded them out West: the Old Settlers who had emigrated over the years before the Treaty of New Echota and the members of the Treaty Party who had moved just prior to forced removal. With an estimated five thousand Old Settlers, about two thousand Treaty Party individuals, and close to fourteen thousand who arrived under Ross's supervision, the new Cherokee Nation had all the makings of a deeply conflicted, dysfunctional political body. While all parties may have sought unity, what they achieved, at least in the first few years, led mostly to dissension and often violence.[9]

Having lived in the West for years, the Old Settlers had fashioned their own simpler means of governance. They had crafted
no constitution and had created only a few laws. Despite some
initial concerns over the reputation of Boudinot and Ridge,
they embraced the Treaty Party settlers. John Brown, the principal chief of the Old Settlers, also welcomed Ross and his "late
immigrants" in the spring of 1839. But Ross and company came
with their own elaborate laws, a written constitution, and a
fierce determination they had made before removal to transfer
their leadership and government intact to the West. And considering that these "late immigrants" outnumbered those already
living in the West two to one, Ross and his supporters felt little
obligation to negotiate.

Soon after arriving in Indian Territory, Ross met with the Old
Settler chiefs, who were concerned about his determination to
transfer his eastern government in the new nation. Such a course,
they cautioned Ross, "would occasion great commotion." According to the missionary Cephas Washburn, Ross denied any such
takeover ambitions, proclaiming that "he & his people were
ready to come under the government and laws already existing here." Others, though, worried about Ross's motives and
expressed alarm at the looming battle. Sophia Sawyer, tutor at
the John Ridge home, noted in May 1839: "The critical situation of the Nation I cannot communicate. It is such a time of
excitement. . . . The atmosphere of the old nation in its most
disturbed state, compared to this was like the peaceful lake to
the boisterous ocean."[10]

In hopes of staving off an internal civil war, Ross proposed
holding a council to unite old and new settlers, which Brown
accepted. On June 3 some six thousand Cherokees, mostly Ross
supporters and Old Settlers, with a sprinkling of Treaty Party

members, arrived at the campgrounds at Takotoka, near the present site of Tahlequah, Oklahoma. Searching for some common ground between the various factions, Brown and others on both sides gave speeches "congratulating each other that they were now reunited as one nation, after having been separated for so long." Invoking a religious theme, Ross's speech pointed to the "mysterious dispensations of Providence" that had called the Cherokee people together again. As Ross told the gathering, "We are all of the household of the Cherokee family and of one blood. Let us kindle our social fire and take measures for cementing our reunion as a nation." Despite the superior numbers of the "late immigrants," Ross insisted he had "no intention nor desire" to dictate terms for the new government. What mattered most, Ross told Brown and the other chiefs, was that the eastern and western Cherokees "become *reunited, and again live as one people.*" And he closed with a prophetic reminder: "Let us never forget this self-evident truth—that a house divided against itself, cannot stand."[11]

While Brown officially welcomed Ross and these sentiments of unity, Ross insisted that the majority of immigrants he represented had not been offered a more explicit, formal reception that clarified "the privileges" to which his people were entitled. So Brown rose again to warmly embrace his eastern brethren: "We joyfully welcome you to our country. The whole land is before you. You may freely go wherever you choose & select any places for settlement which may please you." Brown went on to stress that the new immigrants had full voting and officeholding rights, pointing out that they would be eligible to run for offices ranging from chiefs to legislators, judges, and sheriffs. But, he noted, until the current government and laws were constitutionally repealed, the new settlers would remain subject to the existing laws. As to Ross's ongoing concern to unite the people, Brown claimed that "the two people have already been united. Our chiefs have met their brother emigrants, and made them welcome in the country." Regarding Ross's relentless desire to replace the Old Settlers' government and laws with the far more elaborate system designed back East, Brown was just as adamant: he could not allow Ross's request to take his "original laws, created beyond the Mississippi, to be brought here, brought to life, and to have full force in this nation." Such a move would be "entirely repugnant" to the present government and to the people.[12]

But Ross would not be denied. He understood the significance of the power issue that stood before them: how would this new Cherokee Nation be governed and under what set of laws and chiefs? He announced how critical it was for his party to remain organized as a political body so as to secure itself in all its financial claims regarding the federal government.

And there was the rub. Ross and his supporters feared that the Old Settlers, if they remained in control, might officially accept the Treaty of New Echota and they, rather than Ross and company, would thus gain control of all the funds due to be disbursed to emigrants under the treaty covering the cost of removal, claims for property destroyed or left behind in the East, and per capita payments. In addition to pointing to their numerical majority, then, Ross's party understood full well that money was power, and they were not about to turn it over to what they perceived to be a less sophisticated minority.[13]

Beyond these concerns, the mere presence of the Treaty Party as welcomed allies of the Old Settler group deeply troubled Ross. Having already lost the battle over removal to the likes of the Ridges and Boudinot, the last thing he wanted to confront was the prospect of their enchanced political influence out West. For their part, even though defenders of Boudinot and the Ridges lacked sufficient numbers to take control of the new government, they certainly realized that if Ross gained control they would be completely ostracized and all the treaty privileges they had labored to create would be abolished. So when Ross spotted Major Ridge, John Ridge, Elias Boudinot, and Boudinot's brother Stand Watie showing up one day at the Takatoka Council meeting talking with Old Settler chiefs, Ross's worry turned into alarm—despite the fact that all four of these Treaty Party leaders left the scene the same day in hopes they would not create unnecessary controversy.

But they failed, tragically. Stealing away from the Takatoka Council Grounds after being recognized by Ross, the Ridges, Boudinot, and Watie returned home, but no doubt with restless and worried hearts. They must have known that many of Ross's overwhelming supporters continued to view them as dangerous and despised traitors. And without the armed bodyguards that Ross could marshal for his own protection, the Treaty Party members, simply by being seen in such a politically charged setting, were taking huge risks with their lives. One can only imagine that, in the hours and days after Takatoka, their spirits became engulfed in a growing fear for their safety.

Fueling their increasing worries, ironically, was an element of support: the U.S. government continued to see the Treaty Party as the true patriots among the Cherokees. In contrast, the federal government viewed Ross as a deceptive leader of misguided "savages."[14] Given these underlying stresses, Ross simply would not accept the vague overtures of the Old Settlers. He called for a convention to create a new constitution that would effectively govern the new Cherokee Nation. Brown saw the demand for what it was: a power play. Exasperated, he adjourned the council on June 19. Everyone left the council grounds at that point, but Ross asked his people to stay. Amid more frustration about the impasse in crafting a new government, two prominent figures stepped forward. Sequoyah, the distinguished Cherokee who had been living in the West since 1824, and Jesse Bushyhead, a religious leader among the eastern Cherokees, stood before the assembled crowd on June 20 and spoke about the need for unity. They suggested reassembling as a general or people's council on July 1. The response, rendered in a viva voce vote, was positive. The next day, Ross sent his people home. Most left the council grounds in a state of confusion and unease. That same day Ross gave voice to those frustrations in a note to Montfort Stokes, a federal agent to the Cherokees. Ross complained about the inadequate reception "our western brethren" gave to "the wishes of the whole people." This conduct from the Old Settlers, he noted, served only "to disturb the peace of the community, and to operate injuriously to the best interests of the nation."[15]

While Ross felt thwarted in his attempt to produce unity under his party's controlling leadership, some of his more zealous supporters had become downright angry. Outraged at their inability to take over the government, and convinced that particular leaders in the Treaty Party stood in their path to power, Ross's followers decided to take matters into their own hands. On the night of June 21, more than a hundred Ross supporters who had never left the council grounds met privately to plot their revenge. Among those present were kinsmen of John Ross, including his son Allen Ross. Others were full-bloods and members of the same clans as those who signed the infamous Treaty of

New Echota. This was important because according to traditional clan law only those within the same clan could determine whether blood vengeance was appropriate.[16]

Even though no one heard the Ridges or Boudinot collaborating with the Old Settler chiefs, they were seen "holding private conversations" with them the one day they were in attendance. This was simply too much for the Ross supporters. As one man reported from the secret meeting of the angry Ross contingent, the impulse to action "was the sudden breaking forth of long-smouldering resentment—an ebullition of rage and disappointment occasioned by [the Ridges'] supposed intrigue" in blocking a Ross-led government. Leaders in the secret meeting read the law prohibiting the sale of Cherokee land without tribal approval. The penalty for such a crime was death. Ironically, Major and John Ridge both signed the law in 1829—a law that also required first an indictment of the accused, then a trial with a defense present. In the white hot anger of this moment, however, such formalities were ignored. The plotters then drew up a list of twelve names of leaders from the Treaty Party, men who had illegally ceded tribal land and thus warranted execution. The names scribbled on that list? Major and John Ridge, Elias Boudinot, and his brother Stand Watie. Others likely listed as well were James Starr, John A. Bell, and George W. Adair—all signers of the removal treaty.[17]

Three men representing the clan of each defendant served as judges in this mock trial at the private meeting—with the accused neither aware of, nor present at, the proceedings. Major Ridge, a member of the Deer Clan, was quickly found guilty, like all the other accused. Then a committee arranged for numbered lots for each person present at the meeting to be drawn from a hat—twelve of them containing an *X* mark beside the number to indicate specific executioners. Everyone was asked to draw a lot, but before Allen Ross could do so, he was stopped and informed that "the Committee had another job" for him on that day. He was to stay with his father in order "to keep him from finding out what was being done."[18]

Late in the night of June 22, three assassination parties (composed of the twelve designated executioners and others) galloped off toward their separate targets. Some twenty-five men, loaded with rifles, arrived on horseback around 4:00 AM at the home of John Ridge at Honey Creek. After surrounding the house, three men dismounted, walked up to the front door, and burst inside. Everyone—John, Sarah, their children, along with Sarah's sister and brother-in-law—lay sleeping. One assassin pulled John from his bed and fired a pistol at his head. The pistol jammed, so all three intruders hauled him from his bed and, despite his vigorous struggle, managed to drag him kicking and fighting into the yard. Sarah and the kids tried to rush outside to protect John, but the avengers forced them back into the house at gunpoint. As they looked on in horror, their screams and cries along with John's were drowned out by the shouts of the assassins, who had been "instructed" to make their own noise so they would not have to listen to Ridge's protests, which might weaken their resolve to kill him. With some men grabbing his arms and others holding up his body, the killers stabbed Ridge again and again. Finally, they tossed his body up into the air and let it fall to the ground. Then one by one, all twenty-five men proceeded to stomp Ridge's blood-soaked body. Amazingly, Ridge clung to life and attempted to pull himself up and tried to speak but could make only a blood-gurgling sound. As the avengers galloped away, Sarah and the children rushed to John's side. Sarah sent a messenger to rush to her father-in-law's house to warn him that his life was in danger. John Ridge's lifeless body was brought inside and laid on the bed. His son John Rollin remembered the heartbreaking moment.

> Then succeeded a scene of agony . . . which might make one regret that the human race had ever been created. It has darkened my mind with an eternal shadow. In a room prepared for the purpose lay pale in death the man whose voice had been listened to with awe and admiration in the councils of his Nation, and whose fame had passed to the remotest of the United States, the blood oozing through his winding sheet and falling drop by drop on the floor. By his side sat my mother, with hands clasped and in speechless agony—she who had given him her heart in the days of her youth and beauty, left the home of her parents and followed the husband of her choice to a wild and distant land.[19]

The assassination party rode south to Beattie's Prairie, home of a fervent Ross supporter, Joseph Lynch. There they celebrated their morning of murder by killing a steer and eating it. Among those present were Daniel Colston, John Vann, Hunter, and three Spear brothers, Archibald, James, and Joseph. Joseph Spear bragged that he had been the one who thrust a knife into Ridge's heart.[20]

While John Ridge's avengers feasted after their killing, a second group of armed men rode up to the Park Hill Mission neighborhood of Elias Boudinot. Boudinot's children were away visiting their grandparents in New England. Elias and Delight were living with Samuel and Ann Worcester, about a quarter mile away from their own new house on which carpenters were working to complete. About 9:00 AM, with about thirty men on horseback waiting in the dense woods near the Worcester house, Boudinot left Delight and the Worcesters and headed up toward the new house to talk to the carpenters. From out of the woods walked four men who began calling out to Boudinot. He turned to talk with them. They asked for help; some sick family members needed medicine, they claimed. It was well known that Boudinot and Worcester were in charge of dispensing public medicine to the local community. Boudinot nodded and told the men to follow him. Two of the men walked with Boudinot toward the mission station. A few moments later, one of the men suddenly stopped, pulled out a knife, and plunged it into Boudinot's back. He cried out and dropped to the ground. The other man grabbed his tomahawk and repeatedly smashed it hard into Boudinot's head, gashing and splitting it several times. Seeing the attack, the carpenters ran toward Boudinot but could not catch up to the fleeing killers. Hearing Boudinot's cries, Delight and Samuel rushed out to him. Delight tried to speak to him but to no avail. As Worcester remembered, "He lived a few minutes, till we had time to arrive at the spot, and see him breathe his last—his wife among the rest—but he was speechless, and insensible to surrounding objects. The assassins ran a short distance into the woods, joined a company of armed men on horseback and made their escape. . . . They have cut off my right hand," Worcester said of his loss.[21]

Worcester told a Choctaw Indian who was clearing land nearby to run to the paddock and take Worcester's horse, Comet, to the store about a mile away to warn Stand Watie that his life was in danger. The Choctaw messenger, when he arrived at the store and realized that there were several anti-removal

Stand Watie
Courtesy of the Western History Collections, University of Oklahoma Library

folks inside, whispered the news about Boudinot to Watie over a barrel of sugar. Watie slipped out through the back door, jumped on Comet, and rode straight to Park Hill. He arrived at the Worcester front porch, where he found his brother's corpse and a "milling throng," including some Ross supporters. At which point, according to an eyewitness, Watie reportedly pulled back "the corner of a blood soaked cloth, and uncovered the face" of his mutilated brother. Shocked, he abruptly turned to the crowd and exclaimed, "I'll give $10,000 to anybody who will tell me who made that mark on my brother's face." No one said a word. Seething with rage, Watie replaced the bloody cloth, spun his horse around, and raced away.[22]

That same morning Major Ridge was on his way to visit

some of his sick slaves he had left at the home of Ambrose Harnage in Cincinnati, Arkansas. A third group of avengers, alerted to his location, camped out in the underbrush and behind trees just where the road crossed Little Rock Creek, a mile beyond Cherokee territory and just inside the Arkansas border. Around 10:00 AM, when Major Ridge on horseback, with a slave riding alongside, was crossing the creek, at least ten volleys rang out. The assassins fired five bullets into Ridge's head and body, and he collapsed onto his saddle. The gunfire frightened the horse, which reared up, throwing Ridge to the ground. Seeing that he had been instantly killed, the young black assistant galloped off to spread the news. The messenger Sarah Ridge had sent to warn Major returned to Honey Creek with the somber news of his death.[23]

Upon hearing about the murders, John Ross sent his brother-in-law John G. Ross and some friends over to the Boudinot house to assess the situation. They found Delight Boudinot, who offered a stern warning to Ross: Stand Watie was assembling a posse to exact revenge for the murder of her husband. Ross immediately contacted General Matthew Arbuckle about the incident and asked for protection. Arbuckle strongly advised Ross to ride to Fort Gibson for safety, but Ross's closest friends warned him that traveling from home would be too dangerous; that same day more than two hundred guards were stationed around the Ross house.[24]

———

In the space of a single morning the most prominent leaders of the Treaty Party were assassinated in three different locations. What produced this bloody day of political revenge? The most immediate cause may have been the outrage among zealous Ross supporters over the perceived influence of Boudinot and the Ridges among the western chiefs at the Takatota Council Grounds. Evan Jones, the Baptist missionary and harsh critic of the removal party, speculated that "had Ridge and his friends retired quietly into private life and no more interfered to disturb the peace of the nation, they would no doubt have lived. But having commenced further interruptions" by joining with the Old Settlers against Ross's reunification efforts, "they sealed their own fate." Ross's people were not about to sit idly by as Boudinot and the Ridges blocked the authority of John Ross— especially since it was these very leaders of the removal party who had been ultimately responsible, it was believed, for all the traumas of the trail. Long-simmering personal feuds over removal, then, conspired with ancestral traditions of blood vengeance to end the lives of those who had labored diligently to create a new western home for the Cherokee people.[25]

Who was responsible for the murders? Among the assassins— in addition to those who murdered John Ridge—was James Foreman, whose violent opposition to the removal party had been revealed five years earlier when he murdered the Treaty Party sympathizer John Walker Jr. Others included the Ross supporters Anderson Springston, Bird Doublehead, and Jefferson and James Hair.

Was John Ross involved in the assassination? Despite his own son's role as one of the plotters at the secret meeting and Ross's well-known, deep-seated enmity toward the Treaty Party leaders, the evidence suggests that John Ross did not have advance knowledge of the assassination plan. The federal agent Montfort Stokes, no friend of Ross, apparently viewed him as an innocent as well in the matter: "He is a man of too much good sense to embroil his nation at this critical time; and, besides, his character, since I have known him, which is now twenty-five years, has been pacific." Ross's own statements after the assassination refer to it as an "unhappy occurrence" and focus on how his own life, thanks to Watie's revenge plans, was now endangered. "Why I am thus to be murdered without guilt of any crime—I cannot conceive." Ross told Arbuckle the day after the murders, "I will again repeat that I exceedingly regret the disaster that has happened & if the report of the death of [John] Ridge be true, I assure you that no one will regret the circumstance more than myself." Upon hearing the fate of Major Ridge, Ross reportedly claimed he would have tried to save Ridge had he known of the plot. Regarding the identities of the avengers, Ross insisted, "They are not known to me, nor have they been reported to me, and from the threats which have been made against me personally, I do not know but that I am looked upon as one myself."[26]

We may never know precisely what Ross knew before the morning of June 22, but after the incident he did make sure his own bodyguards protected those who did the killings. And when federal agents confronted Ross about identifying the assassins, Ross responded with a jurisdictional argument: "By what right or sound policy [are] the Cherokee people to be deprived of the exercise of their own legitimate authority over the acts of one Indian against another? . . . How, if the persons charged be Cherokees, they have violated either treaty stipulations or acts of Congress, that they should be held answerable to the courts of the United States, and the military force employed for their arrest?" Meanwhile, Arkansans demanded the murderers be brought to trial.

Federal agents had a list of accused men and were intent on trying them, especially those who killed Major Ridge, since he was murdered on Arkansas soil. The U.S. government sent a police force into Cherokee territory to arrest the accused, using Treaty Party sympathizers as guides. None of the accused was ever found. Ross may not have planned the assassination of his enemies, but he clearly did little to prosecute the murderers, in part, one suspects, because he may have feared the rage of some of his zealous supporters who viewed the killings as warranted, if not heroic.[27]

Settlers near the ambush scene that claimed Major Ridge's life retrieved his body and buried him just inside Cherokee territory in a small cemetery at Piney. A few days after the murders, Reverend Cephas Washburn preached a funeral service for John Ridge at a spot near Ridge's house on Honey Creek. On that same day, Samuel Worcester stood over the coffin of Elias Boudinot in Park Hill offering thanks for "the loveliness, integrity and Christian worth" of his murdered good friend. Boudinot had been executed, Worcester acknowledged, because of his role in promoting removal. "I would that my beloved friend Mr. Boudinot had had no part in that transaction," Worcester observed, "yet I have no doubt of the sincerity of his own conviction that he was doing right, and hazarding his life for the good of his people. He was a great and good man . . . who exhibited the spirit of the Gospel." A simple, hastily cut, unmarked piece of stone was set above Boudinot's grave.[28]

The families of those who were murdered reacted in ways ranging from desertion to defiance. Sarah Ridge abandoned the plantation she and John had built and moved with her children across the border into Arkansas. As an act of further repudiation of her post-removal life, she brought all the store merchandise with them and sold it at auction in Arkansas. Susanna Ridge, Major Ridge's widow, though, demanded that her husband's share of the mercantile goods be returned to the store in Honey Creek, where she insisted the store continue to operate just as Major would have wanted. For Elias Boudinot's brother, Stand Watie, the assassination plunged him into years of plotting revenge. And three years later, he got it: On May 14, 1842, Watie was picking up provisions at a Maysville, Arkansas, bar and grocery store. James Foreman, who had helped assassinate Elias Boudinot, happened to be drinking there. Foreman spotted Watie and began toasting him in mocking tones, then pulled out a horsewhip and flailed away at him. When Foreman grabbed a wooden board, Watie pulled out a knife and stabbed him. Foreman recoiled, saying, "You haven't done it yet." At which point Watie reached for his pistol and shot Foreman. According to court testimony, Foreman died twenty minutes later. In June Watie turned himself in to Arkansas authorities. In May 1843 an Arkansas jury acquitted him on the grounds of self-defense.[29]

No one ever took revenge for the murder of John Ridge. But his son John Rollin certainly dreamed about it. A twelve-year-old boy at the time of his father's murder, John Rollin afterward lived in Arkansas with his widowed mother and other relatives. But he remained in close contact with his uncle Stand Watie, who no doubt helped him nurse ambitions of retaliation. Indeed, John Rollin fantasized about one day stabbing John Ross to death. He also imagined Tom Starr as a brave champion of the Ridge party. A stalwart defender of removal, Starr was rumored to have killed twenty men whom he connected to the assassinations of June 22, 1839. Tom's father, James Starr, who was likely among those slated for assassination in 1839, also relentlessly pursued those who murdered the three Treaty Party leaders.[30]

The murders of Elias Boudinot and John and Major Ridge unleashed several years of chaotic violence and revenge killings throughout Cherokee country. With ongoing violent retaliation over the assassinations of 1839 and Ross under fire as an autocrat, newspapers in the East radically revised their assessment of the Cherokees: what had once been "the most civilized" tribe in America was now "reverting to barbarism" in the West.[31]

To stem the tide of violence, Ross called for a constitutional convention to be held on July 7, 1839. Among the convention's first decisions was to grant pardons to all those accused of murder since the arrival of the "late immigrants," and to declare as "outlaws" all Cherokees pursuing retaliation for the executions of June 22. The Treaty Party vehemently objected, noting that such a declaration turned them all into "outlaws," but Ross insisted he was simply trying to prevent Watie and his friends from perpetuating a private civil war. To monitor the conduct of those bent on revenge, the convention also set up eight companies of provincial police. (Members of the Treaty Party viewed them as vigilante squads propping up Ross's authoritarian rule.) Most critical, at least for Ross and his supporters, was the adoption of the Act of Union, which stated that the eastern and western Cherokees formally agreed "to form ourselves into one body politic under the style and title of the Cherokee Nation." Ross signed the document for the recent emigrants, and Sequoyah and John Looney for the Old Settlers. Excited, Ross wrote Arbuckle and Stokes to emphasize the crucial nature of this Act of Union whereby Cherokees "agreed to unite and live as one people again."[32]

At this point, though, Ross's Act of Union was but a hollow hope. That summer, both the Old Settlers and the Treaty Party held their own conventions to challenge what they saw as the tyrannical ambitions of Ross. Angered by Ross's "outlaw" declaration, supporters of the Treaty Party held their own convention August 20, claiming they would rather fight than cave in to the "mobocracy of John Ross." They informed Secretary of War Joel Poinsett that they feared for their lives under Ross. They requested federal funds for the scores of Treaty Party families exiled in Arkansas as well as for the widows and children of their martyred leaders. And they asked that troops at Fort Gibson round up the men who had executed their leaders and provide protection for Treaty Party signers. Poinsett agreed. He also reminded Matthew Arbuckle that under the Treaty of New Echota he "had the right to arrest Ross" for fomenting civil war against the legitimate authority of the Old Settlers. Arbuckle never tried to arrest Ross largely because of what he termed "the blind attachment" of so many Cherokees to Ross. Poinsett suspended the disbursement of all funds to the Cherokee Nation until peace and order were reestablished. Dispirited about his people's future amid all the chaos and violence, western chief John Brown left for Mexico with family and friends in November 1839.[33]

The Cherokees' trauma of the trail had now become the chaos of civil war. Murderous reprisals on both sides continued for years, with each party blaming the other. Most Cherokees, Ross and his supporters maintained, were law-abiding citizens; Treaty Party members insisted Ross fomented violence to destroy Stand Watie and all his friends. While the Treaty Party could argue, as they did, that it was Ross's supporters who initiated

the cycle of violence with the assassinations of 1839, angry
Treaty Party zealots often practiced their own terrorization of
the Cherokee Nation under the guise of justifiable revenge.
James Starr's sons, the infamous Tom Starr among them, roamed
Cherokee country in the 1840s murdering whites and Cherokees alike. In 1845 the Starr gang broke into the home of John
Ross's daughter, looting and setting fire to the house. In the
aftermath, Jane Ross Meigs wrote her uncle John Ross: "Excitement the most profound reigns around us. More deeds of horror
have been committed. The torch and the deadly weapon have
reeked the vengeance of the dark and hellish band of despera-
does who have so long infested the country." Murderous reprisals on both sides exacerbated the chaotic situation. Stand Watie
staunchly defended himself and his friends from Ross's police
and posse. His brother Thomas had been murdered on November
14, 1845, by a man associated with the Ross party. Fearing for
their safety, some 750 Treaty Party members and 150 Old Settler
families had fled to Arkansas for safety by 1846.[34]

With the Cherokee Nation in disarray and seemingly headed
toward permanent divided loyalties and governments, federal
authorities tried to resolve the conflict. When the House Committee on Indian Affairs introduced a bill in June 1846 to
divide the Cherokee Nation, Ross realized that his relentless
effort to maintain the unity and sovereignty of his people under
his leadership was at a breaking point. He simply could not
abide—nor could the Cherokee people—a divided nation.
Compromise had now become a necessity. In July Ross sent a
delegation to meet with President James K. Polk's commissioners to craft a treaty to work out the Cherokees' internal struggles. On August 6, 1846, a treaty was signed in which Ross

was finally forced to accept the Treaty of New Echota and the $5 million purchase price for Cherokee lands. Ross also had to formally recognize, as legitimate parts of the Cherokee Nation, the Old Settlers, the Treaty Party members, and those who had avoided removal by escaping to the Smoky Mountains and now lived in North Carolina. And as full citizens of the Cherokee Nation, all of these people were to receive their fair share of the federal funds owed the Cherokee people from the sale of ancestral lands. Moreover, Treaty Party families were paid $100,000 for losses suffered in the previous five years while they were forced to live in exile in Arkansas. All who fled to Arkansas could now return to Cherokee country with the expectation of full rights of citizenship and legal protection. Finally, a $5,000 indemnity was paid to each of the families of Major and John Ridge and Elias Boudinot.

Ross did win one very important concession: the Old Settlers could no longer claim to be sole owners of the 7 million acres in the new Cherokee Nation. In effect, the treaty gave control over to the Ross government under the 1839 Act of Union and a new constitution. After ratification by the U.S. Senate on August 7, 1846, Ross and Stand Watie signed it and shook hands in a gesture of unity.[35]

The gesture was not simply symbolic; with the per capita payments now flowing into Cherokees' hands and the reestablishment of law and order, the Cherokees were poised for economic recovery and political stability. Finally—after years of intense political quarrels over removal, a profoundly traumatic and deadly experience on the trail, blood revenge against those who had led the fight for removal, and years of murderous reprisals in the West—finally, in 1846 the removal crisis had ended.

But what, exactly, had been settled? What are the legacies of removal? It was, of course, the tenacity of the Treaty Party—despite the tireless opposition of Ross—that shaped the destiny of the Cherokee Nation in the struggle over removal. Boudinot and the Ridges had no way of knowing that removal would lead to a trail of tears that would cost four thousand lives and enormous suffering. What they did know was that Georgian settlers were invading their country, evicting people from their homes, stealing property, and violently attacking anyone who resisted. Removal offered an alternative to these depredations. But it also produced the misery and death of the Trail of Tears which would linger for generations. Elias Boudinot, John Ridge, and Major Ridge paid the ultimate price for their choice to remove. And that choice was a fervently held vision that in the end nurturing the moral as well as physical condition of their people mattered more than preserving their people's country. Ross lost the battle over removal, but his unflinching commitment to keeping his people together as a unified and sovereign nation remains a powerful legacy of this defining moment in the Cherokee and American past.

For the nation at large, the Trail of Tears offered a devastating commentary not only on white greed and power but also on the increasingly racialized world of Jacksonian America. By the 1830s, only white Americans, especially in the South, could lay claim to citizenship and racial entitlement. Property-owning, well-educated men and women of good character no longer constituted sufficient proof of worthiness for participation in the public realm. One had to be white. In dealing with both African Americans and Native Americans, Andrew Jackson and his southern supporters practiced a form of racial exclusion that hinged on the belief in the permanent inferiority of all non-whites, black and Indian. Most northern whites either looked the other way or agreed with their southern brethren. Elias Boudinot and John Ridge discovered this painful reality behind "civilization" during their wrenching experience at Cornwall. And as the Trail of Tears tragically demonstrates, race remained the key social divide in public life, making much of America a white man's country.[36]

What does the Trail of Tears mean today—both to those who have remained in the ancestral homeland and to those who live in Oklahoma? The Eastern Band of the Cherokees primarily descends from the men and women in western North Carolina who, along with Tsali and his rebellious fellow Cherokees, resisted removal during the roundup in 1838. To the roughly eight thousand Cherokees living in Cherokee, North Carolina, just south of the Smoky Mountains, the Trail of Tears repre-sented a rending of the essential fabric of the Cherokee people. For those who witnessed an entire people violently ripped from their homeland, it signified nothing less than an act of ethnic cleansing. Many Eastern Band Cherokees during the removal crisis and shortly afterward believed that there was only one Cherokee Nation, composed solely of those who remained behind in their eastern home. Therefore, those who moved west in 1838– 39 were sometimes viewed as expatriates and possibly traitors, Cherokees who fell victim to the U.S. government's divide-and-conquer strategy instead of remaining to protect the homeland. Today, such harsh judgments have been replaced by a positive spirit of common origins as fellow Cherokees. And for these contemporary Cherokees, the primacy of place endures, at least in a spiritual sense. As one western Cherokee member put it, "The eastern and western Cherokees are separated only by a short distance and a little time. When you are of a place, you are never separated from it."[37]

Today, the Cherokee Nation, with nearly three hundred thousand members worldwide and seventy thousand within its borders in northeastern Oklahoma, is the second-largest Indian tribe in the United States. For these Cherokees, as well as for those of the Eastern Band, the Trail of Tears remains, among other things, a compelling object lesson in the abuse of power and overwhelming tyranny of greed. For one direct descendant of Chief John Ross, Gayle Ross, the trail still reverberates today with anger: "It is a story of a people who did everything in their power to assert their rights. And still, it came to nothing, in the face of greed. And that's an important lesson." Perhaps the most enduring legacy of the trail is one of survival and hope. As Principal Chief Michell Hicks of the Eastern Band recently observed, "Many things have been taken from us, our homes and our farms, but those people who made that trip, they knew there would be another day. And they knew that we would come back." And as the Eastern Band Cherokee storyteller Freeman Owle noted, "This was a time that people survived insurmountable odds and still remain on this earth today. And this gives a great deal of pride to people who know that their families have gone through such a terrible ordeal."[38]

The adaptability and resilience of the Cherokees are revealed in their successful embrace of the "civilization" program, their unique intellectual and cultural accomplishments thanks to Sequoyah's syllabary and Elias Boudinot's work with the *Cherokee Phoenix*, their democratic constitution of 1827, modeled on the U.S. Constitution, and, most notably, their ability to endure the tragic, wrenching experience of the Trail of Tears, in which they lost one fourth of their people—all of which have become, in the generations since removal, powerful sources of strength and confidence. As Gayle Ross aptly puts it: "We have survived a lot, as a people. But we are still here. We are still Cherokee. We have kept the flame burning."[39]

NOTES

PROLOGUE

1. See, for example, Grant Foreman, *Indian Removal: The Emigration of the Five Civilized Tribes of Indians* (Norman: University of Oklahoma Press, 1932); Gary E. Moulton, *John Ross: Cherokee Chief* (Athens: University of Georgia Press, 1978); Theda Perdue, ed., *Cherokee Editor: The Writings of Elias Boudinot* (Knoxville: University of Tennessee Press, 1983); Theda Perdue and Michael D. Green, *The Cherokee Nation and the Trail of Tears* (New York: Viking, 2007). William G. McLoughlin praised John Ross not only as the Cherokees' unwavering leader but also as "their prophet and eventually their Moses." See his *Cherokees and Missionaries, 1789–1839* (New Haven, Conn.: Yale University Press, 1984), 304. Two other accounts, written by nonhistorians, offer a somewhat more sympathetic treatment of Boudinot and the Ridges: John Ehle, *Trail of Tears: The Rise and Fall of the Cherokee Nation* (New York: Doubleday, 1988), and Thurman Wilkins, *Cherokee Tragedy: The Ridge Family and the Decimation of a People*, rev. ed. (Norman: University of Oklahoma Press, 1986).

2. See Perdue, *Cherokee Editor*, 172; Ralph Henry Gabriel, *Elias*

Boudinot, Cherokee & His America (Norman: University of Oklahoma Press, 1941), 196. See also Susan M. Ryan, *The Grammar of Good Intentions: Race and the Antebellum Culture of Benevolence* (Ithaca, N.Y.: Cornell University Press, 2003), 22; Mary Young, "The Cherokee Nation: Mirror of the Republic," *American Quarterly* 33 (1981), 522.

3. Perdue, *Cherokee Editor*, 157, 215.

4. Theda Perdue adopts an extremely harsh assessment of Boudinot, claiming he "was a tragic figure not just because he made a serious error in judgment or because he paid the ultimate price but because he could not accept his people, his heritage, or himself." Ibid., 33.

1: BECOMING "CIVILIZED"

1. Henry Knox to George Washington, June 15, 1789, and January 4, 1790, in *American State Papers: Indian Affairs* (Washington, D.C.: U.S. Congress, Government Printing Office, 1834), 1: 13, 61.

2. Theda Perdue and Michael D. Green, eds., *The Cherokee Removal: A Brief History with Documents* (Boston: Bedford Books / St. Martin's Press, 1995), 10.

3. David Andrew Nichols, *Red Gentlemen & White Savages: Indians, Federalists, and the Search for Order on the American Frontier* (Charlottesville: University of Virginia Press, 2008), 177–201.

4. Perdue and Green, *Cherokee Removal*, 10–11. See also Francis Paul Prucha, *American Indian Policy in the Formative Years: The Indian Trade and Intercourse Acts, 1790–1834* (Cambridge, Mass.: Harvard University Press, 1962) and Reginald Horsman, *Expansion and American Indian Policy, 1783–1812* (Lansing: Michigan State University Press, 1967).

5. Nichols, *Red Gentlemen & White Savages*, 211.

6. Thomas Jefferson, *Notes on the State of Virginia*, ed. William Peden (Chapel Hill: University of North Carolina Press, 1955), 62–69, 215–18.

7. Thomas Jefferson to Chastellux, June 7, 1785, in Julian Boyd, ed., *Papers of Thomas Jefferson* (Princeton: Princeton University Press, 1950–), 8 (1953): 186.

8. Thomas Jefferson to James Jay, April 7, 1809, in Andrew A. Lip-

scomb and Albert E. Bergh, eds., *The Writings of Thomas Jefferson* (Washington, D.C.: Thomas Jefferson Memorial Association, 1903–4), 12 (1904): 270–71; Francis Paul Prucha, William T. Hagan, and Alvin J. Josephy Jr., *American Indian Policy* (Indianapolis: Indiana Historical Society, 1971), 5–6.

9. Quoted in Anthony F. C. Wallace, *Jefferson and the Indians: The Tragic Fate of the First Americans* (Cambridge, Mass.: Harvard University Press, 1999), 223.

10. Thomas Jefferson to Andrew Jackson, February 16, 1803, in Lipscomb and Bergh, *Writings*, 9 (1905): 357–59; Wallace, *Jefferson and the Indians*, 221, 223.

11. Wallace, *Jefferson and the Indians*, 239, 276, 278.

12. Quoted in Michael Paul Rogin, *Fathers and Children: Andrew Jackson and the Subjugation of the American Indian* (New York: Knopf, 1975), 244.

13. Lewis Cass, "Policy and Practice of the United States and Great Britain in Their Treatment of Indians," *North American Review* 24 (April 1827), 391.

14. William G. McLoughlin, *Cherokees and Missionaries, 1789–1839* (New Haven, Conn.: Yale University Press, 1984), 102–4; William G. McLoughlin, "Who Civilized the Cherokees?" *Journal of Cherokee Studies*, 13 (1988), 65. On Springplace and the Moravians, see Rowena McClinton, ed., *The Moravian Springplace Mission to the Cherokees, 1805–1821*, 2 vols. (Lincoln: University of Nebraska Press, 2007).

15. McLoughlin, "Who Civilized the Cherokees?" 66; Mary Young, "The Cherokee Nation: Mirror of the Republic," *American Quarterly* 33 (Winter 1981), 513; McLoughlin, *Cherokees and Missionaries*, 176.

16. Theda Perdue, "Letters from Brainerd," *Journal of Cherokee Studies* 4 (Winter 1979), 4.

17. Joyce B. Phillips and Paul Gary Phillips, eds., *The Brainerd Journal: A Mission to the Cherokees, 1817–1823* (Lincoln: University of Nebraska Press, 1998), 73–74.

18. Perdue, "Letters from Brainerd," 5.

19. McLoughlin, "Who Civilized the Cherokees?" 66.

20. Phillips and Phillips, *The Brainerd Journal*, 13; Wallace, *Jefferson and the Indians*, 299.

21. Phillips and Phillips, *The Brainerd Journal*, 138.

22. McLoughlin, *Cherokees and Missionaries*, 136.

23. Ibid.

24. Phillips and Phillips, *The Brainerd Journal*, 104, 18.

25. Elizabeth Taylor to Miss Abigail Parker, June 26, 1828, in Perdue and Green, *Cherokee Removal*, 45–46.

26. Phillips and Phillips, *The Brainerd Journal*, 93.

27. Ibid., 135.

28. Ibid., 153.

29. McLoughlin, *Cherokees and Missionaries*, 202.

30. Ibid., 203.

31. Nichols, *Red Gentlemen & White Savages*, 178.

32. Wallace, *Jefferson and the Indians*, 287–88.

33. Phillips and Phillips, *The Brainerd Journal*, 16, 361.

34. Sally M. Reece to Reverend Daniel Campbell, July 25, 1828, in Perdue and Green, *Cherokee Removal*, 46. Lucy McPherson also notes that "a great many of the Cherokees are poor and ignorant and live so poorly that they have scarcely any houses or clothes." Lucy McPherson to Reverend Moses Thatcher, April 23, n.y., in John Howard Payne Papers, Newberry Library, Chicago, Illinois.

35. Phillips and Phillips, *The Brainerd Journal*, 74, 53, 116–17.

36. Quoted in McLoughlin, *Cherokees and Missionaries*, 119.

37. Quoted in Wallace, *Jefferson and the Indians*, 288.

38. McLoughlin, *Cherokees and Missionaries*, 125.

39. Thurman Wilkins, *Cherokee Tragedy: The Story of the Ridge Family and the Decimation of a People*, rev. ed. (Norman: University of Oklahoma Press, 1986), 205–6.

40. McLoughlin, *Cherokees and Missionaries*, 177.

41. Young, "Mirror of the Republic," 517; Wilkins, *Cherokee Tragedy*, 186–89.

42. McLoughlin, *Cherokees and Missionaries*, 183; Wilkins, *Cherokee Tragedy*, 138.

43. Ayer Collection, ms 689, John Howard Payne Papers, Newberry Library, 75–77; see also John Ehle, *Trail of Tears: The Rise and Fall of the Cherokee Nation* (New York: Doubleday, 1988), 152–53, 159.

44. McLoughlin, *Cherokees and Missionaries*, 186, 160–61.

45. Theda Perdue, ed., *Cherokee Editor: The Writings of Elias Boudinot* (Athens: University of Georgia Press, 1996), 5–6.

46. Phillips and Phillips, *The Brainerd Journal*, 36.

47. Ibid., 37.

48. Ehle, *Trail of Tears*, 145–48.

2: OUTRAGE IN CORNWALL

1. Quoted in John Ehle, *Trail of Tears: The Rise and Fall of the Cherokee Nation* (New York: Doubleday, 1988), 146–49.

2. Thurman Wilkins, *Cherokee Tragedy: The Story of the Ridge Family and of the Decimation of a People*, rev. ed. (Norman: University of Oklahoma Press, 1986), 121–22.

3. Ibid., 125–26.

4. Theda Perdue, ed., *Cherokee Editor: The Writings of Elias Boudinot* (Athens: University of Georgia Press, 1966), 6; Theresa Strouth Gaul, ed., *To Marry an Indian: The Marriage of Harriett Gold & Elias Boudinot in Letters, 1823–1839* (Chapel Hill: University of North Carolina Press, 2005), 6; Wilkins, *Cherokee Tragedy*, 122.

5. Elias Boudinot to the Baron de Compagne, January 8, 1821, printed in the *Missionary Herald*, August 1821, in Perdue, *Cherokee Editor*, 44.

6. John Ridge to President James Monroe, March 8, 1822, Ayer Collection, ms 761, Newberry Library, Chicago, Illinois.

7. Quoted in Gaul, *To Marry an Indian*, 7.

8. Ralph Henry Gabriel, *Elias Boudinot, Cherokee, and His America* (Norman: University of Oklahoma Press, 1941), 62–63; Gaul, *To Marry an Indian*, 9.

9. Their correspondence during this period, unfortunately, has not been recovered. Gaul, *To Marry an Indian*, 8.

10. Wilkins, *Cherokee Tragedy*, 130–31.

11. Ibid., 132–33.

12. Ibid., 133.

13. Ibid., 135, 137.

14. Quoted in ibid., 146; "Then and Now," *Fort Smith Herald*, May 21, 1870.

15. Wilkins, *Cherokee Tragedy*, 146–47.

16. Ibid., 147; *Christian Herald,* December 20, 1823.

17. Gaul, *To Marry an Indian*, 8.

18. Gabriel, *Elias Boudinot*, 61–63; Gaul, *To Marry an Indian*, 9.

19. Gabriel, *Elias Boudinot*, 64–65; Gaul, *To Marry an Indian*, 10.

20. Gaul, *To Marry an Indian*, 13.

21. Ibid., 150.

22. Ibid., 14; "Cornwall Mission School," *Gospel Advocate and Impartial Investigator* 3, no. 48 (December 9, 1825), 383.

23. Gaul, *To Marry an Indian*, 81–83.

24. Ibid., 87, 14, 85.

25. Ibid., 18.

26. Wilkins, *Cherokee Tragedy*, 152.

27. Gaul, *To Marry an Indian*, 17.

28. William McLoughlin, *Cherokees and Missionaries, 1789–1839* (Norman: University of Oklahoma Press, 1995), 208; Gaul, *To Marry an Indian*, 19.

29. Gaul, *To Marry an Indian*, 19–20.

30. Ibid., 153.

31. Daniel Brinsmade to Herman and Flora Gold Vaill, June 28, 1824; Reverend Cornelius Everest to Stephen Gold, July 2, 1825, both in ibid., 31, 33.

32. Daniel Brinsmade to Herman and Flora Gold Vaill and Catherine Gold, July 14, 1825, in ibid., 33.

33. Reverend Cornelius Everest to Stephen Gold, July 2, 1825, in ibid., 33.

34. Daniel Brinsmade to Herman and Flora Gold Vaill and Catherine Gold, July 14, 1825, in ibid., 33.

35. Gaul, *To Marry an Indian*, 90. See also Mary Beth Norton, *In the Devil's Snare: The Salem Witchcraft Crisis of 1692* (New York: Knopf, 2002), 58–59.

36. Gaul, *To Marry an Indian*, 91, 94.

37. Herman Vaill to Mary Gold Brinsmade, August 2, 1825, in ibid., 117.

38. Herman Vaill to Benjamin Gold, September 5, 1825, in ibid., 130.

39. Herman Vaill to Mary Gold Brinsmade, August 2, 1825, in ibid., 119–20.

40. Bennett Robert to Herman Vaill, August 1, 1825, in ibid., 115.

41. Flora Gold Vaill to Herman Vaill, September 19, 1825, in ibid., 135.

42. Catherine Gold to Herman and Flora Gold Vaill, July 30, 1825, in ibid., 113.

43. Gaul, *To Marry an Indian*, 44–45.

44. Quoted in Wilkins, *Cherokee Tragedy*, 168, 170.

45. Quoted in ibid., 170.

46. Harriett Gold to Herman and Flora Gold Vaill, January 7, 1831, in ibid., 54.

47. Ibid., 54.

48. Harriett Boudinot to Herman and Flora Gold Vaill, March 29, 1832, in ibid., 55.

49. Ibid., 53.

50. Harriett Boudinot to Herman and Flora Gold Vaill, January 2, 1826, in ibid., 56.

51. Ibid., 55–56.

52. Ibid., 57.

53. Elias and Harriett Gold Boudinot to Herman and Flora Gold Vaill, January 5, 1827, in ibid., 154.

54. Ibid., 157, 159, 160.

55. Gaul, *To Marry an Indian*, 22.

56. Ibid., 22–23.

57. Henry Vaill to Harriett Gold, June 29, 1825, in ibid, 92.

58. Perdue, *Cherokee Editor*, 5–6.

59. Wilkins, *Cherokee Tragedy*, 129; John Ridge to President James Monroe, 1822, in Ayer Collection, ms 761, Newberry Library, Chicago, Illinois.

3: REMOVAL

1. William G. McLoughlin, *Cherokees and Missionaries, 1789–1839* (New Haven: Yale University Press, 1984), 125; Joyce B. Phillips and Paul Gary Phillips, eds., *The Brainerd Journal: A Mission to the Cherokees, 1817–1823* (Lincoln: University of Nebraska Press, 1998), 195; Thurman Wilkins, *Cherokee Tragedy: The Story of the Ridge Family and the Decimation of a People*, rev. ed. (Norman: University of Oklahoma Press, 1986), 194.

2. Francis Paul Prucha, *American Indian Policy in the Formative Years: The Indian Trade and Intercourse Acts, 1791–1834* (Cambridge: Harvard University Press, 1962), 158–60; Return Meigs to William Eustis, October 16 and November 16, 1809, in Clarence E. Carter, ed., *Territorial Papers of the United States* (Washington, D.C.: Government Printing Office, 1934), 5: 739–40.

3. Wilkins, *Cherokee Tragedy*, 197.

4. Ibid., 189.

5. Ibid., 200, 170, 175.

6. Michael D. Green, *Politics of Indian Removal: Creek Government and Society in Crisis* (Lincoln: University of Nebraska Press, 1982), 111, 119, 129, 136; John Ehle, *Trail of Tears: The Rise and Fall of the Cherokee Nation* (New York: Doubleday, 1988), 200–202.

7. Quoted in Ehle, *Trail of Tears*, 203.

8. Theda Perdue, ed., *Cherokee Editor: The Writings of Elias Boudinot* (Athens: University of Georgia Press, 1983), 45–47.

9. Ibid., 90, 67.

10. Ibid., 68.

11. Ibid., 69.

12. Ibid., 72, 80.

13. Ibid., 73.

14. Ibid., 75.

15. Ibid., 77, 76.

16. Ibid., 77–78.

17. Ibid., 78–79.

18. Ibid., 67.

19. Althea Bass, *Cherokee Messenger* (Norman: University of Oklahoma Press, 1936), 93.

20. Wilkins, *Cherokee Tragedy*, 196.

21. Ralph Henry Gabriel, *Elias Boudinot, Cherokee, and His America* (Norman: University of Oklahoma Press, 1941), 112; Benjamin Gold to Herman and Flora Gold Vaill, October 19, 1829, in Theresa Strouth Gaul, ed., *To Marry an Indian: The Marriage of Harriett Gold & Elias Boudinot in Letters, 1823–1839* (Chapel Hill: University of North Carolina Press, 2005), 166.

22. Elias Boudinot and Harriett Boudinot to Herman Vaill, November 21, 1827, in Gaul, *To Marry an Indian*, 159.

23. Ehle, *Trail of Tears*, 216–17; *Cherokee Phoenix*, March 13, 1828.

24. Theda Perdue claims that Boudinot became so Christianized that he did not fully grasp the faith of his own people and how strongly they clung to traditional religion. Perdue, *Cherokee Editor*, 81.

25. Wilkins, *Cherokee Tragedy*, 201, 205.

26. Bass, *Cherokee Messenger*, 99; Wilkins, *Cherokee Tragedy*, 205–6. According to his biographer, Gary E. Moulton, why John Ross married a full-blood "is one of the many mysteries of his life." Moulton, *John Ross, Cherokee Chief* (Athens: University of Georgia Press, 1978), 238; Gary E. Moulton, ed., *The Papers of Chief John Ross* (Norman: University of Oklahoma Press, 1985), 1:3–4.

27. Benjamin Gold to Herman and Flora Gold Vaill, October 29, 1829, in Gaul, *To Marry an Indian*, 165; Moulton, *Papers of Chief John Ross*, 1:5.

28. Ehle, *Trail of Tears*, 205–6; Theda Perdue and Michael D. Green, *The Cherokee Nation and the Trail of Tears* (New York: Viking, 2007), 54–55.

29. McLoughlin, *Cherokees and Missionaries*, 216, 220.

30. Ibid., 231–32; Samuel Worcester to Jeremiah Evarts, March 29, 1827, American Board of Commissioners for Foreign Missions, in Gaul, *To Marry an Indian*, 223.

31. Thomas L. McKenney to James Barbour, February 20, 1827, Bureau of Indian Affairs, M-21, roll 2, p. 390; quoted in McLoughlin, *Cherokees and Missionaries*, 220.

32. Perdue and Green, *Cherokee Nation*, quoting Georgia Assembly, 58.

33. McLoughlin, *Cherokees and Missionaries*, 221.

34. George M. Troup to John C. Calhoun, February 28, 1824, in *American State Papers: Indian Affairs* (Washington, D.C.: U.S. Congress, Government Printing Office, 1834) 2:475–76; Tim Alan Garrison, *The Legal Ideology of Removal: The Southern Judiciary and the Sovereignty of Native American Nations* (Athens: University of Georgia Press, 2002), 24.

35. Andrew Jackson to Rachel Jackson, December 19, December 29, 1813, in Harold D. Moser et al., eds., *The Papers of Andrew Jackson* (Knoxville: University of Tennessee Press, 1980), 2:494–95, 515–16. See also Robert V. Remini, *Andrew Jackson and His Indian Wars* (New York: Viking, 2001), 64.

36. Remini, *Andrew Jackson and His Indian Wars*, 207; Lewis Cass, "Removal of the Indians," *North American Review* 31 (January 1830), 75, chapter 4, 116.

37. Andrew Burstein, *The Passions of Andrew Jackson* (New York: Knopf, 2003), 16; Andrew Jackson to John McKee, May 17, 1794, in Sam B. Smith, ed., *Papers of Andrew Jackson* (Knoxville: University of Tennessee Press, 1980), 1:48–49.

38. Burstein, *Passions of Andrew Jackson*, 185–86; Andrew Jackson to John C. Calhoun, September 2, 1820, in Moser, *Papers of Andrew Jackson*, 4:388.

39. Remini, *Andrew Jackson and His Indian Wars*, 193; Andrew Jackson to John C. Calhoun, August 25, 1820, in W. Edwin Hemphill et al.,

eds., *The Papers of John C. Calhoun* (Columbia: University of South Carolina Press, 1971), 5:336–37; September 2, 1820, John Spencer Bassett, ed., *Correspondence of Andrew Jackson* (Washington, D.C.: Carnegie Institute of Washington, 1926), 3:31–32.

40. See William G. McLoughlin, *Champion of the Cherokees: Evan and John B. Jones* (Princeton, N.J.: Princeton University Press, 1990), 123.

41. Quote is from McLoughlin, *Champion of the Cherokees*, 124; Bass, *Cherokee Messenger*, 102–3, 106–7.

42. *Cherokee Phoenix*, October 10, 1828.

43. Ibid., March 29, 1828.

44. Ehle, *Trail of Tears*, 209–12.

45. Burstein, *Passions of Andrew Jackson*, 170.

46. Quoted in Remini, *Andrew Jackson and His Indian Wars*, 226.

47. Quoted in Samuel Carter III, *Cherokee Sunset: A Nation Betrayed* (Garden City, N.J.: Doubleday, 1976), 83.

48. Ibid., 72.

49. *Cherokee Phoenix*, February 21, 1828.

50. Perdue, *Cherokee Editor*, 48.

51. Michael Paul Rogin, *Fathers and Children: Andrew Jackson and the Subjugation of the American Indian* (New York: Knopf, 1975), 211; U.S. Congress, *Register of Debates* 6 (1829–30), 1088, 1103. Taken nearly verbatim from "On the State of the Indians," *North American Review* 16 (January 1823), 39–40.

52. *Cherokee Phoenix*, June 17, 1829.

53. Ibid., July 15, 1829.

54. Wilkins, *Cherokee Tragedy*, 209.

55. Moulton, *John Ross, Cherokee Chief*, 40; Perdue, *Cherokee Editor*, 21.

56. John Ross to the Senate and House of Representatives, February 27, 1829, in Moulton, *Papers of Chief John Ross*, 1: 154, 155, 157.

57. Ross to Cherokee People, July 1, 1829, in ibid., 166.

58. Ehle, *Trail of Tears*, 221.

59. Quoted in Gaul, *To Marry an Indian*, 53.

60. Benjamin Gold to Herman and Flora Gold Vaill, April 14, 1830, in ibid., 169.

61. *Cherokee Phoenix*, February 10, 1830.

62. Ibid., May 29, 1830.

63. Prucha, *American Indian Policy*, 234; Bassett, *Correspondence of Andrew Jackson,* 2:279–81.

64. John H. Eaton to John Ross, April 18, 1829, in Moulton, *Papers of Chief John Ross,* 1:163.

65. Ehle, *Trail of Tears*, 226.

66. *Cherokee Phoenix*, February 17, 1830. See also John Ross to Hugh Montgomery, February 6, 1830, in Moulton, *Papers of Chief John Ross,* 1:182–83.

67. Quoted in Wilkins, *Cherokee Tragedy*, 212.

68. Ibid., 213; *Cherokee Phoenix*, March 5, 1831.

69. Quoted in Wilkins, *Cherokee Tragedy*, 213.

70. Perdue, *Cherokee Editor*, 23.

71. Ehle, *Trail of Tears*, 234.

72. *Cherokee Phoenix*, August 20, 1828.

73. Remini, *Andrew Jackson and His Indian Wars*, 232.

74. Prucha, *American Indian Policy*, 238–39.

75. Remini, *Andrew Jackson and His Indian Wars*, 232.

76. Perdue and Green, *Cherokee Nation*, 64.

77. Remini, *Andrew Jackson and His Indian Wars*, 234.

78. Rogin, *Fathers and Children*, 206.

79. Remini, *Andrew Jackson and His Indian Wars*, 235.

80. Francis Paul Prucha, ed., *Cherokee Removal: The "William Penn" Essays and Other Writings* (Knoxville: University of Tennessee Press, 1981), 6–7, 22.

81. Ibid., 9–10.

82. Ibid., 249, 240.

83. Gaul, *To Marry an Indian*, 167–68.

84. Perdue and Green, *Cherokee Nation*, 62–63.

85. Prucha, *American Indian Policy*, 242; Garrison, *Legal Ideology of Indian Removal*, 108.

86. Andrew Jackson to Francis P. Blair, June 4, 1838, in Bassett, *Correspondence of Andrew Jackson*, 5:553.

87. Edward Everett to Jeremiah Evarts, February 21, 1831, quoted in Prucha, *Cherokee Removal*, 37.

88. John Ross to Jeremiah Evarts, July 24, 1830, in Moulton, *Papers of Chief Ross*, 1:195–96.

89. Elias Boudinot to Herman and Flora Gold Vaill, January 7, 1831, in Gaul, *To Marry an Indian*, 174.

90. Ibid., 173.

91. *Cherokee Phoenix*, March 20, 1838.

92. Ibid.

93. Quoted in Garrison, *Legal Ideology of Removal*, 106–7.

94. Quoted in Bass, *Cherokee Messenger*, 129.

4: THE "WHITE MAN'S WEAPON"

1. *Cherokee Phoenix*, January 7, 1829; William G. McLoughlin, *Cherokees and Missionaries, 1789–1839* (New Haven, Conn.: Yale University Press, 1984), 243, 248.

2. McLoughlin, *Cherokees and Missionaries*, 252, 267; William G. McLoughlin, *Champions of the Cherokees: Evan and John B. Jones* (Princeton: Princeton University Press, 1990), 124.

3. *Cherokee Phoenix*, October 1, 1830; McLoughlin, *Cherokees and Missionaries*, 292.

4. McLoughlin, *Cherokees and Missionaries*, 255; "Resolution and Statement of the Missionaries," *Missionary Herald* 27 (1831), 80–84.

5. John Howard Payne Papers, vol. 9, 1, Newberry Library, Chicago; McLoughlin, *Cherokees and Missionaries*, 255.

6. Ralph Henry Gabriel, *Elias Boudinot, Cherokee, and His America* (Norman: University of Oklahoma Press, 1941), 128; *Cherokee Phoenix*, January 8 and January 1, 1831; quote by Jones is from McLoughlin, *Champions of the Cherokees*, 128.

7. McLoughlin, *Cherokees and Missionaries*, 257.

8. *Cherokee Phoenix*, February 19, 1831.

9. Jeremiah Evarts to Samuel Worcester, February 1, 1831, quoted in McLoughlin, *Cherokees and Missionaries*, 259.

10. George R. Gilmer to John H. Eaton, April 20, 1831; Gilmer to William T. Barry, April 19, 1831, in Gilmer, *Sketches of Some of the First Settlers of Upper Georgia* (Baltimore, Md.: Genealogical Publishing, 1965), 302–8; Gary E. Moulton, *John Ross: Cherokee Chief* (Athens: University of Georgia Press, 1978), 45; Tim Alan Garrison, *The Legal Ideology of Removal: The Southern Judiciary and the Sovereignty of Native American Nations* (Athens: University of Georgia Press, 2002), 171–72.

11. Garrison, *Legal Ideology of Removal*, 172–73.

12. Ibid., 173.

13. Althea Bass, *Cherokee Messenger: A Life of Samuel Austin Worcester* (Norman: University of Oklahoma Press, 1936), 137; Garrison, *Legal Ideology of Removal*, 173–74.

14. McLoughlin, *Cherokees and Missionaries*, 262; Garrison, *Legal Ideology of Removal*, 174.

15. John Ehle, *Trail of Tears: The Rise and Fall of the Cherokee Nation* (New York: Doubleday, 1988), 252; "Imprisonment of the Missionaries to the Cherokees," *Vermont Telegraph*, December 13, 1831, reprinted in *Journal of Cherokee Studies*, 4 (1979), 86; Gilmer is quoted in Garrison, *Legal Ideology of Removal*, 174–75.

16. Lucy Butler to John Howard Payne, January 25, 1837, in John Howard Payne Papers, Ayer Collection, ms 689, Newberry Library, vol. 5, 25; Bass, *Cherokee Messenger*, 138–39, 150; *Missionary Herald* 27 (1831), 395, reprinted in *Journal of Cherokee Studies* 2, no. 4 (1977), 372.

17. Quoted in Bass, *Cherokee Messenger*, 146–47; Moulton, *John Ross*, 46.

18. *Cherokee Phoenix*, August 27, 1831, September 17, 1831.

19. Ibid., September 17, 1831.

20. McLoughlin, *Cherokees and Missionaries*, 265; Garrison, *Legal Ideology of Removal*, 176.

21. John Ross, "Annual Message," October 24, 1831, in Gary E. Moulton, ed., *The Papers of Chief John Ross* (Norman: University of Oklahoma Press, 1985), 1:225, 227–28.

22. Moulton, *John Ross*, 47.

23. "Report of Attempted Assassination," January 21, 1832, Moulton, *Papers of Chief John Ross*, 1:236, 238; Moulton, *John Ross*, 48.

24. John Ross to William Wirt, November 11, 1831; Ross to John Martin, John Ridge, and William S. Coodey, December 1, 1831, in Moulton, *Papers of Chief John Ross*, 1:231–32.

25. John Ridge to John Ross, January 12 and January 13, 1832, in Moulton, *Papers of Chief John Ross*, 1:235; *Cherokee Phoenix*, December 21, 1832.

26. *Cherokee Phoenix*, November 17, 1831.

27. John Ridge to John Ross, January 12 and January 13, 1832, in Moulton, *Papers of Chief John Ross*, 1:235; Ehle, *Trail of Tears*, 254.

28. John Ridge to John Ross, January 12 and January 13, 1832, in Moulton, *Papers of Chief John Ross*, 1:235–36.

29. *Cherokee Phoenix*, February 18, 1832; Ehle, *Trail of Tears*, 254.

30. Garrison, *Legal Ideology of Removal*, 177.

31. Ibid.

32. Ibid., 178–81.

33. *Cherokee Phoenix*, May 12, 1832; Ehle, *Trail of Tears*, 255; John Ross to Cherokee delegation, March 30, 1832, in Moulton, *Papers of Chief John Ross*, 1:241; Elias Boudinot to Stand Watie, March 7, 1832, quoted in Barbara Luebke, "Elias Boudinot, Cherokee Editor: The Father of American Indian Journalism" (Ph.D. diss., University of Missouri, 1981), 270–71. Back home in Cherokee country, Harriett Boudinot was moved as well by the Marshall ruling, though she worried that Worcester and Butler "[might] yet have to stay another year in their confinement." Harriett also noted that Ann Worcester remained "very cheerful. You don't know what a good Sister she is to me. We are as one family." Harriett Boudinot to Herman and Flora Gold Vaill, March 29, 1832, in Theresa Strouth Gaul, ed., *To Marry an Indian: The Marriage of Harriett Gold & Elias Boudinot in Letters, 1823–1839* (Chapel Hill: University of North Carolina Press, 2005), 182.

34. "Report of the Committee on the State of the Republic," December 15, 1831, in Gilmer, *Settlers of Upper Georgia*, 313, 335–43;

Wilson Lumpkin, "Annual Message," November 6, 1832, in Wilson Lumpkin, *The Removal of the Cherokee Indians from Georgia* (reprint, New York: Augustus M. Kelley, 1971), 103–7; *Macon (Ga.) Advertiser*, March 13, 1832; George M. Troup, "The Sovereignty of the States: An Open Letter to the Georgia Journal," *Niles Register*, March 5 and March 31, 1832.

35. Andrew Jackson to John Coffee, April 17, 1832, in John Spencer Bassett, ed., *The Correspondence of Andrew Jackson* (Washington, D.C.: Carnegie Institute of Washington, 1926), 4:430.

36. John Ridge to Stand Watie, April 6, 1832, in Edward Everett Dale and Gaston Litton, eds., *Cherokee Cavaliers: Forty Years of Cherokee History as Told in the Correspondence of the Ridge-Watie-Boudinot Family* (Norman: Oklahoma University Press, 1939), 7–10; Ehle, *Trail of Tears*, 255–56; Thurman Wilkins, *Cherokee Tragedy: The Ridge Family and the Decimation of a People*, rev. ed. (Norman: University of Oklahoma Press, 1986), 229.

37. Theda Perdue argues that, given Boudinot's change of heart in favor of removal, he should have followed "traditional Cherokee ethics" and "withdrawn and maintained silence." Theda Perdue, ed., *Cherokee Editor: The Writings of Elias Boudinot* (Athens: University of Georgia Press, 1983), 26. Perdue also speculates that John Ridge's change of heart on removal happened later—after the council canceled elections in 1832 in which Ridge planned on defeating Ross and becoming chief. Ibid., 231.

38. Ehle, *Trail of Tears*, 256–58; Theda Perdue and Michael D. Green, *The Cherokee Nation and the Trail of Tears* (New York: Viking, 2007), 96.

39. John Ridge to John Ross, April 3, 1832, in Moulton, *Papers of Chief John Ross*, 1:241.

40. Ehle, *Trail of Tears*, 257.

41. Perdue and Green, *Cherokee Nation*, 95–96.

42. John Ridge to Stand Watie, April 6, 1832, in Dale and Litton, *Cherokee Cavaliers*, 7–10; Ehle, *Trail of Tears*, 258.

43. Ehle, *Trail of Tears*, 258.

44. Perdue, *Cherokee Editor*, 167.

45. John Ross to Elias Boudinot, May 17, 1832, in Moulton, *Papers of Chief John Ross*, 1:244; *Cherokee Phoenix*, July 20, 1833.

46. *Cherokee Phoenix*, August 4, 1832. The historian William G. McLoughlin argues that the Treaty Party, in its "paternalistic" perspective, believed the treaty was a good bargain for the Cherokee people, but it was, in fact, "so transparently illegal by Cherokee law and so overwhelmingly repudiated by the vast majority of chiefs and Cherokee citizens that the Ross Party foolishly believed that the United States Senate would never ratify it." See McLoughlin, *Cherokees and Missionaries*, 308.

47. Perdue, *Cherokee Editor*, 161.

48. Ibid., 177, 162.

49. Ibid., 162.

50. John Ross to General Council, August 4, 1832, in Moulton, *Papers of Chief John Ross*, 1:250; Perdue, *Cherokee Editor*, 226, 175.

51. *Cherokee Phoenix*, August 11, 1832; Perdue, *Cherokee Editor*, 163, 166, 168.

52. Perdue, *Cherokee Editor*, 174.

53. Ibid., 174, 172.

54. Ibid., 173.

55. McLoughlin, *Cherokees and Missionaries*, 307; Perdue, *Cherokee Editor*, 176–77.

56. Garrison, *Legal Ideology of Removal*, 192.

57. Lucy Butler to John Howard Payne, January 25, 1837, Payne Papers, Ayer Collection, ms 689, Newberry Library, vol. 5, 29–30; McLoughlin, *Cherokees and Missionaries*, 297–98; Garrison, *Legal Ideology of Removal*, 195–96.

58. "Apologia of Worcester and Butler," in Jack Frederick Kilpatrick and Anna Gritts Kilpatrick, eds., *New Echota Letters: Contributions of Samuel A. Worcester to the Cherokee Phoenix* (Dallas, Tex.: Southern Methodist University Press, 1968), 124. See also McLoughlin, *Cherokees and Missionaries*, 298–99; Garrison, *Legal Ideology of Removal*, 196. Garrison claims that in contrast to Evarts's expectation, "the Cherokees had demonstrated greater 'long continued courage' than had his own missionaries" (196).

59. John Ridge to John Ross, February 2, 1833, in Moulton, *Papers of Chief John Ross*, 1:259–60.

5: NEW ECHOTA

1. Thurman Wilkins, *Cherokee Tragedy: The Ridge Family and the Decimation of a People*, rev. ed. (Norman: University of Oklahoma Press, 1986), 246.

2. John Ridge to John Ross, February 2, 1833, in Gary E. Moulton, ed., *The Papers of Chief John Ross* (Norman: University of Oklahoma Press, 1985), 1:260.

3. John Ehle, *Trail of Tears: The Rise and Fall of the Cherokee Nation* (New York: Doubleday, 1988), 268.

4. Theda Perdue and Michael D. Green, *The Cherokee Nation and the Trail of Tears* (New York: Viking, 2007), 100–101; Ehle, *Trail of Tears*, 283.

5. Gary E. Moulton, *John Ross: Cherokee Chief* (Athens: University of Georgia Press, 1978), 52, 55.

6. Ehle, *Trail of Tears*, 269.

7. Quoted in ibid., 269–70.

8. Moulton, *John Ross*, 57; Ehle, *Trail of Tears*, 271.

9. Moulton, *John Ross*, 58.

10. Ibid.; Ehle, *Trail of Tears*, 271.

11. Moulton, *John Ross*, 58.

12. Theda Perdue, ed., *Cherokee Editor: The Writings of Elias Boudinot* (Athens: University of Georgia Press, 1983), 178.

13. Ehle, *Trail of Tears*, 273.

14. Moulton, *John Ross*, 60–61; Perdue and Green, *Cherokee Nation*, 106.

15. Moulton, *John Ross*, 62.

16. Edward Everett Dale and Gaston Litton, eds., *Cherokee Cavaliers: Forty Years of Cherokee History as Told in the Correspondence of the Ridge-Watie-Boudinot Family* (Norman: University of Oklahoma Press, 1939), 13.

17. *Allegheny Democrat*, March 16, 1835.

18. Moulton, *John Ross*, 62; Perdue and Green, *Cherokee Nation*, 105.

19. Perduc and Green, *Cherokee Nation*, 105.

20. Althea Bass, *Cherokee Messenger* (Norman: University of Oklahoma Press, 1936), 176; Moulton, *John Ross*, 63; Perdue and Green, *Cherokee Nation*, 111.

21. John Howard Payne Papers, Ayers Collection, ms 689, Newberry Library, vol. 1, 133–36; Ehle, *Trail of Tears*, 281–82; Moulton, *John Ross*, 64.

22. Payne Papers, vol. 1, 138; Moulton, *John Ross*, 64–65.

23. Ross's Annual Message, October 12, 1835 and Benjamin F. Currey to John Ross, September 9, 1835, both in Moulton, *Papers of Chief John Ross*, 1:353, 357–58.

24. Wilkins, *Cherokee Tragedy*, 268.

25. Moulton, *John Ross*, 66.

26. Ross to the National Committee, October 24, 1835, in Moulton, *Papers of Chief John Ross*, 1:365; Perdue and Green, *Cherokee Nation*, 107.

27. John Schermerhorn to John Ross and other members of the Cherokee delegation, October 27, 1835, in Moulton, *Papers of Chief John Ross*, 1:370.

28. John Schermerhorn to John Ross, October 30, 1835, and John Ross to John Schermerhorn, October 30, 1835, both in ibid., 370, 372.

29. Quoted in Wilkins, *Cherokee Tragedy*, 283; Samuel Carter III, *Cherokee Sunset: A Nation Betrayed* (Garden City, N.J.: Doubleday, 1976), 184–85.

30. John Ross to George Gilmer, November 13, 1835, in Moulton, *Papers of Chief John Ross*, 1:373; Wilkins, *Cherokee Tragedy*, 275.

31. Gary Moulton argues that Ross's fear of a conspiracy between Schermerhorn and Currey in his arrest was unwarranted; the Georgia Guard simply overreached. See *John Ross*, 69.

32. Ibid., 69–70; John Ridge to John Ross, December 4, 1835, and John Ross to John Ridge, December 4, 1835, both in Moulton, *Papers of Chief John Ross*, 1:377–78.

33. Perdue and Green, *Cherokee Nation*, 110.

34. Quoted in Wilkins, *Cherokee Tragedy*, 286; *Cartersville (Ga.) Courant*, March 26, 1885.

35. James J. Trott to John Ross, January 6, 1836, in Moulton, *Papers of Chief John Ross*, 1:379.

36. Perdue and Green, *Cherokee Nation*, 112–13.

37. Quoted in Wilkins, *Cherokee Tragedy*, 287.

38. Quoted in ibid.

39. Ibid., 289, 295; quote is from *Little Rock Arkansas Gazette*, October 2, 1839. In a joint letter with Boudinot and Stand Watie, Ridge told Schermerhorn: "[Some Cherokees] may be secretly induced to assassinate, by John Ross & his friend, but it will be done so secretly that only one or two may fall. What will that be to the joy which the treaty will ultimately give to the Indians? the thousands who will emigrate and be happy? the thousands who will be relieved from the lowest state of wretchedness and who, now reduced almost to nakedness and starvation; buffeted and lacerated by the settlers among them; driven, with their women and little ones, from their cabins and their fields, to the woods and mountains, stripped of the little property they once possessed, [are now] wandering outcasts . . . dependent on the cold charity of their new oppressors?" Wilkins, *Cherokee Tragedy*, 293.

40. James J. Trott to John Ross, January 6, 1836 and George Lowrey to John Ross, February 11, 1836, both in Moulton, *Papers of Chief John Ross*, 1:379, 387.

41. John Ross to John Howard Payne, January 7, 1836, in Moulton, *Papers of Chief John Ross*, 1:382.

42. John Ross to Lewis Cass, February 29, 1836 and John Ross to John Howard Payne, March 5, 1836, both in ibid., 388–91; Perdue and Green, *Cherokee Nation*, 111–12.

43. Perdue, *Cherokee Editor*, 199.

44. Moulton, *John Ross*, 77.

45. Quoted in Wilkins, *Cherokee Tragedy*, 294–95.

46. Ehle, *Trail of Tears*, 298.

47. John Ross to Senate and House of Representatives, June 21, 1836, in Moulton, *Papers of Chief John Ross*, 1:427–28.

48. Ibid., 1:428–29.

49. Perdue, *Cherokee Editor*, 213, 214, 216.

50. Ibid., 215, 223–24.

51. Ibid., 224.

52. Ibid.

53. Ibid., 224–25.

54. Elias Boudinot to Benjamin and Eleanor Gold, August 16, 1836, in Theresa Strouth Gaul, ed., *To Marry an Indian: The Marriage of Harriett Gold & Elias Boudinot in Letters, 1823–1839* (Chapel Hill: University of North Carolina Press, 2005), 184, 186, 189; "The Death of Harriett Gold Boudinot," *Journal of Cherokee Studies* 4, no. 2 (1979), 102–7.

55. Elias Boudinot to Job Swift Gold, October 26, 1836, in Gaul, *To Marry an Indian*, 196–97; "Death of Harriett Gold Boudinot," 102–3.

56. Harriett Boudinot to Herman and Flora Gold Vaill, March 29, 1832, in Gaul, *To Marry an Indian*, 180–81.

57. Elias Boudinot to Benjamin and Eleanor Gold, August 16, 1836 and Elias Boudinot to Herman and Flora Gold Vaill, August 28, 1836, both in ibid., 189, 194–95.

6: ROUNDUP

1. Evan Jones to John Ross, February 6, 1837, cited in William G. McLoughlin, *Champions of the Cherokees: Evan and John B. Jones* (Princeton, N.J.: Princeton University Press, 1990), 139–40.

2. Quoted in Grant Foreman, *Indian Removal: The Emigration of the Five Civilized Tribes of Indians* (Norman: University of Oklahoma Press, 1932), 271–72.

3. General John E. Wool, Proclamation to the Cherokee People, March 22, 1837, Tennessee State Library and Archives, Nashville, Tenn., State Library Cherokee Collection, box 3, folder 9, document: ch078.

4. Gary E. Moulton, *John Ross: Cherokee Chief* (Athens: University of Georgia Press, 1978), 82; Theda Perdue and Michael D. Green, *The Cherokee Nation and the Trail of Tears* (New York: Viking, 2007), 113–14.

5. John Ross to the Senate and House of Representatives, June 21, 1836, in Gary E. Moulton, ed., *The Papers of Chief John Ross* (Norman: University of Oklahoma Press, 1985), 1:433–34.

6. John Ross in answer to inquiries from a friend, July 2, 1836, in ibid., 1:448, 454, 456.

7. John Ross to Senate and House of Representatives, September 28, 1836, in ibid., 1:458–59.

8. Ibid., 1:460.

9. John Ehle, *Trail of Tears: The Rise and Fall of the Cherokee Nation* (New York: Doubleday, 1988), 311–12; Moulton, *John Ross*, 81; Lewis Ross to John Ross, March 22, 1838, in Moulton, *Papers of Chief John Ross*, 1:615; John Ross to Job R. Tyson, January 19, 1838, in ibid., 1:583. "My course has been a steady one," Ross told some friends. "It will continue." John Ross to Joseph Gales and William W. Seaton, March 29, 1838, in ibid., 1:618.

10. Quoted in Moulton, *John Ross*, 84–85.

11. Ehle, *Trail of Tears*, 307.

12. Ibid., 363.

13. Quoted in Thurman Wilkins, *Cherokee Tragedy: The Ridge Family and the Decimation of a People*, rev. ed. (Norman: University of Oklahoma Press, 1986), 294, 292; Ehle, *Trail of Tears*, 366.

14. Elias Boudinot to Job Swift Gold, October 26, 1836 and Sophia Sawyer to David Green, n.d., both in Theresa Strouth Gaul, ed., *To Marry an Indian: The Marriage of Harriett Gold & Elias Boudinot in Letters, 1823–1839* (Chapel Hill: University of North Carolina Press, 2005), 196–98.

15. Elias Boudinot to Benjamin and Eleanor Gold, May 20, 1837, in ibid., 200.

16. Ehle, *Trail of Tears*, 366; Wilkins, *Cherokee Tragedy*, 309–10.

17. John Ross to Lewis Ross, April 5, 1838, in Moulton, *Papers of Chief John Ross*, 1:623.

18. John Ross to Job R. Tyson, May 6, 1837, in Moulton, *Papers of Chief John Ross*, 1:496; John Ross to Lewis Ross, November 6 and November 11, 1837, in ibid., 1:541; John Ross to William S. Coodey,

December 1837, in ibid., 1:573; George Lowrey to John Ross, January 5, 1838, in ibid., 1:578.

19. John Ross to Lewis Ross, January 13, 1838, in ibid., 1:579; Evan Jones to John Ross, March 20, 1838, in ibid., 1:614.

20. John Ross to Samuel Webb and John M. Truman, May 14, 1838, in ibid., 1:637–38.

21. Lewis Ross to John Ross, March 5, 1838, in ibid., 1:604–5.

22. John Ross to John M. Ross, April 10, 1838, in ibid., 1:626; Lewis Ross to John Ross, April 29, 1838, in ibid., 1:633.

23. John Ross to Lewis Ross, April 5, 1838, in ibid., 1:623; John Ross to Samuel Webb and John M. Truman, May 3, 1838, in ibid., 1:635. See also "John Ross and Cherokee Resistance," *Journal of Southern History* 44, no. 2 (May 1978), 211.

24. Moulton, *John Ross*, 86; Theda Perdue, ed., *Cherokee Editor: The Writings of Elias Boudinot* (Athens: University of Georgia Press, 1983), 158.

25. Moulton, *John Ross*, 86; Perdue and Green, *Cherokee Nation*, 123.

26. General Scott's address of May 10, 1838, in the *Journal of Cherokee Studies* 3, no. 3 (1978), 145.

27. Ibid., 146; Perdue and Green, *Cherokee Nation*, 123.

28. Ehle, *Trail of Tears*, 328.

29. Ibid., 330.

30. James Mooney, *Myths of the Cherokee and Sacred Formulas of the Cherokees* (Nashville: Charles and Randy Elder, 1982, reprint), 130–31.

31. Ibid.; Moulton, *John Ross*, 96.

32. The Neugin quote is from Grant Foreman, *Indian Removal: The Emigration of the Five Civilized Tribes of Indians* (Norman: University of Oklahoma Press, 1932), 302–3; Daniel S. Butrick, *The Journal of Rev. Daniel S. Butrick, May 19, 1838–April 1, 1839* (Park Hill, Okla.: Trail of Tears Association, Oklahoma Chapter, 1998), 2, 8.

33. Evan Jones, June 16, 1838, letter quoted in McLoughlin, *Champions of the Cherokees*, 171.

34. Perdue and Green, *Cherokee Nation*, 126, 133; John B. Finger, *The Eastern Band of Cherokees, 1819–1900* (Knoxville: University of

Tennessee Press, 1984), 20–40. See also John B. Finger, "The Impact of Removal on North Carolina Cherokees," in William L. Anderson, ed., *Cherokee Removal: Before and After* (Athens: University of Georgia Press, 1991), 103–4.

35. "R. H. K. Whiteley's Journal of Occurrences," August 1, 1838, found at www.mindspring.com/~wayne.gibson/JP1.gif.

36. J. W. Lide to Captain John Page, July 20, 1838, in Vicki Rozema, ed., *Voices from the Trail of Tears* (Winston-Salem, N.C.: John F. Blair, 2003), 128–29; McLoughlin, *Champions of the Cherokees*, 173.

37. Butrick, *Journal of Rev. Daniel S. Butrick*, 6.

38. Quoted in Ehle, *Trail of Tears*, 341–42.

39. For a discussion of Ross's role in self-removal, see Moulton, *John Ross*, 101–6.

40. Perdue and Green, *Cherokee Nation*, 131; Moulton, *John Ross*, 98; Grace Steele Woodward, *The Cherokees* (Norman: University of Oklahoma Press, 1963), 211.

41. Moulton, *John Ross*, 103.

42. Perdue and Green, *Cherokee Nation*, 6, 134.

43. William Shorey Coodey to John Howard Payne, August 13, 1840, John Howard Payne Papers, Newberry Library, Chicago, Illinois.

7: THE TRAIL OF TEARS

1. Thurman Wilkins, *Cherokee Tragedy: The Ridge Family and the Decimation of a People*, rev. ed. (Norman: University of Oklahoma Press, 1986), 299.

2. Ibid., 297–99.

3. Ibid., 300; John Ehle, *Trail of Tears: The Rise and Fall of the Cherokee Nation* (New York: Doubleday, 1988), 369.

4. George Hicks to John Ross, November 4, 1838, in Gary E. Moulton, ed., *The Papers of Chief John Ross* (Norman: University of Oklahoma Press, 1985), 1:687.

5. Lieutenant H. L. Scott to General Winfield Scott, October 11, 1838, in Vicki Rozema, ed., *Voices from the Trail of Tears* (Winston-Salem, N.C.: John F. Blair, 2003), 132–33; William Shorey Coodey to John Howard Payne, August 13, 1840, John Howard Payne Papers, Newberry Library, Chicago, Illinois.

6. Theda Perdue and Michael D. Green, *The Cherokee Nation and the Trail of Tears* (New York: Viking, 2007), 117–21.

7. For an insightful account of each detachment's journey, see David G. Fitzgerald and Duane King, *The Cherokee Trail of Tears* (Portland, Ore.: Graphic Arts Books, 2007).

8. Ibid., 127; *Journal of Occurrences on the Route of a Party of Cherokee Emigrants by Lt. E. Deas*, in Rozema, *Voices*, 104.

9. The third detachment that embarked four days later proved even more rebellious. Rozema, *Voices*, 110; Perdue and Green, *Cherokee Nation*, 129; Grant Foreman, *Indian Removal: The Emigration of the Five Civilized Tribes of Indians* (Norman: University of Oklahoma Press, 1932), 295.

10. Gary E. Moulton, *John Ross: Cherokee Chief* (Athens: University of Georgia Press, 1978), 99.

11. Ibid., 100; Perdue and Green, *Cherokee Nation*, 133.

12. Daniel Butrick, *The Journal of Rev. Daniel S. Butrick, May 19, 1838–April 1, 1839* (Park Hill, Okla.: Trail of Tears Association, Oklahoma Chapter, 1998), 57.

13. Desertion rates ranged from 1 to 18 percent. Moulton, *John Ross*, 104. John Ross to Winfield Scott, November 12, 1838, in Moulton, *Papers of Chief John Ross*, 1:692; Perdue and Green, *Cherokee Nation*, 133, 135, 137. Butrick speculated that the local litigant may in fact have been the man who killed the Cherokee.

14. John Benge, George C. Lowry, and George Lowrey to John Ross, September 19, 1838, in Moulton, *Papers of Chief John Ross*, 1:673; Jesse Bushyhead to John Ross, October 21, 1838, in ibid., 1:683.

15. Quoted in Fitzgerald and King, *Cherokee Trail of Tears*, 50.

16. Winfield Scott to John Ross, October 3, 1838, in Moulton, *Papers of Chief John Ross*, 1:677; John Ross to Winfield Scott, October

6, 1838, in ibid., 1:679; John Ross to Winfield Scott, November 12, 1838, in ibid., 1:691–92; Moulton, *John Ross*, 101.

17. Jesse Bushyhead and John Powell to John Ross, October 26, 1838, in Moulton, *Papers of Chief John Ross*, 1:685.

18. Gary Moulton calls the suspicions about John Ross's profit-taking from the removal "largely indeterminable," while admitting that he may indeed have shared in his brother's largesse. Moulton, *John Ross*, 105–6; Thomas Clark Jr. to John Ross, November 15, 1838, in Moulton, *Papers of Chief John Ross*, 1:694.

19. Perdue and Green, *Cherokee Nation*, 135; Butrick, *Journal of Rev. Daniel S. Butrick*, 51; William G. McLoughlin, *Champions of the Cherokees: Evan and John B. Jones* (Princeton: Princeton University Press, 1990), 184; Evan Jones to John Ross, October 27, 1838, in Moulton, *Papers of Chief John Ross*, 1:686.

20. Rebecca Neugin, "Memories of the Trail," *Journal of Cherokee Studies* 3, no. 3 (1978), 176.

21. Fitzgerald and King, *Cherokee Trail of Tears*, 71, 97, 101.

22. Quoted in Foreman, *Indian Removal*, 305–6.

23. Ibid., 295.

24. Butrick, *Journal of Rev. Daniel S. Butrick*, 22.

25. Perdue and Green, *Cherokee Nation*, 137; Ehle, *Trail of Tears*, 353; Foreman, *Indian Removal*, 302–3; McLoughlin, *Champions of the Cherokees*, 187.

26. Elijah Hicks to John Ross, October 24, 1838, in Moulton, *Papers of Chief John Ross*, 1:684.

27. Quoted in McLoughlin, *Champions of the Cherokees*, 184.

28. Butrick, *Journal*, 52. Butrick also records the story of tending to a ten- to twelve-year-old boy, "sick with a bowel complaint": "He extended his emaciated hand to take mine and then pointed to the place of his extreme pain. Before our meeting was closed he was a corpse." Ibid., 61.

29. Quoted in Ehle, *Trail of Tears*, 358.

30. Thomas N. Clark Jr. to John Ross, November 15, 1838 and December 17, 1838, in Moulton, *Papers of Chief John Ross*, 1:694.

31. Moulton calls this story "probably apocryphal." Moulton, *John Ross*, 100–101.

32. Russell Thornton, "The Demography of the Trail of Tears Period: A New Estimate of Cherokee Population Losses," in William L. Anderson, ed., *Cherokee Removal: Before and After* (Athens: University of Georgia Press, 1991), 75–95.

33. Michael F. Doran, "Population Statistics of Nineteenth Century Indian Territory," *Chronicle of Oklahoma* 53 (1975–76), 492–515; Moulton, *John Ross*, 100. The Mooney quote is from Thornton, "Demography of the Trail of Tears Period," 78.

34. Elijah Hicks to John Ross, October 24, 1838, in Moulton, *Papers of Chief John Ross*, 1:684–85; Fitzgerald and King, *Cherokee Trail of Tears*, 74.

35. Quoted in McLoughlin, *Champions of the Cherokees*, 184.

36. Butrick, *Journal of Rev. Daniel S. Butrick*, 52.

37. Ibid.

38. Ibid., 50.

8: BLOOD REVENGE

1. Washington Irving, *A Tour of the Prairies*, ed. John Francis McDermott (Norman: University of Oklahoma Press, 1956), 50–51; Daniel Butrick Journal, John Howard Payne Papers, Newberry Library, Chicago, Illinois, 94.

2. Althea Bass, *Cherokee Messenger* (Norman: University of Oklahoma Press, 1936), 252.

3. Ibid., 219, 225, 226, 248; William G. McLoughlin, *Champions of the Cherokees: Evan and John B. Jones* (Princeton: Princeton University Press, 1990), 187.

4. Bass, *Cherokee Messenger*, 255.

5. Ibid., 219.

6. Susanna Ridge quoted in John Ehle, *Trail of Tears: The Rise and Fall of the Cherokee Nation* (New York: Doubleday, 1988), 363, 366; Thurman Wilkins, *Cherokee Tragedy: The Story of the Ridge Family and*

the Decimation of a People, rev. ed. (Norman: University of Oklahoma Press, 1986), 311.

7. Ehle, *Trail of Tears,* 371; *Arkansas Gazette,* October 2, 1839.

8. George Hicks and Collins McDonald to John Ross, March 15, 1839; John Ross to Montfort Stokes, April 5, 1839; John Ross to Matthew Arbuckle, April 23, 1839; all in Gary E. Moulton, ed., *The Papers of Chief John Ross* (Norman: University of Oklahoma Press, 1985), 1:701, 702, 704; Theda Perdue and Michael D. Green, *The Cherokee Nation and the Trail of Tears* (New York: Viking, 2007), 143–45; William G. McLoughlin, *After the Trail of Tears: The Cherokees' Struggle for Sovereignty, 1839–1880* (Chapel Hill: University of North Carolina Press, 1993), 7. For a useful detachment-by-detachment analysis of provisioning numbers, see David G. Fitzgerald and Duane King, *The Cherokee Trail of Tears* (Portland, Ore.: Graphic Arts Books, 2007), 114–22.

9. McLoughlin, *Champions of the Cherokees,* 191.

10. Perdue and Green, *Cherokee Nation,* 146–47; Wilkins, *Cherokee Tragedy,* 319; Marion L. Starkey, *Cherokee Nation* (New York: Knopf, 1946), 305.

11. John Ross to General Council, June 10, 1839, in Moulton, *Papers of Chief John Ross,* 1:712–13; Gary E. Moulton, *John Ross: Cherokee Chief* (Athens: University of Georgia Press, 1978), 110.

12. Wilkins, *Cherokee Tragedy,* 332; John Brown, John Looney, and John Rogers to John Ross and George Lowrey, June 14, 1839, in Moulton, *Papers of Chief John Ross,* 1:714.

13. Wilkins, *Cherokee Tragedy,* 332.

14. Perdue and Green, *Cherokee Nation,* 148.

15. McLoughlin, *After the Trail of Tears,* 14; John Ross to Montfort Stokes, June 21, 1839, in Moulton, *Papers of Chief John Ross,* 1:716.

16. McLoughlin, *After the Trail of Tears,* 15.

17. Wilkins, *Cherokee Tragedy,* 334; Ehle, *Trail of Tears,* 375; McLoughlin, *After the Trail of Tears,* 16.

18. Allen Ross deposition in Grant Foreman, "The Murder of Elias Boudinot," *Chronicles of Oklahoma* 12 (1934), 23.

19. Samuel Worcester to Daniel Brinsmade, June 26, 1839, in The-

resa Strough Gaul, ed., *To Marry an Indian: The Marriage of Harriett Gold & Elias Boudinot in Letters, 1823–1839* (Chapel Hill: University of North Carolina Press, 2005), 202–3. John Rollin Ridge quote is from John Rollin Ridge, *Poems* (San Francisco: Henry Payot & Company, Publishers, 1868), 7–8.

20. Ehle, *Trail of Tears*, 376.

21. Samuel Worcester to Daniel Brinsmade, June 26, 1839, in Gaul, *To Marry an Indian*, 202–3.

22. Ehle, *Trail of Tears*, 377; Watie's quote is from Kenny A. Franks, *Stand Watie and the Agony of the Cherokee Nation* (Memphis: Memphis State University Press, 1979), 1; Wilkins, *Cherokee Tragedy*, 338.

23. Samuel Worcester to Daniel Brinsmade, June 26, 1839, in Gaul, *To Marry an Indian*, 202–3; Wilkins, *Cherokee Tragedy*, 340.

24. Moulton, *John Ross*, 113.

25. Evan Jones to John Howard Payne, June 24, 1839, John Howard Payne Papers, vol. 5, 76, Newberry Library, Chicago; McLoughlin, *Champions of the Cherokees*, 194.

26. John Ross to Matthew Arbuckle, June 22, June 23, and June 24, 1839, in Moulton, *Papers of Chief John Ross*, 1:717–20; Edmund Schwarze, *History of the Moravian Missions among Southern Indian Tribes of the United States* (Bethlehem, Pa.: Times Publishing, 1923), 191. Regarding the assassins, William G. McLoughlin claims that "they had only carried out tribal law and probably the majority will." McLoughlin, *After the Trail of Tears*, 17.

27. Tim Alan Garrison, *The Legal Ideology of Removal: The Southern Judiciary and the Sovereignty of Native American Nations* (Athens: University of Georgia Press, 2002), 232; Ehle, *Trail of Tears*, 379.

28. Samuel Worcester to Daniel Brinsmade, June 26, 1839, in Gaul, *To Marry an Indian*, 203; Wilkins, *Cherokee Tragedy*, 338–40.

29. George Paschal, "The Trial of Stand Watie," *Chronicles of Oklahoma* 12 (1934), 305–39; Franks, *Stand Watie*, 64–66, 80–88; Ehle, *Trail of Tears*, 379. For conflicting evidence on the Foreman-Watie fight, see Garrison, *Legal Ideology of Removal*, 232–33.

30. McLoughlin, *After the Trail of Tears*, 50, 41.

31. Ibid., 43.

32. Ibid., 18–20; John Ross to Creeks, July 19, 1839, in Moulton, *Papers of Chief John Ross*, 1:738.

33. McLouglin, *After the Trail of Tears*, 20, 23.

34. Ibid., 49, 51–56.

35. Ibid., 57–58.

36. See Lacy K. Ford Jr., "Making the 'White Man's Country' White: Race, Slavery and State-Building in the Jacksonian South," *Journal of the Early Republic* 19 (Winter 1999), 736–37; William G. McLoughlin, "Who Civilized the Cherokees?" *Journal of Cherokee Studies*, 13 (1988), 77.

37. Tom Belt, quoted in the documentary film *The Trail of Tears: Cherokee Legacy* (Rich-Heape Films, 2006).

38. The Hicks, Ross, and Owle quotes are from ibid.

39. Ibid.

ACKNOWLEDGMENTS

This book began as a movie. Not the usual genesis of a book, I admit, but in 2004 I began researching and writing narration for a documentary film about the Cherokees and the Trail of Tears. And in doing research and conducting many of the interviews for the film, it occurred to me that the story I was uncovering did not square with what I had read about the Cherokees during removal. What I discovered was that there was a powerful drama over removal going on inside Cherokee country, just as corrosive and revealing as the one that was dividing the country at large—a story of competing notions of patriotism and the future of the Cherokee Nation. I want to thank the producers of that film (*The Trail of Tears: Cherokee Legacy*), Steve Heape and Chip Richie, for trusting my instincts in helping to conceive the documentary. And getting James Earl Jones and Wes Studi to host and narrate the film certainly didn't hurt.

Working on that film soon prompted thoughts on writing a narrative story about the Cherokee odyssey during the removal crisis. It was invigorating to return to the spirited debates and superb scholarship that inform so much of the work on the Trail of Tears. I witnessed some of the informed enthusiasm about exploring the meaning and history of the removal crisis when I gave a talk before the National Trail of Tears Association at its annual meeting in Metropolis, Illinois, in September 2010. And I have profited immensely from insightful critiques from several outstanding scholars of Native American history. Fay Yarbrough at the University of Oklahoma offered a smart critique of my manuscript, especially on matters of race. Rowena McClinton at Southern Illinois University at Edwardsville not only read the book with insight but also made innumerable primary sources available to me from her deep knowledge of Cherokee culture. And in her inimitably good-humored way, she warmly welcomed me as a newcomer into the St. Louis area. Vicki Roz-ema at the University of Tennessee kindly gave of her time to make instructive suggestions regarding the trail experience as well as critical encouragement for the project as a whole. While it may be a commonplace observation in acknowledgments, it bears repeating here: whatever is good about the book, these kind readers deserve some of the praise; whatever flaws remain, that's all my doing.

Books on Native American history are, alas, not necessarily an easy sell in the world of commercial publishing. So I want to thank my agent, Geri Thoma, for working hard to find a good home for *An American Betrayal*. She remains a forceful and inspir-ing advocate for my work, for which I am very grateful. And it is a repeat pleasure to be in the hands of a major pro in the world of editing; Jack Macrae at Henry Holt loves books about history, and I would like to believe that this book adds to his rich legacy of memorable explorations of the past. Also at Henry Holt,

Assistant Editor Kirsten Reach thoughtfully responded to my many questions and helped shepherd the project through the production process. And Senior Production Editor Rita Quintas ably supervised the transition from manuscript to book. Finally, I am indebted to Vicki Haire, who copyedited the manuscript with a keen and thorough eye.

My wife, Lorri Glover, herself a superb historian and gifted writer, encouraged me to pursue this subject in book form. But in addition to the example of her remarkable work ethic, she has always offered a loving spirit that in the larger scheme of things makes writing books a joyful irrelevance.

INDEX

Page numbers in *italics* refer to illustrations.

ABOUT THE AUTHOR

DANIEL BLAKE SMITH is the author of *The Shipwreck That Saved Jamestown*, *Inside the Great House: Planter Family Life in 18th-Century Chesapeake Society*, and many articles on early American history. Formerly a professor of early American history at the University of Kentucky, Mr. Smith now lives in St. Louis, where he also works as a screenwriter and filmmaker.